Backroads of
ONTARIO

5th Edition — Expanded and Updated

Backroads of ONTARIO

RON BROWN

FIREFLY BOOKS

A FIREFLY BOOK

Published by Firefly Books Ltd. 2019

First Printing

Library of Congress Control Number: 2019930195

Library and Archives Canada Cataloguing in Publication
Title: Backroads of Ontario / Ron Brown.
Names: Brown, Ron, 1945- author.
Description: 5th edition, expanded and updated. | Includes index.
Identifiers: Canadiana 20190053976 | ISBN 9780228101888 (softcover)
Subjects: LCSH: Rural roads—Ontario—Guidebooks. | LCSH: Automobile
travel—Ontario—Guidebooks. | LCSH: Ontario—Description and travel. |
LCSH: Ontario—Guidebooks. | LCGFT: Guidebooks.
Classification: LCC FC3067.6 .B76 2019 | DDC 917.1304/5—dc23

Published in the United States by
Firefly Books (U.S.) Inc.
P.O. Box 1338, Ellicott Station
Buffalo, New York 14205

Published in Canada by
Firefly Books Ltd.
50 Staples Avenue, Unit 1
Richmond Hill, Ontario L4B 0A7

Interior design: Gareth Lind, LINDdesign
Cover design: Noor Majeed

Printed in China

Canada ▮◆▮ We acknowledge the financial support
of the Government of Canada.

Opposite: Inglis Falls Conservation Area near Owen Sound.

Contents

9 Introduction: The Story of Ontario's Backroads

12 Section 1 — Southwestern Ontario
14 Route 1. Climbing Neptune's Staircase
22 Route 2. The Tranquility of the Grand River Road
30 Route 3. To the Source of the Grand
42 Route 4. The Hidden Treasures of the Erie Shore Road
50 Route 5. The Face of Farm Country
60 Route 6. The Bruce Peninsula Road
68 Route 7. Cuestas and Valleys

78 Section 2 — Central Ontario
80 Route 8. Those Surprising Simcoe County Highlands
88 Route 9. The Lake Simcoe Steeple Chase
96 Route 10. The Ridge Road West
102 Route 11. The Ridge Road East
110 Route 12. The Rice Lake Road
118 Route 13. The Quinte Shore Road

128 Section 3 — Eastern Ontario
130 Route 14. The Napanee River Road
140 Route 15. Island Roads
152 Route 16. The Perth Road
162 Route 17. The Rideau River Road
170 Route 18. The Ottawa River Road
176 Route 19. The Opeongo Pioneer Road
184 Route 20. The Remarkable Highlands of Hastings

192 Section 4 — Northern Ontario
194 Route 21. Algoma's Scenic Dunn's Valley Road
200 Route 22. The Nipissing: A Road of Broken Dreams
212 Route 23. Manitoulin's Haweater Trail
222 Route 24. Boomtown Backroads: The Cobalt Circle
228 Route 25. The Trail of the Sleeping Giant
238 Route 26. The Silver Mountain Road

246 Index of Cities, Towns, Villages and Hamlets
249 Index
255 Photo Credits

A lookout point on Manitoulin Island. See Route 21.

The Story of Ontario's Backroads

The road was scarcely passable; there were no longer cheerful farms and clearings, but the dark pine forest and the rank swamp crossed by those terrific corduroy paths (my bones ache at the mere recollection) and deep holes and pools of rotted vegetable matter mixed with water, black bottomless sloughs of despond! The very horses paused on the brink of some of these mud gulfs and trembled ere they made the plunge downwards. I set my teeth, screwed myself to my seat and commended myself to heaven.

Today's backroad adventures are a far cry from 1837, when traveller Anna Jameson wrote the above words. Indeed, thanks to those who flee the hustle of freeways and the tedium of suburban sprawl to seek the tranquility of an uncluttered countryside, backroad driving is North America's most popular outdoor activity.

This book leads you from Ontario's main highways onto its backroads. Before 1939 the province had no expressways. That was the year King George VI and Queen Elizabeth opened the Queen Elizabeth Way. In 1929 Ontario had less than 2,000 km of hard-surface highway. Before 1789 it had no roads at all. European settlement of Ontario began with the arrival of the United Empire Loyalists from the war-torn colonies that had become the United States of America.

Opposite: Indian Head at Ouimet Canyon Provincial Park near Dorion, Ontario — see Route 23.

The Loyalists settled on the shorelines of the St. Lawrence River, Lake Ontario and Lake Erie, and they had no need of roads. But the governor of the day, John Graves Simcoe, casting a wary eye on the restless neighbour to the south, embarked on the building of military roads. In 1793 he ordered a road from Montreal to Kingston, and Ontario soon had its first road. (You can follow it even today as County Road 18 through Glengarry County.) This he followed with Yonge Street and Dundas Street, which also survive and have retained their names.

Despite the slow pace of settlement through the early years of the 19th century, the pattern of Ontario's road system was taking shape. From the Loyalist ports roads led inland to bring out lumber and farm products. They were useless quagmires in spring and little better in summer. Only in winter, when frost and snow combined to create a surface that was hard and smooth, did farmers haul their wheat to port.

Settlement roads connected the main towns of the day. Among the more important were the Danforth Road, replaced soon after by the Kingston Road (portions of both survive), linking York (now Toronto) with Kingston; the Talbot Trail that followed the shores of Lake Erie; and roads to the northwest, such as the Garafraxa Road, the Sydenham Road and Hurontario Street.

As settlement progressed, surveyors made their way through the forests, laying out townships and

Fall scenic highway in northern Ontario.

surveying each into a rigid grid of farm lots and concessions. Along each concession they set aside a road allowance, linked at intervals of 2 to 5 km by side roads. And so Ontario's road network became a checkerboard that paid no attention to mountains, lakes and swamps.

One of the first problems was that there was no one to build the roads. Although each settler was required to spend twelve days a year on road labour, settlers were few at first.

In the 1840s, the government turned road-building over to private companies and to municipalities. Some of the companies tried such improvements as macadam and planks. But rather than being grades of crushed stone, the macadam was often little more than scattered boulders, while the planks rotted after a few years. When the railways burst on the scene in the 1850s, road companies and municipalities both turned their energies to railway-building.

Despite the railways, the government tried one more road-building venture, the colonization road scheme. This was in the 1850s, when lumber companies were anxious to harvest the pine forests that cloaked the highlands between the Ottawa River and Georgian Bay. Although early surveyors had dismissed the agricultural potential of the upland of rock and swamp, the government touted the region as a utopia for land-hungry settlers. What the politicians didn't reveal was that the main aim of the scheme was to provide labour, horses and food for the timber companies. Once the forests were razed and the timber companies had gone, the settlers who had moved to the area were left to starve. By 1890 most of them had fled, and the roads in some cases were totally abandoned. Nevertheless, a few of them retain their pioneer appearance and have become some of the backroads in this book.

In 1894 the Ontario Good Roads Association was formed to lobby for better roads, and in 1901 the government passed the *Highway Improvement Act* to subsidize county roads. Finally, in 1915 the government got back into the business of road-building and created the Department of Highways. The first 60 km of provincial road was assumed east of Toronto in 1917.

But for decades afterward, northern Ontario remained railway country. Most towns and villages north of the French River owed their existence to the railways, and what roads there were stabbed out from the railway lines to the lumber and mining camps.

The years following the Second World War saw the arrival of the auto age, and during the 1950s and 1960s Ontario embarked on a spate of road improvements unequalled in the entire previous two centuries. Road-building continues unabated, and as it does it destroys much of the province's traditional landscape. As rows of maple and elm, cedar rail fences, and roadside buildings fall before the bulldozer, Ontario is left with a legacy of endless asphalt. Despite enlightened planning, countryside sprawl continues to engulf Ontario's once pastoral landscapes. It is not surprising, therefore, that Ontarians, overwhelmed with the tedium of an omnipresent suburbia, are travelling farther afield to seek the tranquility of backroad Ontario.

The backroads in this book are special. Each has a story of its own. Some follow the unhappy colonization roads, some the more prosperous settlement roads; some explore rural areas that have retained their century-old landscapes, others follow the shores of lakes or rivers. Some plunge into deep valleys and mount soaring plateaus. Others take you into northern Ontario to logging areas old and new, to once-booming silver fields and to the fringes of the province's last frontiers.

Although the maps at the start of the four major parts of the book, along with those that accompany the 22 that guide you through each chapter, contain basic information, you will also need to bring along more detailed road maps or a quality GPS device. And don't overlook the driving and walking tours offered by many local counties and municipalities.

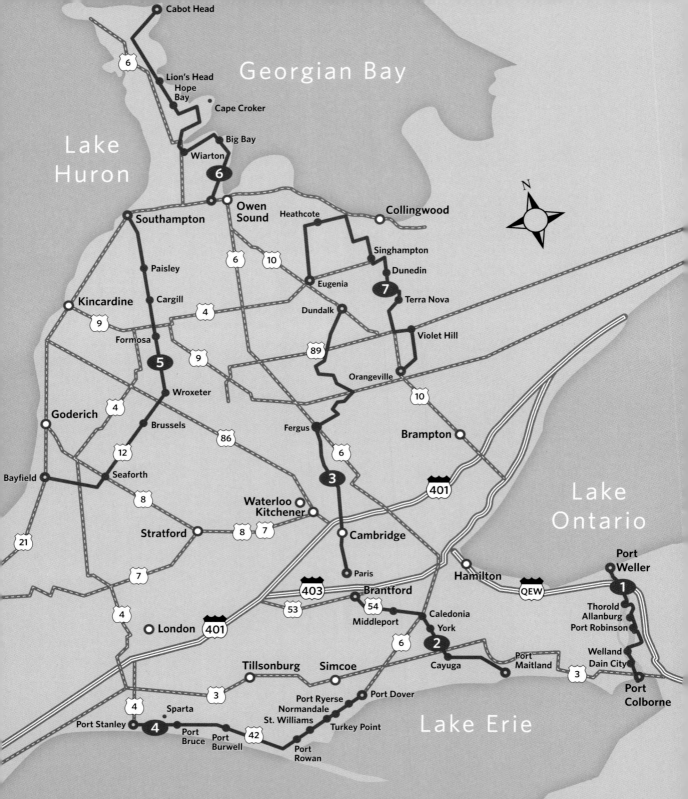

Section 1
Southwestern Ontario

ROUTE 1   Climbing Neptune's Staircase   14

ROUTE 2   The Tranquility
of the Grand River Road   22

ROUTE 3   To the Source of the Grand   30

ROUTE 4   The Hidden Treasures
of the Erie Shore Road   42

ROUTE 5   The Face of Farm Country   50

ROUTE 6   The Bruce Peninsula Road   60

ROUTE 7   Cuestas and Valleys   68

1 Climbing Neptune's Staircase

A freighter makes its way towards Lock 1 on the Welland Canal.

SOME FUNDAMENTAL FACTS:
- The first seven locks carry the boats over an elevation of 99.1 m within a distance of just 11.2 km.
- The locks are more than 260 m long and nearly 25 m wide with a depth of over 8 m.
- Tolls could range from $10,000 to $30,000, depending on the size of the boats, which could be as many as 3,000 in a year.

n 1824 William Hamilton Merritt saw there was profit to be made by building a canal that would cut through the Niagara Escarpment from his mills on Twelve Mile Creek on Lake Ontario to Lake Erie. He formed the Welland Canal Company and began digging. His route followed the creek and tributaries to the Welland River at Port Robinson, the canal's original southern terminal. From there the canal route led along the Welland River into the Niagara River and on towards Lake Erie. However, the Niagara River proved too turbulent and so a cut was made southward from Port Robinson to Port Colborne. The new canal began carrying ships in 1833.

To mount the Niagara Escarpment, more than 40 locks were needed; those that led up the cliff face itself were nicknamed "Neptune's Staircase." The canal's length was 44 km with 40 wooden lock stations. However, those first locks soon proved too small for the larger ships and in 1841 construction began on a new canal with new locks that were larger and made of stone, replacing the earlier wooden structures. In addition, a "feeder" canal was dug from Welland to the Grand River is order to bring in more water whenever it was needed. Remains of the feeder canal remain visible in the small community of Wainfleet and near Dunnville as well. But soon, steamships began replacing the schooners and barges, and by 1870 a still bigger canal was being built. This time a straighter route was used, reducing the number of locks to 26.

The lake ships kept on getting bigger, so the fourth Welland canal opened its gates to the larger ships in 1932. The route was altered significantly with a completely new point of entry on Lake Ontario known as Port Weller and the number of locks was reduced to seven, with an eighth lock in Port Colborne to adjust the water level to the changing levels in Lake Erie. Then in 1933, a new alignment re-routed the canal around the City of Welland.

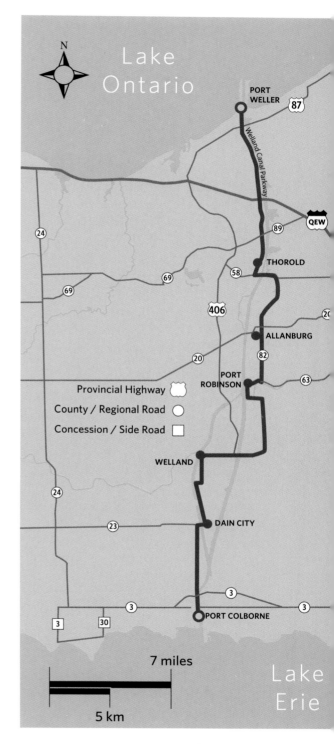

When the new alignment opened in 1933, engineers from around the world hailed what they called an engineering marvel, and with all the re-routing and the unusual bridges, it still is. This route follows the canal for 45 km from Lock 1 to Lock 8.

Lock 1 to Lock 3

This route begins in Port Weller. While the community lacks any kind of heritage townscape, a heritage townscape lies further west in the community of Port Dalhousie. Here is where the canal began and here Lock 1 remains preserved on both the second and third canals, along with a wooden lockmaster's cabin. The historic Main Street, with its hotels and tiny two-cell gaol, reflects the busy and often boisterous days of sailors and town boys who often duked it out on the old Main Street, only to keep close company overnight in the lock-up.

In Port Weller, two roads lead from Lakeshore Road north to the Lake Ontario shore: the Welland Canals Parkway on the west side of the canal (the one you will be taking south), and the Seaway Haulage Road on the east. For the most part, a chain link security fence keeps visitors from the canal's edge.

Two features mark Lock 1: the heavy duty bascule style jackknife lift bridge, where the deck rises from the east side, and the historic dry dock on the east side, which continues to service even the largest of the ocean-going ships.

The Welland Canals Parkway continues as Bunting Road south of Lakeshore Road, the site of Lock 1. After a short distance look for the Welland Canals Parkway again and turn left onto it. Here it hugs the canal up to Lock 2. The parkway then crosses Carlton Street and continues along the canal bank. Industrial St. Catharines intrudes upon the landscape as the Parkway swings away from the canal to pass under the Garden City Skyway, built in 1963 to replace the congested Queen Elizabeth Way lift bridge. The traffic lights at Queenston Road mark the original route of the QEW and a double deck jackknife lift bridge. Continue south on the Parkway. From here it is a short distance to the Lock 3 Viewing Station and St. Catharines museum.

Lock 3 Viewing Station

This is the place to pause and not just learn about the canal but also see it in action. The viewing station is built specifically to allow the public to watch the massive freighters inch their way into the lock with often only a few centimetres to spare, and then see the water level in the lock either rise or lower depending upon which way the vessel in proceeding. You can climb the 3-level viewing platform located immediately beside the lock. Should the weather be unfavourable, there is also an indoor viewing area. If there is no boat in the lock, check the board for the arrival time and name of the next vessel to arrive. Don't expect anything between December and April, as that is when the canal is closed for the winter and yearly maintenance.

The St. Catharines museum is located here as well and offers an informative 15-minute video that tells the story of the canal. A room full of displays depicts the history of the entire region with a focus on the canal. The parking area has ample room for vehicles and tour buses too. At the far south end of the lot, there is a wooden lockmaster's cabin like the one that still stands in Port Dalhousie.

Lock 3 to Lock 7

This is where the engineering of the canal really gets interesting. From the parking lot continue south on the Welland Canals Parkway. This brings you to a traffic light at Glendale Road

Spectators can easily watch ships at the Lock 3 viewing station.

and one of those vertical lift bridges where the deck rises between two steel columns. Turn right here, followed by an immediate left to bring you back onto the Parkway. As you proceed you will come face-to-face with the Niagara Escarpment, the greatest hurdle that the canal builders had to conquer. To mount the cliff, the builders used three twin-flight locks, Locks 4, 5 and 6. A flight lock means that the locks basically sit right next to each other with no channel between. The twin aspect means that inbound and outbound boats can lock simultaneously through the side-by-side locks, a much more efficient way to mount the cliffs than the 28 locks on the original canal. While there is no designated viewing area to watch the action, there is enough space beside the roadway to pull over.

But there is another viewing area at Lock 7. A small parking area and information building are situated there, as is the locally famous "Kissing Rock," which is where the Longest Kiss Contest for the *Guinness Book of World Records* is held, and a popular place to be married. There is also a small amount of accommodation here from which to view the canal activity. Although it is to all intents and purposes part of St. Catharines, this is the industrial town of Thorold.

Thorold to Welland

The next section takes you away from the canal itself but not away from some of the canal's more interesting features. The Parkway ends at the Lock 7 viewing station at a T intersection with Chapel Street where you turn left and then take an immediate right onto Portland Street. From the next T intersection with Ormond Street, turn left again and follow Ormond (which turns into Richmond Street) to Pine Street and turn left. This takes you over the bridge that crosses Regional Road 58. Turn left to take the ramp onto 58. Here you will enter a tunnel built beneath the canal in the 1970s. You are now below those massive freighters.

After emerging from the tunnel, turn right at the traffic light onto Davis Road (CR 58). Follow it to the traffic light at Lundy's Lane. If you wish to digress a bit, you can turn right here and drive into Allanburg and the site of the sod turning for the canal. Otherwise, continue straight ahead to follow what is now Allanport Road (CR 82) south to where it ends at Canby Street/Chippewa Road and turn right.

Port Robinson

This will lead you into the historic and near ghost town of Port Robinson, for it was here that the first canal originally terminated with the vessels turning into the Welland River on their way to the Niagara River.

After you cross the railway tracks and follow the bend in the road to the left, park and wander into the Port Robinson Park on your left to see the remains of that early lock, now overgrown. A little further on, the ghostly Main Street with its few remaining places of business tells you that the village's busy days are behind it. The lift bridge that once crossed the canal at this location was taken out in 1974 when the freighter *Steelton* hit the bridge. The bridge was never rebuilt and today only a small ferry connects the two sides of Port Robinson. Continuing south the canal crosses over the Welland River, which is diverted beneath the canal.

Continuing by car on River Street, turn left onto the second Biggar Road, then right on Darby Road. Follow it until you hit the stop sign at East Main Street—make a right to get to the centre of Welland.

Welland

With its canal-side location and its junction of several rail lines, Welland became a centre for quite a few foundries and heavy industries. It also earned the role of county seat. The county court house and adjacent jail still stand on the north side of East Main Street. Today it is known for its many historic murals, but first you go into the Main Street Tunnel and once again beneath the waters of the canal. To best enjoy this outdoor art gallery, park your car on East Main Street and walk the few blocks it takes to see most of the murals.

The collection of outdoor murals begins in earnest at Burgar Street where you see on the northwest corner a mural called "Upbound at Midnight." In the adjacent parking lots on each side of Main Street, five murals depict various historical images of early Welland including "Welland Fair" by John Hood, and "Tell Me About the Olden Days" and "Little Helper," both by famed muralist Dan Sawatsky.

As you approach the lift bridge at King Street, you will encounter "Tugboats" and "Where Water Meets Rail" as well as one above the entrance to the Main Street Gaming Centre ironically called (although maybe not intentionally so), "Women at Work" showing life in a textile factory. Several others line Division Street and Niagara Street on the opposite side of the former canal.

From East Main Street you should turn left to follow King Street along the side of the landscaped former canal where you will find more murals, with the waterway hosting regattas and recreation activities. (Information on the entire collection of murals is on the website www.inforniagara.com.) Head back to your car to continue the journey to Port Colborne.

The "Women at Work" mural is just one of many located in Welland.

Welland to Port Colborne

King Street eventually leads past the large regional hospital and into the rugged industrial community of Crowland. Here is where many of Welland's heavy industries once stood, but the large fields of overgrown cement pads and collapsing fencing show that the industries have gone, leaving a bleak wasteland. The community itself consists of older shops selling second hand goods and rows of what were formerly boarding houses for the workers.

King Street ends at Ontario Road where you turn right and then left at Canal Bank Road. This follows the bank of the canal, where recreational activities now take place.

After you cross Towline Tunnel Road, you go over the railway bridge, and if you look left you can see where the rail lines have all been brought together to pass beneath the canal.

Canal Bank Road brings you into Dain City, a one-time workers' community for the now-vanished factories. The historic Dain City House

Tavern still serves customers as it did when the trains on the nearby tracks once called.

Once in Dain City turn right onto Forks Road, passing through a steel truss bridge over the former canal. To your right you will see a railway lift bridge that is no longer required to rise for the passage of boats. After crossing the bridge turn left at the stop sign for Elm Street to take you into Port Colborne where you can park and enjoy the community on foot.

Port Colborne

This breezy lakeside community marks the southern terminus of the Welland Canals, old and new. In fact, you can see both canals converging beside the Clarence Street lift bridge that lies at West Street, three blocks east of Elm. West Street's stores line the side of the canal and include cafes and gift shops. The remains of a railway swing bridge lie to the north of the lift bridge and to the west is the former CNR station, which has been re-purposed as a restaurant. Across King Street from the station is the Port Colborne Historical and Marine Museum—well worth a visit.

A walkway leads along the canal south on West Street from Clarence Street where you might hear the siren and see the lift bridge rise high into the air to allow a mighty freighter to pass beneath. Down on the lake itself, at the foot of Elm Street, is the town's revitalized waterfront where you can have a dip, pause for a picnic and see the still active grain elevators offloading grain from the mighty lakers and onto the waiting rail cars.

While in Port Colborne, hop back in your car and drive west on Sugarloaf Street for two and a half blocks from Elm to visit Tennessee Avenue, where a few homes built by wealthy Americans during the 1880s still line the lakeside street. Once a gated community, the stone gates themselves are now a heritage site.

Locals might also tell you how to see the "shrinking" grain elevator. To do that, turn left from Tennessee Avenue onto Lakeshore Road, follow it west to Cement Road and turn around. As you drive back east, the distant elevators are framed by a tunnel of trees and appear to shrink as you proceed. It is actually an optical illusion, for it is the trees that get larger as you pass beneath them, while the distant elevators remain roughly the same size.

A ship arrives in Port Colborne, traveling for 43 km from Port Weller.

2 The Tranquility of the Grand River Road

The Grand River is one of Ontario's most historic water-ways. From its humble swampy beginnings far to the north of Kitchener, it rushes through a rock-walled canyon at Elora before meandering through a gentle countryside to its outlet into Lake Erie.

This route follows the portion south of Brantford—that is, the most historic part of the river. Here, the Grand's links to the First Nations are the strongest, and here it was tamed and confined between the walls of a long-forgotten canal.

The route is relatively short, requiring a mere half-day, and should appeal to almost everyone. It offers history and Native lore, handsome 19th-century homes and mills, and opportunities to fish, photograph or just relax in a riverside park.

The valley of the Grand River near Brantford.

The story of the Grand River reflects the frustrations of Ontario's Native peoples as few others do. In 1784 Mohawk Chief Joseph Brant and his Six Nations followers from New York State were granted all the lands along the river as a reward for having fought and died beside the British in several valiant victories in the American Revolutionary War. But when settlers made their way up the Grand, clamouring for land, the British began to reduce Brant's holdings. Today, Brant's descendants retain a fraction of that land.

Settlement remained light, however, until 1829, when William Merritt and Absalom Shade decided to construct a canal along the Grand and pressured for even more of the Native lands. The first ships passed through the canal in 1835, and lock-side towns soon burst into life. Sawmills and gristmills flourished. But during the 1850s, as railways began to snake their way across the countryside, river traffic dwindled. The last vessel passed through the locks in 1890, only 55 years after the waterway was first opened. An era had quickly passed.

Some of the towns that had depended on the river traffic shrunk to hamlets; others vanished entirely. Following the Second World War, a recreation boom brought new life to the banks of the Grand. The river sprouted cottages and buzzed with motorboats. Parks replaced lock stations, new dams replaced old ones. Today, virtually no trace remains of the original canal.

Yet the banks of the river remain steeped in history, and the roads that follow it are lined with pioneer farms, tall forests and historic hamlets, all providing an unusual backroads drive.

Brantford to Newport

The first portion of the trip leads to three historic sites and takes you along the high scenic banks of the river. From Highway 2 in Brantford, turn south onto Lock Street and follow the yellow and

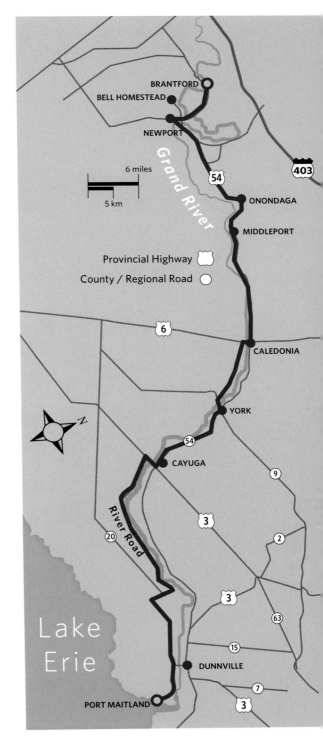

blue directional signs to the Mohawk Chapel, about 1.5 km distant. Sitting in a grove of trees that shade an ancient cemetery, this chapel is Ontario's oldest Protestant church and the only Royal Native chapel in the world.

It was on this site that Chief Joseph Brant in 1784 settled his band. They built a school, 24 houses and a small log chapel. The following year they added St. Paul's Chapel, the gleaming white building that you see here. Your next historic site is close at hand, but has a decidedly different story to tell. It is the birthplace of the telephone.

Across from the chapel stands a horrific legacy, the former Mohawk Indian Residential School. Operated from 1828 to 1970, the school deprived First Nations children of their families and their culture. Today it is open as part of the Woodland Cultural Centre, a museum and First Nations educational centre.

From the Mohawk Chapel, drive left out of the parking lot to Birkett Lane and turn left. Continue for 2 km and turn left again onto Erie Avenue, which becomes County Road 4. After 1 km, you will cross the Grand River and continue to Tutela Heights Road, where you turn right. The yellow and blue signs will direct you to the home of Alexander Graham Bell.

The landscaped grounds provide ample parking as well as washrooms, picnic tables, paths for strolling and superb views over the Grand Valley. In the white frame homestead, the rooms are furnished as in Bell's day, and some of his personal effects are on display. Beside the Bell Homestead is the Henderson Building. It was Canada's first telephone exchange and houses a display of interesting and odd early telephones.

The next leg of your journey leads to another historic site with an indigenous theme to it, the

birthplace of Canadian poet Pauline Johnson. From the Bell Homestead, return to the intersection of Tutela Heights Road and County Road 4. As you cross the latter, you are on the Newport Road, which lurches down into the valley and follows the river for 2 km to the first of the riverside settlements that you will visit, Newport. The hamlet began life as Burtche's Landing, a shipping point for pine and grain. But as the canal declined so did Newport. Today, the only real vestige is a yellow brick community centre.

From the community centre, turn right and drive the short distance back to County Road 4; turn right and drive to County Road 18, where you turn right again. Cross the bridge and continue to Salt Springs Road and turn right. This quiet country lane wanders along the north bank of the river, past the historic Salt Springs Church and farms that date from the time of the earliest settlements.

After 5 km you will come to a stop sign at Highway 54, known as the Grand River Scenic Parkway. Turn right here, passing through the village of Onondaga, a one-time shipping point on the river. Three km east of Onondaga is Chiefswood, the birthplace of Pauline Johnson. In 1845 Emily Howells, a young English immigrant, met Six Nations chief George Johnson, then a government interpreter. In 1853 they married and Johnson built her this Georgian mansion called Chiefswood, a home that entertained such dignitaries as the Prince of Wales. Their daughter, Pauline Johnson, became an internationally celebrated poet and performer. Today, her birthplace is a museum (open daily in the summer) devoted primarily to Johnson and her works.

Middleport, the next village on your tour, lies a short distance eastward on Highway 54.

Opposite: Brantford's Royal Mohawk Chapel.

The board-and-batten church at Middleport dates from the forgotten canal era.

Middleport

This small and picturesque village began, as the name suggests, as a landing on the Grand River Canal. For a time it shipped timber and grain, and eventually a town plot was laid out. But once canal traffic began to decline, the community dwindled. On the tiny main street, shaded by the trees of the river bank, is an early board-and-batten church. Surrounded by a white picket fence and a spacious cemetery, it dates from the time of the canal.

Opposite: The Grand River near Caledonia.

Middleport to Caledonia

From Middleport your route continues southeast along Highway 54. In this area, the river's banks recede and become gentle hills, among which are several handsome riverside homes dating back more than a century. After 10 km, you pass under the Highway 6 bridge and enter the town of Caledonia, with its many historic structures. Beneath the railway bridge is the site of one of Caledonia's three canal locks and, opposite the lock, a trio of early canal buildings including the lock master's house and a former hotel.

Few towns of 2,500 can claim as many historic 19th-century buildings as Caledonia. Most of these buildings are within a few blocks of the main intersection. From that intersection go north on Argyle Street to the railway tracks, where the 1904 Grand Trunk railway station has been restored and houses the Chamber of Commerce. The town hall stands two blocks east of the intersection of Argyle and Caithness Streets. This tall brick structure with embedded columns was built in 1857 and has appeared in books featuring Ontario's architectural highlights. With the creation of regional government, the town hall became redundant and is now the Edinburgh Square Heritage and Cultural Centre.

A few paces from the town hall is 46 Caithness Street. This 1847 building was the home of Dr. William McPherson, one of the town's first physicians, and it still retains its second-storey balcony. Dumfries Street runs beside the town hall. Look there for 7 Dumfries, a small frame building covered now with stucco. Originally the Ryan Hotel, it was built in 1854. At 22 Dumfries is a building that once served as a stagecoach inn. Constructed in 1836, it is Caledonia's oldest still-standing building.

The year 1872 marked the coming of the railway, and Caledonia boomed. Many of the buildings in

the downtown core date from those boom years, including the old Opera House. Another, the toll-keeper's house at the eastern end of the bridge, was built in 1857 during a period when toll roads were common, though unpopular.

Before leaving Caledonia, cross the magnificent concrete arch bridge to the south bank, where the oldest mill on the Grand, built in 1863, stood until 2017, when a misguided council allowed a developer to remove it and replace it with condos and a parking lot.

Caledonia to York

To continue on your route, return to Argyle Street, and turn right to take you to Haddington Street and there turn left. Haddington becomes River Road and leads past farms that date back more than a century. The road, which follows a high bank about 1 km from the river, offers views of the wide, gentle valley of the Grand. After 6 km, the road comes to an intersection with County Road 9. About 1 km to the left, across the river, lies the sleepy village of York.

Although York is small, it is rich in buildings that date from the canal period. It was located at the site of the second lock on the canal and developed quickly. At its peak it had 450 residents along with several hotels, stores and mills. But when the canal closed and the railways passed York by, its population plummeted to 175 and it became the quiet residential hamlet that you see today.

Cross the bridge and turn right onto Highway 54, which is the main street through the village. Beside the road, at the site of the lock and mill, you will find a small park. Across the road from the park is a red brick structure—a former hotel and just one of the many village buildings that owe their origins to the forgotten canal.

York to Cayuga

To leave York, continue along Highway 54. After 8 km, you reach a brick gatehouse that marks the entrance to the stunning mansion known as Ruthven Park. This pillared castle, which overlooks the Grand, was built by canal promoter David Thompson in 1845 and contains 36 rooms. A short distance away stood the town of Indiana with its 300 residents and various mills, as well as lock station 1 on the canal. Ruthven remained in the Thompson family until 1994. It was then deeded to the Grand River Land Trust, which has opened it for tours. The furnishings are all original to the Thompson family.

A short drive farther along Highway 54 takes you to Cayuga.

Cayuga

Another of the canal villages, Cayuga, boomed when the railway reached town, but then it stagnated. Although it was named the county seat in 1850, it remained smaller than its upstream rival, Caledonia, and its current population of 900 is an increase of just 200 over its peak in the 19th century.

As you enter town you pass the courthouse and historic jail beside. Cayuga Street, a once-bustling main street, may be short, but it offers a delightful collection of early brick and stone buildings including a tall, red brick one that housed the post office.

Cayuga to Port Maitland

To continue to Port Maitland, turn right from the main street onto Highway 3. Drive across the Grand River bridge to the River Road, then turn left. As you cross the bridge you will see off to the right the steel truss railway bridge built by the Canada Southern Railway and now no longer in use.

Port Maitland's historic lighthouse marks the confluence of the Grand River with Lake Erie.

South of Highway 3, River Road bends east and the river banks disappear as the back shore becomes low, in places swampy. Riverside farms mingle with country homes and rows of cottages. Wide and sluggish, the river is suddenly alive with motorboats and fishermen. After 10 km, the road bends away from the river to Haldimand Road 20. Turn left here. For the last 7 km the land is low, and the views of the river few. A stop sign tells you that you are in a community once known as Byng. Although still known locally as such, its identity has merged with the larger town of Dunnville on the opposite shore of the river. You may wish to visit Dunnville with its busy main street, a riverside park and a variety of fast food restaurants.

From Byng, turn onto County Road 11 and follow it to the mouth of the Grand and the historic port of Port Maitland. More a lake port than a river town, Port Maitland was settled in 1820. Although much is new, you may still see some late 19th-century buildings, including one-time inns, and fishermen's homes along the river. The road ends at the lake. Here, you can park your car and read the historical plaque, which describes the port's early role as a naval depot, or stroll out on the breakwater to the historic Port Maitland lighthouse. You can see by the fishing tugs that Port Maitland retains its link with the past.

3 To the Source of the Grand

O
ntario's Grand River, a national heritage waterway, is really two rivers. The portion below Brantford is wide and sluggish, made navigable to Lake Erie by the Grand River Canal. (This section is covered in Route 2.) However, there is another Grand, one which tumbles through glacial hills, foams through steep canyons and has carved a scenic valley through Ontario. From its headwaters in a dank swamp in faraway Grey County, a network of tributaries gradually feeds the river until it contains enough water to have powered grist and saw mills. Dozens of mill towns grew up along its banks, some of which have boomed into sizable cities while others have faded and, in some cases, become ghost towns.

This route begins in Paris, Ontario, and follows the river northward to Breslau before taking to a network of farm roads that crisscross the river on the way to its headwaters.

Paris

Start your journey in the heart of Paris, where Grand River Street crosses the Nith River. On the right side of the road, you can see the confluence of the Nith with the Grand, a site known as the "Forks of the Grand." Just south of the bridge stand two outstanding examples of the unique cobblestone architecture for which Paris has become famous. At the corner of Grand River Street and Burwell is a two-storey building erected in 1845-51 as a dispensary for Samuel Sowden, a local druggist. Across the intersection stands St. James Anglican. Built in 1839, it was the first building made of cobblestone in Ontario.

Paris is the only city in Canada where this building technique was used. An American, Levi

Opposite: The historic core of Galt exhibits a decidedly European flavour.

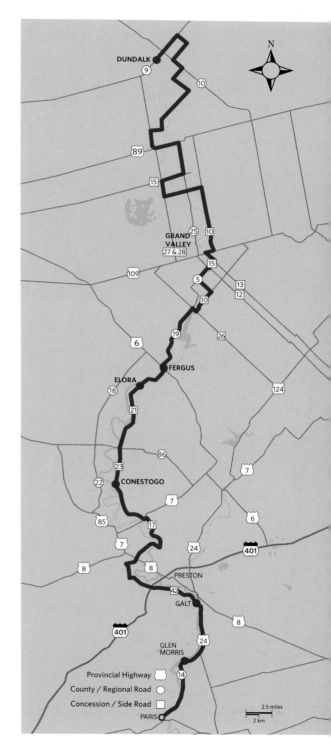

Cobblestone is a distinctive feature of Paris' architecture.

that owe their legacy to those heady days abound and can be viewed using a local walking-tour guide. Dominating the main intersection is the grand three-storey Arlington Hotel, now a popular restaurant.

Paris to Galt

To continue on the Grand River route, cross the Grand on William Street and turn left at Willow. This brings you to the historic high-level Grand Trunk Railway bridge and the start of the Galt to Paris Rail Trail. As you travel along what has become County Road 14, on your left the banks of the Grand become increasingly steeper and are covered with rare Carolinian forest.

When you enter the hamlet of Glen Morris, turn left on Forbes Street to reach the rail trail and the site of the Glen Morris station, now gone. Back on County Road 14, with the river on the left, you pass through gently rolling farm fields on your right, interspersed with some fine new country homes. Turn left when you come to a stop sign at Highway 24, which will take you into the revitalized mill town of Galt.

Galt

Laid out in 1816 by Absolom Shade, Galt's abundant waterpower brought in enough settlers to construct some 60 buildings, including its first mills, in just four years. By the 1880s, Galt had several rail lines radiating out from it, turning it into a busy industrial town. Although most of the mills have long since closed, local heritage enthusiasts have worked hard to preserve the town's industrial heritage.

You enter town on Water Street, where you will pass the Galt Woollens Mill (36-38 Water Street), built in 1843 and now converted into offices. Mill

Boughton, brought the cobblestone style to Paris in the late 1830s. From his first commission, the Anglican Church, he went to build or inspire more than a dozen similar buildings in Paris and the surrounding countryside. It was a style devised by the builders of the Erie Canal in the 1820s, and thanks to the bountiful supply of the rounded stones found in the banks of the Grand River, one that became common in Paris.

But it was another material from the riverbanks that gave Paris its economic impetus, gypsum. These chalk-like layers turned Paris into a leading producer of plaster, earning its name after the plaster resources near Paris, France. By the 1880s, the railway had turned Paris into a leading manufacturing town.

Paris was also the recipient of the world's first long distance phone call, placed by its inventor, Alexander Graham Bell, from his lab near Brantford in 1874.

Today most of the industries have closed, and Paris has become a quieter place. Yet buildings

Opposite: Galt offers many pleasing trails, here with Knox Presbyterian Church in the background.

Race Park, which began as a flood works following the damaging flood of 1974, was created from the rubble of the Turnbull Woollen Mill. Not only does the levee hold back the river but it also offers a hiking trail and amphitheatre.

The area bounded by Main, Ainslie, Dickson and Water Streets is the heart of Galt, its many heritage structures now forming a designated heritage district. While you will need a local walking-tour brochure to appreciate them all, among the more prominent are the old town hall at 46 Dickson Street built in 1857, the 1887 Market Building at 40 Dickson Street and the Dando commercial block on Ainslie Street.

From downtown Galt, cross the river on the historic twin-arch Main Street bridge. This brings you to Queens Square at Grand Avenue and Main Street. It has been the town square since 1864. The Hume Block at 14-16 Queen's Square, built in 1856, is the last of the original buildings which once enclosed the square. (Devotees of the television series "The Handmaid's Tale" will recognize some locations from that show.)

Galt to Doon

Turn right onto George Street. As you leave the built-up area, George Street becomes Blair Road with views across the wide gentle valley, which the river has formed.

Blair is another community worth visiting, especially if you have one of the Cambridge walking-tour guides. From Lamb's historic inn built in 1837, you can follow Old Mill Road to the site of the Blair mills. The building was built in 1931 after the original mill was destroyed by fire. In the woods across the road, you can follow a short trail to Blair's restored sheave tower. Resembling a miniature mining headframe, it provided supplementary waterpower to the mill using a system of pulleys.

After you have explored Blair, another historic mill village awaits, Doon. Continue on Blair Road to the roundabout at Fountain Street and turn left. Fountain Street becomes Homer Watson Boulevard as it carries you across the 401 to Conestoga College Boulevard, where you turn right. Turn left onto Doon Valley Drive. Follow it a short distance to Pinnacle Drive and turn right. At the stop sign for Old Mill Road, turn left and drive to the Homer Watson house, which is a short distance up the hill, on your right.

As you will have observed, this area has been enveloped by Kitchener's growing urban fringe. Nevertheless, Doon is a nicely preserved historic oasis. One of Kitchener's most famous homes, the Homer Watson house was originally built in 1834. In 1881 painter Homer Watson bought it to use as a studio. By age 25, Watson had achieved international acclaim with several of his works hanging in Windsor Castle. Following his death in 1936, the house became an arts centre and, from 1948 until 1975, housed the Doon School of Fine Art. Today it is a gallery that celebrates the work of one of Canada's most celebrated artists. Behind the house stands the Doon Presbyterian Church dating from 1854.

As you walk down the hill from the Watson house, you will come to the stone remains from the Doon Mills. Built in 1839, the mill stood five stories tall and was briefly the centre of an industrial empire run by Adam Ferried. Following a fire in 1915, it was left vacant, crumbling over the decades until only a meager shell survives.

Doon to Conestogo

To reach the next segment of your journey, return to Homer Watson Boulevard and follow Fountain Road across the Grand River and into Preston. Here turn left onto Shantz Hill Road, which becomes Highway 8. Follow the Parks Canada

Blair's restored sheave tower historically provided supplementary power to the town's former grist mill.

signs for a side trip to the historic pioneer tower. Built under the inspiration of William Breithaupt in 1924, it was a tribute to the area's German heritage at a time when the wounds of World War I needed healing. From its lofty riverbank perch, you have lengthy vistas along the river.

Back on King Street, continue left to Riverbank Drive at Fairport and turn right. The six-span bowstring bridge that crosses the river here is the second longest of many similar structures built across the Grand, and one of the most beautiful. (The longest is in Caledonia on the lower Grand.) Continuing along Riverbank Drive, you will catch occasional glimpses of the river and the wide valley to your left. Turn right onto Fairview Drive, and then keep to your left when you reach the roundabout for Regional Road 17.

When you pass the Waterloo Wellington Airport, turn left onto Woolwich Street South and pass through the suburban community of Breslau, which was once a scenic mill town. Here you will cross the tracks of the historic Grand Trunk Railway (now CN), and at the traffic lights for Highway 7, continue straight ahead. On Regional Road 17, you are travelling through the neat fields and sturdy farm homes that mark Mennonite country. At the almost-vanished crossroads hamlet of Rosendale, keep right on Regional Road 17.

As you drive through the one-time mill town of Bloomingdale, note the former general store and hotel, two standard features of Ontario's country villages. After passing Regional Road 23, you come back to the riverbank, which is much lower here. Watch for the confluence of the Grand and Conestogo Rivers.

Historic Elora has become a popular destination for a day trip.

Conestogo to Elora

Conestogo remains a busy farmers' village, with its still functioning feed mill. After you pass through the village, come to the stop sign for Regional Road 22, Northfield Drive, and turn right. This brings you into the heart of Mennonite country. Most of the farms you pass here belong to the conservative Old Order Mennonites. Then after you pass through a steep gully, watch for Jiggs Hollow Road and turn right, keeping to the left at the bend. Here you pass one of the parochial schools run by the Old Order Mennonites. After you climb a hill, you encounter a vista of the Grand River on your right, with one of Ontario's last surviving covered bridges in the distance.

At the stop sign for Hill Road, turn right. West Montrose, which you then enter, is a little picture-postcard village tucked around the covered bridge.

Cross through the structure and turn left, where you will find a small parkette where you can leave the car. The road along the river here offers you some good photo opportunities, but take care to respect the many private property signs.

From the park, continue along the riverside road to the stop sign. Turn left and then left again onto Regional Road 86. As you cross the river, note on the right the old bridge abutments for the abandoned Galt and Goderich branch of the Canadian Pacific Railway. When you come to Middlebrook Road, turn right. Here you follow the gentle west bank of the river, passing old stone farmhouses and another bowstring bridge. When you come to the stop sign for Wellington Road 7, you can turn right and then make another right turn onto Regional Road 21, which will take you to the entrance to the popular Elora Gorge Conservation Area.

The Grand River reflects the buildings of Elora's main street.

One of the Grand River's geological highlights, this deep crevice features unusual rock formations, trails and opportunities to float down the mild rapids on an inner tube, a popular summer pastime. Trail guides are available at the gate.

Elora

To enter Elora instead, continue straight ahead from the stop sign at Wellington Road 7 and continue to Geddes Street, where you turn right. After Geddes becomes Metcalfe Street, you are in downtown Elora. The many heritage stores and the old mill have turned this once sleepy farm town into a major tourist attraction. Pubs and gift shops now line the roads. The row of heritage buildings along Mill Street is reminiscent of an English country village.

Heritage buildings abound. St. John's Anglican church dates from 1842. The Iroquois Hotel, once known as the Dalby House, has been serving customers since 1865, while the 1859 Royal Hotel is now the home of the local Legion. The most prominent building is, of course, the mill. Built in 1843 by Charles Allan, it was converted to a restaurant and inn in 1974 and is the only five-storey mill left in Ontario.

Public access to the river is frustratingly limited, however. If it is open, you can view the waterfalls from a viewing area beside the mill. Here the water foams around a rock pillar known as the "Tooth of Time." Alternatively, Church Street leads to a small park with trails to Lover's Leap, a rock cliff that juts out between the gorges of the Grand River and Irving Creek.

To leave Elora, follow Mill Street east. A couple of parks on your right, including Bissell Park and the Elora Quarry Conservation Area, allow you to view the river in this area. Once you leave the built-up area, you will pass the Wellington County Museum and Archives on the left, housed in what is called "Ontario's oldest house of industry."

The railway bridge just beyond the museum is now a trail along which you can find some striking views of the river from the old railway bridge that spans the water.

Fergus

You then enter the main street of Fergus, with its striking resemblance to a Scottish town. This should be no surprise, as the community was established to attract Scottish settlers. One of the most prominent of its many heritage structures is the market that is housed in the 1870s Beatty Bros farm-implement factory. The Theatre on the Grand, which attracts thousands of theatre lovers each season, plays to sold-out crowds in a restored 1928 movie house. The Breadalbane Inn and restaurant is housed in a grand stone mansion which dates to 1860

Continue through Fergus on St. Andrews Street, the main thoroughfare, until you come to the Mill Tower condos, situated in an early mill. Just beyond the mill complex, turn right onto Gartshore Street, cross the river and turn right. This brings you to a delightful riverside park with trails that lead to a waterfall. This is a good place to take photographs of the mill on the opposite bank.

Fergus to Grand Valley

Return to St. Andrews Street and turn right where a collection of historic stone and brick homes, built in conjunction with the mill, cluster around the intersection. When you come to the stop sign at Anderson Street, return left. Drive to the stop sign for Wellington Road 19 and turn right. The highway leads to the partially-flooded former

mill town of Belwood. The lake that stretches out beside it was formed by the flood control dam and inundated part of community.

At Belwood turn right onto Concession Road 26 and cross the lake. On the south shore, you will encounter the abandoned roadbed of the Elora Branch of the Credit Valley Railway, now a rail trail.

From Concession Road 26, turn left on Side Road 10, which briefly follows the shore of Belwood Lake. A short distance along on the left, look for the top of a drowned bridge that marks the pre-lake road. Drive to the stop sign at the 10th Line and turn left to cross the river. At the stop sign for County Road 5, turn right. When County

Templin Gardens beside Grand River, Fergus.

Road 5 bends left for the second time, turn right onto the 12th Line and drive to the river to a quiet pastoral setting beside the bridge.

Return along the 12th Line to the 15th Side Road and turn right. Turn right again when you reach the 13th Line. This little side trip returns you to the river and an historic steel truss bridge that spans it here.

Follow the 13th Line back the way you came and continue all the way to the stop sign for Highway 109 and turn right.

When you come to the first crossroad, the 10th Line, turn left to reach Waldemar. Now the site of newer homes, the older section of the one-time mill village is but a relic of its heyday, with its church, former general store, hotel and blacksmith shop all being put to other uses. Past Waldemar you follow the bank of the river through a valley, which is wide and pastoral. You will notice that the flow in the river is considerably less than that which you saw below the Belwood dam.

At Side Road 5, turn left. Keep left again at Amaranth-East Luther Town Line. Then turn right onto Concession Road 2-3, which leads you into the village of Grand Valley. Had you stood on this road in 1984, you would have witnessed a scene of incredible destruction. It was here that a vicious tornado roared along the road ripping to shreds the many old homes that once stood here. Newer homes now stand in their place.

You enter the village on Amarath Road 8. When you reach the main street, turn left. While the twister raged just meters away, the historic stores of the main street were left unscathed and offer the traditional range of businesses for a farm town. The river crosses through the village at the south end of the main street.

Grand Valley to the Headwaters

From Grand Valley drive north on the main street, County Road 25, to Concession Road 7, and turn left. Continue to Sideroad 21-22 and turn right to reach the Luther Marsh Conservation Area.

This wildlife management area of 5200 hectares was created when a dam was built across Black Creek, a tributary of the Grand River. The reservoir is home to wide range of floral species, as well as 35 species of mammals, 11 species of reptiles and more than 237 different bird species. Canoe routes, trails and observation towers give you a chance to count them for yourself.

From the conservation area, continue north on Sideroad 21-22 to Concession Road 15 and the one-time farm hamlet of Monticello. Drive east to Sideroad 27-28 and the hamlet of Colbeck, where the once proud river looks more and more like a simple creek. Turn left and drive through flat farmlands to the stop sign at Highway 89. A short distance to the left is the riverside village of Keldon, now nearly a ghost town with its three old houses.

From Highway 89, turn north onto County Road 8, and then right onto Southgate Road 8. Turn left onto Melancthon-Proton Townline Road. Keeping right onto 260 Side Road leads you into the sleepy hamlet of Riverview, the last of the upstream mill villages on the Grand River. From Riverview continue on 260 Sideroad to the second

intersection, the 2nd Line SW, and turn left. Turn right onto 250 Sideroad and drive to Highway 10. Here you can see the river has become little more than a trickle wending its way through flat farmlands.

Follow Highway 10 to the left until you reach County Road 9 and turn right. As you cross a few rivulets, you are approaching the headwaters of not only the Grand River but also the Saugeen River, which flows west; the Mad River, which flows east and a tributary of the Beaver River, which flows north. Because drainage flows in all directions from this high swampland, it is known as the "Roof of Ontario," and the little hamlet of Shrigley, with its church and school, is its "capital." To reach this two-building hamlet, continue on 240 Sideroad to the 8th Line NE.

Then to discover the Grand River's starting point, the object of this quest, after you cross 6th line NE, a dank waterlogged swamp closes in on both sides of the road. Incredible as it may seem, the little waterways that percolate through the swamp here mark the humble beginnings of the journey for a river that has carved gorges, formed valleys and spawned mill towns. It has earned a Canadian Heritage River designation.

To return home from your trip, simply return along County Road 9, which brings you out to Highway 10, your main route south. A convenient stop before you head south is the town of Dundalk, which lies a short distance ahead along County Road 9.

Opposite: The headwaters of the mighty Grand River lie in a vast swamp know as the "Roof of Ontario."

4 The Hidden Treasures of the Erie Shore Road

This route winds along Ontario's most underrated and perhaps most maligned shoreline, that of Lake Erie. Following a pioneer trail along the lake's shores and bluffs, it begins at Port Dover, 60 km southwest of Hamilton, and runs 95 km westward to Port Stanley.

This trip will delight the water lover, the birdwatcher and the history buff. Public wharves in most towns provide opportunities to cast for Lake Erie's popular yellow perch or to watch squat-fishing tugs chug to their berths. Here, too, are clifftop lookouts, more public than on any comparable length of Great Lakes shoreline, marshes that abound in bird and plant life, and some of Ontario's best-preserved early towns.

Many of Port Dover's historic harbourside buildings have been preserved.

Lake Erie's first settlements were founded by the United Empire Loyalists, refugees from America's post-revolutionary persecutions. But no sooner had they begun to get established than the War of 1812 burst upon them, bringing with it a devastating raid that laid waste to farms, homes and industries. However, settlement revived after the war, spurred on by Thomas Talbot, a retired army officer who sold his land grants to any settler meeting his stringent standards. Busy villages developed around the mills and small harbours, and, as the homesteaders moved up the creeks and crude trails, the backlands began to fill. The railway age ushered in even greater prosperity to those towns fortunate enough to be on a rail line. The little ports thrived and the fishery flourished. Then, in the 1920s, just as farming appeared to be declining, tobacco crops were introduced to the infertile sands and gave agriculture a much-needed boost.

Port Dover

Port Dover, the start of this route, was until recently Ontario's fishing capital and the home of the world's largest freshwater fishing fleet. (That fleet now calls Wheatley, Ontario, home.) It began as a mill town called Dover Mills, but in 1812, as the Yankee invaders ignited their fiery trail across the countryside, Dover Mills was reduced to ashes. To take advantage of the growing trade in lumber and grain, the townspeople rebuilt closer to the lake. Later, after the coming of the railways, commercial fishing boomed and Port Dover grew quickly. Most of the town's historic buildings date from those heady years in the late 19th century.

The town has several fascinating sights, and most of them can be seen on foot. If you follow St. Andrew Street from Highway 6 to Harbour Street, you will come to the Port Dover Harbour Museum. Housed in a restored fisherman's shanty,

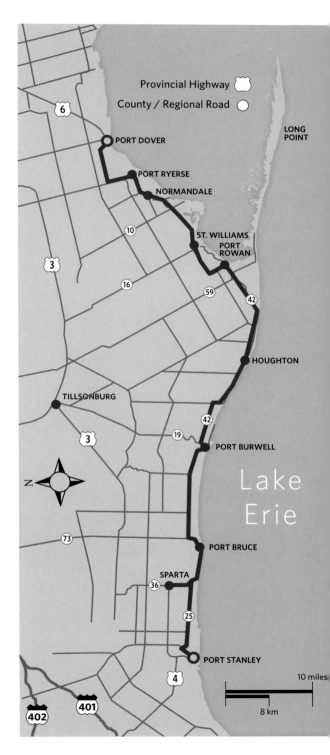

built about 1890, it displays old-time fishing equipment and graphically depicts the tribulations of fishing on Lake Erie.

Farther along the west side of the harbour, the former net sheds and shanties of the old fishermen's quarter have become homes, craft shops and restaurants. At the end of the street, you come to the public wharf. No matter when you visit, you will see local residents casting a line in the water or just watching the fishing tugs glide behind the breakwater and manoeuvre for space in the more recent harbour on the east side.

Port Dover to Normandale

To leave Port Dover, turn left from Highway 6 onto Nelson Street at the north end of the commercial core. This part of the route is marked by signs announcing the "Talbot Trail." For the first 2 km the route treats you to bluff-top views over Lake Erie; then it heads inland across a flat farmland of pastures, orchards and a few commercial greenhouses. After 6 km turn left at Port Ryerse Road, and 2 km farther on you will come to Port Ryerse.

Named for Colonel Sam Ryerse, an early mill owner, this wooded narrow gully has gone from busy shipping centre to quiet cottage community, and it has some of the oldest buildings on Lake Erie. Atop the east side of the gully stands the picturesque white frame Memorial Anglican Church, c.1869. The church has witnessed many changes, as has a large brick hilltop mansion, the former Ryerse family home.

Your next stop after Port Ryerse will be another former centre of activity, Normandale. To get there, continue 1 km west until you come to a fork in the road. Keep left on Front Road, a winding farm road, and, after 5 km, you will come to a T intersection. Turn left, and, after about half a kilometre, you will be in the cottage community of Fishers Glen. Once in this wooded gully, keep right, drive 2 km to a T intersection; turn left and drive less than 1 km to Normandale.

Normandale

As you descend the hill into this quiet valley, you may find it hard to refer to Normandale as "yesterday's Hamilton." Yet for three decades in the 19th century, Normandale was Ontario's foremost iron producer, thanks to Joseph Van Norman. The production of iron was launched here in 1815 by John Mason, who simply burned a mixture of charcoal and bog ore from the many local swamps. Van Norman acquired the operation in 1828 and turned it into a major industry.

A town plot of five streets and 42 lots was laid out, and by 1846 the town had a population of 300, a gristmill, and a main street full of businesses. However, by 1848 the timber and ore were gone. Joseph Van Norman moved on, and Normandale became a ghost town. Today it exists as a cottage and country-living community.

Yet you may still see vestiges of its glory years. At the foot of the hill is a T intersection where, on the southeast corner you will see a two-storey frame building with a front gable. This is the former Union Hotel built by Van Norman himself, and it has been restored. Adjacent to it, the small building with the "boomtown" facade served as the village post office. Near the lake, down Mill Lane, lies the site of Van Norman's foundry, commemorated by a historical plaque. So thoroughly was the industry abandoned that Van Norman's blast furnaces lay buried and forgotten until their rediscovery by Royal Ontario Museum archaeologists in 1968. One of the furnaces is now in Upper Canada Village in eastern Ontario, and the other is in the Eva Brook Donly Museum in Simcoe, just 17 km north of Normandale on Highway 24.

The water-powered Backus Mill near Port Rowan is Ontario's oldest.

Normandale to St. Williams

To continue on the pioneer trail, drive west from the Union Hotel up the wall of the gully and, after 1 km, stay left on Front Road. This scenic section of the route winds through woods and fields for 1 km to a stop sign at Regional Road 10. South of the intersection, at the foot of Lake Erie's cliffs, lies Turkey Point. Atop the bluff a golf course covers the sites of Fort Norfolk and Charlotteville. They were built as a fortified administrative district seat during the last decade of the 18th century, when the threat of an American invasion loomed large. But the fort was never finished and instead the district seat was relocated to Vittoria, a safer inland location. Charlotteville and Fort Norfolk quickly vanished from the landscape, and today only a historical plaque marks the spot. Turkey Point is a peninsula of shifting sand which extends 5 km into the lake and encloses a vast marsh. A popular public beach lines the lake.

As you drive west from Regional Road 10, the trees of a forest form a leafy tunnel. About 3 km from Regional Road 10, the route skirts a high bluff offering a vista across the grassy Turkey Point marsh to the wooded spit beyond. Here, too, you pass fields that are flat and sandy, with long rows of leafy crops and lined with square wooden barns painted green and red. This is Ontario's tobacco country and one of Canada's richest agricultural communities. Yet a little over half a century ago it was a wasteland.

Originally, Norfolk's sand plains, as they are called, were a park-like savannah of oaks and grasses. The first settlers, attracted by the light, stone-free soils, quickly cleared the area of its sparse forest. However, a few bountiful crops

Cliffs of clay mark the Lake Erie shore near Port Bruce.

depleted the soil, and, one by one, the farms were abandoned, leaving Norfolk a desert of blowing sand, good for little other than pine plantations. Then, in 1923, agricultural scientists Henry Freeman and William Pelton carefully studied the soils and decided to introduce tobacco. Their foresight paid off, and Norfolk became Canada's leading tobacco region. However, high cigarette prices and the growing concern over tobacco-induced cancer have once more sent the area into an economic downspin. A few former tobacco producers have begun planting peanuts and ginseng, while others have reverted to more traditional crops such as wheat and oats.

St. Williams

From the cliff-top the road ventures inland through the periphery of tobacco country and,

after 5 km, stops at the farm village of St. Williams. This community was originally called Neals Corner but the name was changed to honour William Gellassy, a local landowner and religious leader. Located just 1 km from the lake, St. Williams was in its early years a shipping and milling centre. But with the arrival of the South Norfolk Railway and, later, the growth of the tobacco industry, it became a busy farm-service town of about 200. Although it is quieter now and many of its early businesses have folded, you can still find a few older houses and a church from those heady times.

St. Williams to Port Rowan

At the stop sign, turn left, drive a few metres and turn right. For 5 km this road winds through the farm fields and along the cliff to the busy resort town of Port Rowan. From the stop at County Road 42, the main street of Port Rowan lies to your right. A disastrous fire in 1919 destroyed most of the downtown area, leaving few historic buildings. At the north end, however, the blaze stopped short of the Baptist church, which stands as it has since 1856, with its white steeple rising above its brick walls.

The main attraction of Port Rowan is its shoreline. Turn left and descend the hill to the Lions Club Park, a small treed picnic area wedged between the harbour and a curving beach. Once a bustling port and fishing centre, the harbour is now home largely to pleasure craft.

From Port Rowan you can take a side trip to see Ontario's oldest mill. Follow County Road 42 north through the town for 3.5 km, and follow the signs to the Backus Heritage Conservation Area. The wooden mill that you see here was the only mill on Lake Erie to survive the scorched earth devastation of the American attack in 1812. It grinds grain today just as it has since it was built in 1798. The conservation area also offers 20 restored pioneer buildings, including an unusual octagonal schoolhouse that dates from 1866. You may also camp, fish or follow the 12 km nature trail through one of southern Ontario's most extensive Carolinian forests.

Port Rowan to Port Burwell

Return to Port Rowan and follow County Road 42 through town and then carry on for 2 km until you arrive at a stop sign for Highway 59. Six km south lies Lake Erie's longest sand spit, Long Point, a UNESCO World Biosphere Reserve that extends 32 km into Lake Erie. A small provincial park is situated at the end of the highway, but most of the point is privately owned. Nevertheless, the peninsula is a major port of call for birdwatchers.

The next section of your route passes through a string of faded hamlets and long-gone schooner ports—some that have come back to life as country living quarters and others that have vanished altogether. From Highway 59, continue west on County Road 42. After 2 km, you will come to a wide swampy inlet and a small string of houses, the village of Port Royal. The marshlands that now clog the creek belie its early role as a bustling schooner port.

From Port Royal, your route crosses an area of fertile farms until, after 8 km, a handful of buildings announces the former schooner port of Clear Creek. Once a busy lumber port, Clear Creek lost its unprotected wharf to Erie's waves after just a few decades.

Continue along County Road 42. After 4 km, a small range of hills looms on the left. Known as the Sand Hills, the ridge marks the sudden appearance of shoreline sand hills. A private park, the Sand Hills have camping and picnic facilities as well as a beach. For your best view of these remarkable sand cliffs, pay your park admission and follow the trail down the 100-metre-high sand pile to the beach.

For 14 km the road continues along the shore, passing through villages such as Jacksonburg, Houghton and Hemlock, as farm fields spread straight and flat into the distance.

Port Burwell

Another of Erie's once busy ports, Port Burwell is quiet now, more popular for its beaches and its 1840 lighthouse that sits right in the middle of town. The marine museum displays an extensive nautical collection. In 2013, the Elgin Military Museum relocated here from St. Thomas and displays the submarine, *Ojibwa*.

A few fishing tugs still make Port Burwell their home and offer fish for sale. Cross the bridge and continue on County Road 42 where you can pause in Iroquois Beach Provincial Park for a swim or a stroll on one of Lake Erie's longest beaches.

Port Burwell to Sparta

Continue west along County Road 42. Thanks to the shoreline's moderate climate, this is not only prime tobacco country but also greenhouse and orchard territory. Some of the peach and cherry orchards offer the opportunity to pick your own fruit; others have retail booths by the roadside.

For the next 17 km the road follows a straight line about 2 km inland. The farmland is flat and prairie-like. Prosperous rural communities such as Lakeview and Grovesend dot the route. Then, at County Road 73, County Road 42 ends. Turn left here, then follow the highway 3 km through a series of deep wooded gullies to the once busy Port Bruce.

Erosion has left a series of hills and gullies that were once the shore bluff. It was around these hills that the village grew. It too started as a lumber port and then boomed with the growth of commercial fishing. But Port Bruce never attracted a railway, and the fishermen soon moved on to ports that did. The cliffs and valleys, however, did not go unnoticed, and Port Bruce has become a popular cottage and recreation centre. Beside the river mouth is a small treed park, and the long sandy beach is now a provincial park.

To leave Port Bruce, follow County Road 73 back to the bridge and turn left onto County Road 24. For 4 km this road carries on past cliff-top views before it swings inland. After 2 km, watch for the intersection with County Road 36 and turn right. Drive along this road for 3.5 km and you will arrive in Sparta, Ontario's oldest and best-preserved Quaker village.

Sparta

Although new homes have been built around Sparta, the original village core surrounding the main intersection has survived almost intact. On the southeast corner is the general store (now a craft shop), which was built in 1842 of handmade bricks. On the northwest corner stands the old Sparta House Hotel, with its long wooden porch. It too was constructed in 1842 and stood empty for several years before receiving new life as a tea room. Next to it is the Forge and Anvil Museum and the old village smithy, but one with a difference: it was made from adobe brick. About 1 km west of the intersection stands one of Ontario's oldest and best examples of Quaker architecture, the Haight-Zavitz house. Indeed, much of the main street survives as it appeared a century ago, and it is proudly preserved. A short distance north of the intersection, the Quaker Meeting House still survives. You may pick up a walking-tour guide in almost any shop.

Return south along County Road 36 to County Road 24 and turn right. The flat, prosperous farmlands here seem endless. Farm homes, which might more appropriately be termed mansions, testify to the bounty. One outstanding example is just 2 km south of Sparta on the east side of the road.

After continuing west for 9 km on County Road 24, you will come to County Road 23. Follow this road a short distance to St. Joseph Street in Port Stanley and to the centre of town. Port Stanley is a town of 2,000 that still lives off shipping and the lake.

Port Stanley

The area was first settled in 1818, several years after the shoreline farther east was opened. The harbour at Port Stanley was not ready until 1823, and the place remained a small shipping port until 1857, when the railway reached town. Built jointly by the counties of Middlesex and Elgin, the London, St. Thomas & Port Stanley Railway was one of Ontario's shortest lines.

Port Stanley is a fitting place to end this particular tour, a busy modern community that retains

The memorial to Port Dover's fishermen.

its historic links to the lake—and even to the railway—and harbours a rich collection of historic buildings. At the junction of Bridge and Main Streets you will find downtown Port Stanley, with its shops, taverns and restaurants. Main Street follows the east bank of the harbour, and along it are Port Stanley's oldest buildings. No. 211 is the Russell House, a brick inn constructed in the 1850s and later repurposed as a bank, a butcher's shop and offices. No. 207 is unarguably Port Stanley's most historic building, for it was built in 1822 by the town's founder, Colonel John Bostwick. Originally a warehouse, it is now a private home. Next to it stands a yellow brick house, considered by many to be the port's most handsome structure. It was built in 1873 by Manuel Payne, who served variously as postmaster, telephone operator and customs officer. Farther along are net sheds,

ice-houses and other buildings from the early days of fishing.

On the west side of the bridge, you will find the efforts of local railway enthusiasts to keep alive the community's railway links. The station for the Port Stanley Terminal Railway is the point of embarkation for rail excursions to a replica station in downtown St. Thomas.

It is wise to pick up a brochure that guides you on a walking tour of the place and then meander along the beach, enjoy a meal or perhaps even stay overnight.

To return home via Highway 401, simply follow Highway 4 north from Port Stanley to its junction with that freeway.

5 The Face of Farm Country

This is a route for anyone who is out of touch with their rural roots and craves rolling pastures and "Old Ontario" scenery. The trip starts at Southampton on Lake Huron and follows the fertile farmlands of Bruce and Huron Counties south for 120 km to Bayfield. Along the way, you will encounter some of Ontario's best-preserved 19th-century main streets plus enough farmscapes, riverscapes and old buildings to delight any photographer.

This backroad leads through Ontario's farming heartland.

These are not the hobby farms of the wealthy urban commuter, but of those for whom farming is more than a livelihood—it is their life. This area is rural Ontario as it used to be.

There are two chapters to the settlement of Bruce and Huron Counties. The first belongs to energetic land colonizers John Galt and William "Tiger" Dunlop. In 1824 they chartered the Canada Company and advertised extensively in the United Kingdom the bounties of the Huron Tract, the territory that would become Huron County. Most of the land was level and stone-free, and it quickly attracted settlers. By 1850 most of Huron County's farms were taken and the government looked north to Bruce County, then a dark and mysterious forest known as the Queen's Bush.

Farms were surveyed and roads cut through the forest. The first was the Huron Road from Guelph to Goderich on Lake Huron. Then, in 1851 the Elora Road followed, leading from Guelph to Southampton. Before long, the two counties were crisscrossed with a network of farm roads. Villages grew up at important intersections and where the roads crossed water-power sites.

The next chapter belongs to the railways. In 1864 the Wellington, Grey & Bruce Railway began construction from the south, followed by three other lines from the south and east. As usual, towns wily enough to lure the railway burgeoned into important manufacturing centres, while those that were bypassed stagnated. In time even the railways lost their importance. Towns and villages that eventually lost their industries nevertheless continued to serve the farmers, and many retain 19th-century streetscapes of brick stores and shady residential lanes.

Southampton

The trip starts in the tree-lined streets of South-hampton, on Highway 21. Southampton began as a fishing village and became a busy port when the Elora Road was opened in 1851. But its real boomtime began with the completion of the Wellington, Grey & Bruce Railway in 1872 and

Paisley's main street buildings are among Ontario's most historic.

with the growth of several furniture factories. Most of Southampton's buildings date from those years. The main street, only two blocks long, runs west from Highway 21 and ends pleasantly at a long sandy beach. Here, the municipality has developed a small, landscaped rock garden.

On an island about 2 km southwest of the harbour is the Chantry Island lighthouse. This 30 metre stone tower was built in 1859 and is one of the oldest on Lake Huron. The harbour is located a few blocks north of the business district, and here you can launch or rent a boat to visit the historic tower.

On Highway 21, also at the north end of the town, is the Bruce County Museum and Cultural Centre. Large for a town this size, it contains 11 rooms of artifacts, documents and photographs.

At the south end of town, at the corner of

Grosvenor and Morpeth Streets, is the attractive brick station built by the Grand Trunk after its takeover of the Wellington, Grey & Bruce Railway. But trains haven't called here for more than 25 years, and the tracks have been lifted. Still, you can almost hear that distant whistle.

Southampton to Paisley

This portion of your route follows the broad, fertile Saugeen River Valley. Drive out of Southampton south on Highway 21 and turn left onto County Road 3 (the alignment of the old Elora Settlement Road). Three km from the turn, you cross the Saugeen River, where it has carved a rugged gorge into the clay cliffs. (The abandoned iron bridge is worth a look.) The road then bends south and follows a straight course for 14 km. After 2 km you will pass the old road village of Burgoyne, and, after a farther 6 km, the one-time hamlet of Dunblane. Here, set in a grove of willows, is the Dunblane School. It has been altered slightly to become a residence but, with its yellow brick and its bell tower, is one of the most photogenic places on this trip.

Continue for 4 km beyond the school to the turnoff to the Saugeen Bluffs Conservation Area. Its 200 hectares offer camping, fishing, hunting in season and a few short hiking trails. Four km farther on, in a shallow valley where the Teeswater River flows into the Saugeen, is a village in which you will want to linger—the village of Paisley.

Paisley

Although Paisley dates from 1851, its boom time began 20 years later, with the arrival of the Wellington, Grey & Bruce Railway. By 1890 Paisley had a population of 1,500 and several factories and mills. Today, it claims only two-thirds of that population, while the industries have nearly all vanished.

Thanks to the efforts of interested citizens and a Province of Ontario grant, the main buildings of this attractive village have been preserved and its streets beautified. In the middle of town, on the south side of the bridge, stands the town hall with its delicate bell tower and its sidewalks redone in interlocking brick. Built in 1876, the hall remains the focus of the community. Beside it is the green hose tower of an 1891 fire hall, and across the road looms the 1885 Fisher woollen mill, while on the banks of the river you will see the preserved sawmill. South of the town hall, a string of commercial buildings climb the hillside, most of them dating from 1880–1910.

A short distance west on Mill Drive brings you to Nature's Millworks gift and craft shop, which occupies the five-storey wooden Stark's Mill dating from 1885. Close by is the high-level trestle, which now carries a rail trail high above the river.

Paisley to Cargill

To leave the village and continue the trip, continue west on Mill Street (County Road 1). The road crosses the bridge and climbs up the wall of the Teeswater River Valley. Stay on this road to where it bends sharply right. At this point you turn left onto Concession Road 20. Drive another 1 km and turn right onto Town Line Road. Here you are on a quiet country road that parallels the busier County Road 3, which lies 2 km to the east. This farm road is the original alignment of the Elora Settlement Road. That is why the old villages are found on this backroad rather than on the county road.

The road takes you south through Ontario's prime beef country. Green pastures and blowing cornfields are level and stone-free; many of the old wooden barns now sport gleaming aluminum silos. After 6 km, you will meet County Road 15. To follow it on a side trip to the small valley village of Pinkerton, turn right. After 1 km, the road winds into the valley of the Teeswater River and enters Pinkerton.

Cargill

From Pinkerton, return to the Elora Road, turn right and drive 1.5 km to Cargill. This was until recently a traditional mill town. It dates from 1879, when Henry Cargill bought 1,600 hectares of timber and built a sawmill, a gristmill, a planing mill and a store. Although most of the industries have vanished, the village (population about 100) has retained its collection of yellow brick buildings. As you enter Cargill, turn right onto County Road 32 and cross the bridge. Here you will find the Bailey factory (now abandoned), a brick store that is a block deep, a crescent of identical yellow brick houses, and the Village Inn, located in the old Cargill Hotel.

Return to the Elora Road and turn right. This brings you to a small park where, beside Henry Cargill's millpond, you can picnic or fish.

Cargill to Formosa

Continue south on Townline Road. For 10 km the road takes you through prosperous farm country. Beef cattle graze lazily on rolling pastures, while in late summer hay and oats waft in the wind. Most farmhouses are large and constructed of yellow or red brick, some elaborately mixing the two colours.

Cross Highway 9 and continue on south. After 1 km, the old Elora Road, here Tower Road, leaves your route and angles southeast. Drive instead straight ahead onto County Road 12, the old Wroxeter Stage Road, which was built to link Wroxeter with the Elora Road.

Formosa

At 3 km from the intersection, nestled in the wide valley of Formosa Creek, lies the little town of Formosa, settled originally by a colony of Roman Catholic Germans. The location not only spawned the usual mills, but also the trademark of any good German town—a brewery. Formosa's present population of 200 is down from the 350 of its peak years, but it still retains its stores and hotels—and even a descendant of the original brewery.

Although the creek is small, the valley is steep and wide. As you begin your descent, you have a striking view of the village rooftops below. To your left is the Immaculate Conception Church with its soaring steeple—a landmark since 1885. Drive down the hill and follow the main street past the taverns and stores.

Formosa to Wroxeter

Continue south through the village on County Road 12 as it climbs out of the valley and onto the rolling plain above. At the south end of the village stands the Formosa Springs Brewery. Ontario's traditional small-town beer-making is a tradition that has resurfaced in other small towns across the province. In 1968 this brewery gained national fame as the only such establishment in southern Ontario to defy a long beer strike and stay open. Thirsty customers drove from all parts of central Ontario to line up, some for an entire day, to buy their favourite drink.

For 20 km the road takes you past more fertile farmlands and through forgotten crossroad hamlets with names like Ambleside and Belmore. After crossing Highway 87, you will come to Wroxeter, a "former ghost town" that is coming back to life.

Wroxeter

Wroxeter dates from 1854, when the Gibson family arrived from Scotland and bought a large tract of land around a water-power site on the Maitland River. Within ten years, Wroxeter had three stores. Twenty years later, when the Toronto, Grey & Bruce Railway arrived, it boomed to five hotels and five blocks of stores, with mills and factories along the Maitland River. But after the turn of the century, Wroxeter's industries began to close. Then, after the First World War, Wroxeter's population began a slow but steady decline and one by one Wroxeter's stores closed. By the late 1940s it had fallen so low that it ceased to be a separate municipality.

Along the wooded river banks, you will find no trace of the old industries that marked Wroxeter's heyday. In the early 1980s Wroxeter's main street resembled that of a ghost town. For three blocks stores sat closed and shuttered. Some have since been demolished, others spruced up to the point where a highway sign proudly announces that Wroxeter is now a "Former Ghost Town."

At the south end of the business section, at the corner of Centre and Ann Streets, five roads

Brussels' old railway station was saved and moved to a lawn bowling club.

converge. To continue on your route, cross Ann and then immediately fork right. This will take you through another small neighbourhood and out of the village.

Wroxeter to Brussels

Drive to the T intersection with County Road 12 and turn left. After 4 km, you will come to Highway 86. Cross it, remaining on County Road 12. Two km from Highway 86 you pass through a nondescript collection of houses known as Jamestown. For the next 8 km you cross farmlands that are flat and so clear of trees that they appear almost prairie-like.

Brussels

Brussels lies 8 km beyond Jamestown and is another town that shows the scars of decline. It began in 1852 when William Ainley arrived and laid out a town plot, and William Vanstone erected mills on the Maitland River. In 1864 the rails of the Wellington, Grey & Bruce were laid and turned

Brussels into a busy shipping and factory town. The early years of the 20th century were unkind to Brussels, and its population plummeted from 1,800 to today's 1,000. If it weren't for the prosperous farms that surround it yet, it too would have become a ghost town.

Despite the setbacks, Brussels has preserved some of its more important buildings. The bridge over the Maitland River marks the north limit of the business section where the Graham Block is a well-preserved 19th-century commercial building. North of the bridge, the former railway station now sits on the grounds of a lawn bowling club. If you follow the signs from the main street for two blocks to the Brussels Conservation Area, you will see a picturesque Logan gristmill.

Brussels to Seaforth

Continue south on County Road 12 for 8 km to County Road 25 and the pioneer village of Walton. One of its two original hotels is the handsome red brick Walton Inn Bed and Breakfast. Drive left on

The Cardno tower dominates the main street of Seaforth.

County Road 25 for a few metres and then resume your route right onto County Road 12. Once more you pass farmlands that are flat and fertile, and Georgian-style farm homes that were built in the 1840s. Fifteen km from Walton you enter Seaforth, the largest town on this route. Its streetscapes, mansions, and commercial buildings were built in the 19th century, so plan for a prolonged stop here.

Surprisingly, Seaforth is younger than its two suburbs, Egmondville and Harpurhey. Named for Constant Van Egmond, one of the builders of the Huron Road (Highway 8), Egmondville sits on the banks of Silver Creek, 2 km south of the heart of town. The place became a busy village with taverns, shops, three stores and Van Egmond's sawmill and gristmill. In 1839, 3 km northwest of Egmondville, on the Huron Road, landowner Dr. William Chalk opened a post office and surveyed a townsite. With

traffic on the Huron Road heavy, the site was ideal for a village. Harpurhey, as he called it, soon contained two hotels and three blacksmith shops, plus a store and several other shops. Meanwhile, the intersection of the Bayfield Road (as County Road 12 was called then) and the Huron Road itself, where Seaforth would later grow, remained a swamp.

When the railway arrived in Seaforth and the Bayfield Road was extended to it, the intersection sprang to life. It boomed even more when in 1870 it got a railway of its own. By 1900 Seaforth's population had soared to 2,500 and overshadowed its pioneer predecessors. Although most of the town's early factories have long since gone, Seaforth remains a major regional shopping town. Its commercial core extends about four blocks and is one of western Ontario's most striking.

Guarding the main street like sentries are three towers. On the east are the towers of the town hall (built in 1893) and the post office. On the west side is the tower of the Cardno Opera House, built in 1877. On the back streets are several 19th-century mansions, such as 99 Goderich Street West, built within the first half-decade of Seaforth's existence; 38 Louisa Street, at John, another of Seaforth's oldest homes; and 88 Goderich Street East, which dates from the 1860s and was built by Dr. T. Coleman, the village's first reeve.

Seaforth's most historic building can be seen on your way out of town. Drive south on Main Street, and after 1.5 km, you will come to the brick mansion that Constant Van Egmond built in 1846. Preserved and restored by the Van Egmond Foundation, it is open to the public during the summer.

South of it, County Road 3 (the old Bayfield Road) forks from County Road 12 and leads west toward the Lake Huron port of Bayfield, the oldest village on this trip, and the last.

Side Trip: From Seaforth, follow Highway 8 west to Clinton and then Highway 4 south to the signs for the "Clinton School Car." This refurbished passenger coach is that last surviving school car which brought education to the isolated railway communities in northern Ontario between 1928 and 1966.

Seaforth to Bayfield

Follow County Road 3 for 8 km across Huron County's flat clay plains. A stop sign marks Highway 4, and here you pass through the tiny village of Brucefield. Sadly, insensitive highway widening has removed many of Brucefield's early crossroads buildings. After a farther 6 km on County Road 3 you will come to another small crossroads hamlet, Varna. Here, an old general store and feed mill hug the intersection and carry on the hamlet's traditional role as a farm service village. A further 9 km brings you to the end of your trip, and to the remarkable village of Bayfield.

Bayfield

Through a gap in the high clay bluffs, the Bayfield River swirls into Lake Huron and forms a small but protected harbour. Bayfield is remarkable in many ways. It is one of Lake Huron's earliest communities, its streets radiate from a central park, and its tree-lined main street is one of the best preserved in the province.

Many Ontario villages were raw forest in 1836, when Bayfield was already a busy port, and settlers departed daily along the Bayfield Road to their lands in the interior. But the railways went elsewhere and, by the end of the century, Bayfield was in decline. Although a small fishing fleet and the productive farmlands of Bayfield's hinterland prevented it from becoming a ghost town, it was only when Lake Huron's shore became a popular recreation mecca that the town revived.

On Bayfield's outskirts, County Road 3 ends at Highway 21. Turn right here and drive 1 km to Clan Gregor Park, the main square where the streets converge. Turn left at the park and follow its perimeter to Main Street.

Bayfield is best enjoyed on foot. Its main street is a wide avenue two blocks long, where the stores and businesses occupy separate buildings cooled by large shade trees. As you walk north from the park the first building on the left is the Albion Hotel, which was built in 1840 and still provides food and drink. Across from the hotel, on the east side, is a trio of early buildings, including the Village Store (now a hair salon) and the Rogers House, built in 1834 and one of the town's oldest structures.

The Little Inn, built in 1847 and the street's most prominent structure, is surmounted by a cupola. Its wraparound porch has recently been

Bayfield's strollable main street.

reconstructed. Inside, the rooms have been refurbished in the style of the 19th century, including the licensed dining room.

From the north end of Louisa Street, Long Hill Road winds down the wall of the steep ravine that forms the harbour. At the end of the street are a parking lot and the beach. Although the beach is stony, it offers a pleasant view south along the steep shore bluffs of Lake Huron. At the marina the slender masts of the pleasure craft form a thick forest, while on the opposite side of the harbour you may see the few remaining tugs of the Bayfield fishing fleet. From the bluff atop the west end of Bayfield Terrace, enjoy the spectacular sunsets for which Lake Huron is famous.

If you are returning to central or eastern Ontario, retrace your steps to Seaforth and follow Highway 8 east, leading you to Kitchener and Highway 401. To reach the London area, return on County Road 3 to Brucefield and take Highway 4 south. For the Windsor area, take Highway 21 south from Bayfield.

Opposite: The Lake Huron shoreline at Bayfield.

6 The Bruce Peninsula Road

Winding beneath brooding limestone cliffs and past the remains of pioneer farms and lumber camps, this backroad probes what is probably Ontario's best-known backwater, the Bruce Peninsula. Starting in the town of Owen Sound, on Provincial Highway 10, it twists and bumps along 130 km of quiet old farm roads, climbing up the east side of the Bruce Peninsula and ending at a remote point of rock called Cabot Head.

If you are coming from Toronto, Kitchener or farther away, you may wish to consider spending the night. Owen Sound abounds in good motels and campgrounds, though there are few at the other end of the route. Wherever you stay, reserve ahead. During the summer, the morning ferry to Manitoulin Island from Tobermory is so popular that motels are usually full.

A long limestone finger, the Bruce Peninsula divides Lake Huron from Georgian Bay. On its eastern side, the high cliffs of the Niagara Escarpment plunge into Georgian Bay's clear waters. The west side of the peninsula is a marked contrast. Amid a shoreline of swampy coves, the limestone plain slips quietly beneath Lake Huron.

This is a trip for every outdoors person. For spelunkers and geologists, there are caves and the strange rock pillars known as flowerpots. Plant lovers can rummage around the swamps for the rare calypso orchid and other unusual flowers and plants, while hikers can clamber over some of the roughest portions of the famous Bruce Trail. And for divers, there is Ontario's only underwater park, Fathom Five National Marine Park, with its treasure trove of wrecks.

A typical waterfall along the Niagara Escarpment.

ettlement on the Bruce has always been sparse. Archaeologists claim that, despite a few small fur posts, the Native population was light. When the townships of the Bruce were surveyed into farm lots in the 1850s, the few settlers were more interested in selling the timber than in farming.

Sawmilling was the primary industry of the peninsula throughout its early years. At one time or another, most of the protected west coast coves housed a mill and a small community, but there were few settlements on the exposed shoreline of the east coast. Inland from the coasts, the bedrock and boulders discouraged the few pioneer farming communities that did start up, and today only two remain.

Tourists have now replaced the farmers and lumbermen; and campers, hikers, divers, nature lovers and cottagers flock to the peninsula.

Owen Sound to Wiarton

Owen Sound sits at the head of a deep bay bordered by the cliffs of the Niagara Escarpment. It contains a full range of shops, most of them downtown, on or near 16th Street, the street that the highway follows. Begin the route at a fitting site, the Marine Rail Heritage Centre on 1st Avenue West which is housed in a preserved CNR railway station on the west side of the harbour. Continue north on 1st Avenue West to 14th Street West and turn left. At 2nd Avenue West, turn right. It will become County Road 1.

At 6 km from the downtown core is the Indian Falls Conservation Area. In late spring and early summer, Indian Creek falls veil-like into a 20 metre gorge. An easy 1 km wooded walking trail follows the gorge to the falls. Unfortunately, unless the weather has been rainy, the river is usually dry by midsummer.

North of the falls, the route passes farms and

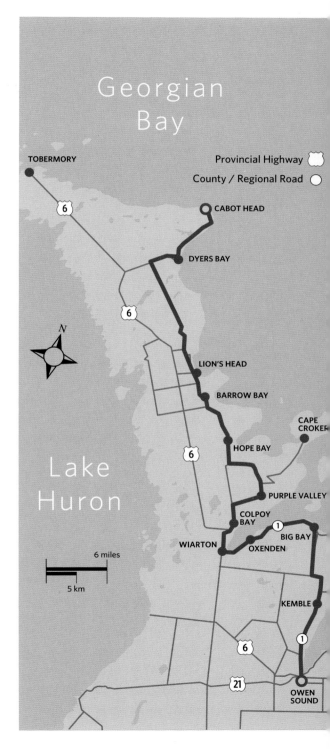

pastures. Small hamlets, which once catered to the needs of the local farmers, cluster about most crossroads. East Linton, 3 km from the park, still has its landmark, the 100-year-old brick United church just west of the intersection. Some 4 km farther on, at the next crossroads, the hamlet of Hogg contains a one-room schoolhouse, now a private residence. Here County Road 1 goes right, but instead you should continue north on Kemble Rock Road. Another 5 km bring you to the larger crossroads village of Kemble, where its historic brick church stands on the main corner.

In this area, the escarpment lies about 4 km from the water's edge. The road itself is about 1 km from the water, and the plain between is a fertile and prosperous farming area. From Kemble, drive north. After 2 km the road grinds up a wooded outlier of the Niagara Escarpment, where, to the right, the view extends across the waters of Owen Sound Bay. Continue 2 km, follow the road left for another 1 km, and turn right at Big Bay Road.

The view that greets you is sudden and panoramic. Here, at the brink of the cliffs, the ground drops to a flat pastoral plain that stretches 2 km to the blue waters of Colpoys Bay and its green, wooded islands. Extending out of sight on the horizon is the long, white cliff line of the Bruce Peninsula.

Drive down the hill and across the plain. On the shoreline sits the hamlet of North Keppel, shown on today's maps as "Big Bay." A former shipping village, it still contains a general store and several original houses. Here you rejoin County Road 1. Turn left and follow the shore road for 5 km. This road skirts the water, squeezing a string of cottages against the shore. Then, as the road swings inland, it climbs a shore cliff. Continue for a few metres and look for a small park and lookout, the Colpoy Lookout, where you can pause and enjoy the view across Colpoys Bay or have a picnic. Here, the

Owen Sound's Grand Trunk station is preserved as a museum.

escarpment consists of two bluffs—the 50 metre shore cliff in front of you and, behind you, Skinner Bluff. On the narrow plain, early settlers tried to farm. But the soil was shallow and rocky, and most farms failed. As you follow the plain, you can see the remains of these farms, though many of the houses are more modern.

Another 4 km from the little park, the road eases inland and up the second cliff to a yawning limestone cave. At the brow of the hill, watch for the sign to Bruce's Cave Conservation Area. There is neither a gate fee nor any facilities. But from the dirt parking lot you can follow the trail through the woods for half a kilometre to the cave. It has no passages but is a deep ballroom-like cavern in the rock wall, its opening divided by a high rock pillar. A second, smaller cave lies a few metres away.

From the conservation area, resume your route

Wiarton's Grand Trunk station has been moved to a waterside campground.

along County Road 1. After 1 km, you will cross a small bridge over a tumbling stream and enter the hamlet of Oxenden. There are two buildings of historic note here. One lies beside the stream and is the gristmill, built in 1866, when Oxenden was a busy landing and farm-service village. The mill is now covered with stucco and has been converted to a private dwelling. The other building of note is the village store at the northwest corner of the intersection. Although the store is no longer in business, it retains many of the century-old architectural features that typified the general store of a century ago.

Your next stop, Wiarton, lies 3 km farther along.

Wiarton

Wiarton offers a combination of heritage buildings and waterside recreation. Located at the head of Colpoys Bay and nestled beneath the cliffs of the escarpment, the town is a relative latecomer to southern Ontario's urban scene. It began around 1870 with the lucrative trade in lumber, and only ten years later had eight sawmills. When the railway arrived, not only did the fishing industry boom, but furniture factories became Wiarton's main industry. Meanwhile, the town's population swelled to more than 2,000. Today, sleek yachts have replaced the fishing tugs, and a campground and park have replaced the factories.

The road from Oxenden enters Wiarton from the east on Frank Street. Follow it to Highway 6 (Berford Street) and turn right. This is the main street and it takes you to the commercial core, where you will find a few small restaurants. If you need to replenish your picnic supplies, there are grocery and variety stores.

There are a few historic buildings in Wiarton that are worth a look. Among these are the two former hotels in the downtown area, which were built before the turn of the century. One is near William Street and the other at Boyd. Farther north, the three-storey stone feed mill, which supplied local farmers since 1903, has been renovated for commercial uses. At the campground, Bluewater Park, lies one of the town's most important heritage buildings, its 1904 railway station.

If you turn right past the feed mill and follow Division Street to its end, you come to the yacht basin and Wiarton's restored waterfront.

Leave Wiarton north on Highway 6 and take a detour into the Spirit Rock Conservation Area to see the shell of the "castle" Corran, home of Member of Parliament Alexander McNeill from 1881 to 1901. After 3 km, turn right onto County Road 9. This road soon descends the escarpment to the shore and enters the village of Colpoys Bay, an early sawmill village that predates Wiarton by two decades.

From Colpoys Bay, the route follows a network of pioneer concession roads that crisscross the flat, table-like top of the escarpment. Sometimes they swoop down to hug the shore; other times, they soar to the brink of the cliff, providing views of distant headlands and sparkling bays. Short side trips lead to caves, coves and quiet beaches.

Stay on County Road 9 as it swings inland from Colpoys Bay. Drive north for 4 km and then turn right onto Purple Valley Road. Continue for 5 km through a few pockets of pastureland and turn left. Here, you will come upon a small collection of buildings in the colourfully named Purple Valley, an important centre for early pioneers.

Continue north for another 5 km. The second road right from Purple Valley, McIver Road, leads to the Cape Croker Indian Reserve. With its campgrounds, village, historic lighthouse and one of the peninsula's oldest churches, it makes an interesting side trip.

To continue on your route, carry on north from McIver Road. The road bends left and soon reconnects with County Road 9. Turn right to Hope Bay. The side road from County Road 9 to Hope Bay is only 1 km long, but as it descends the escarpment it provides you with a picturesque vista over the bay, walled on both sides by limestone bluffs. A century ago, Hope Bay was a busy shipping centre for lumber, but today cottages have replaced the workers' homes on the narrow streets, and a public beach and campground have replaced the docks and the wood piles. At the beach, you can stretch your legs and have a picnic before resuming your trip.

Hope Bay to Lion's Head

From Hope Bay, continue north on County Road 9. This road, which runs as straight as the terrain permits, was surveyed as a farm road, part of a system of concession roads that enabled settlers to travel to their farm lots. But in this area, as through much of the Bruce, the soils were rocky and the farms short-lived. You will pass fields that are overgrown—many reclaimed entirely by the forest—and the gaunt shells of cabins and barns that peer from the bush.

About 4 km from the Hope Bay turnoff, watch for signs pointing to the Greig's Caves. A road on the right leads you 3 km to the site. The caves are a popular attraction on private property, and there is a charge for a tour. These caves were home to prehistoric cave dwellers in the movie *Quest for Fire*. Shortly after the movie was filmed, one unsuspecting stroller discovered, to his horror, a fur-clad body lying on the ground. Not until he learned that it was a discarded dummy used during a fight scene in the movie did he breathe a heavy sigh of relief.

From the Greig's Caves turnoff, County Road 9 twists northward through a rocky woodland for 2 km and suddenly emerges onto a wide plain. Originally a swamp, the Eastnor Plain was drained to produce the most prosperous farming community on the peninsula. It is now a treeless landscape of green fields, grazing cattle and blowing hay.

Most large farming areas have their mill towns, and here that is Barrow Bay. After travelling 1 km over the plain and across a bridge, you will see a pair of unusual old buildings on the left side of the road. The first one, a simple board-and-batten affair, is the former office of the Barrow Bay Lumber Company, and it dates back more than 100 years. Beside it is a general store. If you look downstream from the bridge, you will see a stone wall. This is all that remains of Barrow Bay's mill dam. The foundations of the mill (which burned in 1947) now support a modern cottage.

Continue north across the plain for a farther 4 km and you will come to Lion's Head, the largest town north of Wiarton on the peninsula.

Lion's Head

This town of 600, located on a small sheltered harbour, began as a centre for shipping and fishing. The prosperity of the farming community elevated it to a busy commercial centre at the turn of the century, and tourism has helped to keep it that way.

You enter the town on the main street, where there are shops, motels, restaurants and a bank. The municipal beach offers camping, picnicking, bathing and access to the Bruce Trail. Extending into the harbour is a long public wharf, from which you can see everything from luxury yachts to simple runabouts. Looming over the harbour, the great wall of the Niagara Escarpment reaches out to a craggy headland. Before it eroded, the rocky profile resembled the head of a lion, the feature that gave the village its name.

The historic Cabot Head lighthouse is now a museum.

Lion's Head to Cabot Head

This last section of the route traces little-used concession roads through some of the emptiest parts of the peninsula and then follows a rocky shoreline beneath looming limestone cliffs to a remote headland.

Leave Lion's Head by driving north on the main street, which before long swerves down to the water and to the wide expanse of Whippoorwill Bay. During the next 2 km, after passing a string of cottages, you will find several opportunities to pull over to the roadside. Wander along the rocky shore or cast a line into the surf. From the northern head of the bay, the road bends inland where you follow the Forty Hills Road north. This rugged limestone ridge continues to defy road-building and forces the gravel road to snake precariously around each outcropping. The bends are sharp, there is no winter maintenance.

After 3 km, the road emerges from the hills into the one-time farming community of Cape Chin.

Most of the farms have been abandoned, leaving behind the ruins of their log cabins.

At the next intersection, continue straight ahead and, a kilometre later, look for a stone church standing alone in an empty field. This is the widely known and much-photographed St. Margaret's Chapel, which was completed in 1930. It took three years to finish and was a community effort. The area's determined farmers hauled stone from the fields and little quarries to erect the solid church. The stained-glass windows were donated by a factory in London, Ontario, and the oak pews from a local parishioner. The bell came from a Canadian Northern Railway steam locomotive.

North of the church, the road bends sharply right. Keep left on East Road. For the next 9 km, follow another old concession road through swamps and around rock outcrops. A few pioneers tried to carve out farms here, but the overgrown fields and derelict barns testify to the futility of their efforts. After 10 km, the road ends abruptly at a T intersection at Brinkman's Corners with the Dyers Bay Road. Turn right and travel 4 km to another T intersection. Turn right again and descend the hill into the little waterside village of Dyers Bay—and to a vista that you will be unlikely to forget.

Once a thriving lumber town, Dyers Bay now consists of a store, a restaurant and a string of cottages. Here you start the last and most scenic portion of the route. From the village, the road winds along the narrow beach 10 km to Cabot Head. After 3 km the cottages begin to thin out, until there is just no more room at the base of the huge cliff.

Roughly 2.5 km from the last cottage, the road crosses a small culvert. If you are a hiker, stop here and explore the remains of one of Ontario's more ingenious sawmill efforts. In 1881 Horace and Robert Lymburner acquired rights to the timber that covered the mesa atop the bluffs. There, Gillies Lake empties down a cascading stream into Georgian Bay, 100 metres below. Down on the beach, where tugs could haul the lumber off to the south shore and the railways, the Lymburners built a mill and a town. At first the logs were simply hurled down the cliff into a small pond on the beach. But the damage to the logs was so enormous that the Lymburners decided to build a log slide. By damming the outlet from Gillies Lake and periodically allowing great gushes of water and rock to plummet down the steep gully, erosion soon carved a natural flume, which was then lined with planks. But by 1905 the timber was gone and the Lymburner mill fell silent.

From the mill site, a drive of 5 km brings you to Cabot Head, one of the most placid points of land in Ontario. Here, at the northeasterly point of the peninsula, a lonely lighthouse is the sole remaining building of what was once a bustling sawmilling and fishing village. Dating from 1896, the restored wooden light tower and keeper's dwelling is now a museum. Here, too, you will find Wingfield Basin, a former port but now a wildlife area with a board-walk and the hull of a wrecked ship.

This is the end of the road. Here, the escarp-ment changes direction and runs westward in a wild, rocky and unsettled shoreline. By following Dyers Bay Road back out to Highway 6, you can drive north to Tobermory, home of the *MS Chi-Cheemaun* (the car ferry to Manitoulin Island), boat tours to remarkable Flowerpot Island, and Fathom Five National Marine Park. Highway 6 south returns you to Wiarton.

Opposite: Flowerpot Island.

7 Cuestas and Valleys

The Hockley Valley is one of many beautiful valleys in this region.

This route guides you through the valleys and to breathtaking vistas of Ontario's most unusual and scenic geological feature, the Niagara Escarpment. The route begins at Orangeville, 60 km northwest of Toronto, and for 80 km it follows backroads northward over old concession roads, plunges into wide valleys and soars onto rocky cuestas. (A cuesta is a long, low ridge with a gentle slope on one side and a steep cliff on the other.) It ends in the Beaver Valley, one of the province's most beautiful valleys.

With its windswept lookouts, pastoral lowlands and tumbling streams, this trail will appeal to the recreational driver. The hiker can gain access to the Bruce Trail at several points, and the aficionado of Ontario's rural vernacular architecture will discover outstanding 19th-century farm homes, churches, schools and even Orange lodges.

The villages along the route are small and few contain gas stations or restaurants, so you would be advised to stock up at Orangeville before starting out.

Before 1850 the area between Orangeville and Georgian Bay was still a land of silent pine forests. The lack of roads and navigable rivers held settlement at bay. However, a few hardy settlers forged their own trails, and by 1830 they had built sawmills on the tumbling brooks. But these were the exception, and it was not until 1850 that three roads finally breached the wilderness: Hurontario Street, from Port Credit on Lake Ontario to Collingwood on Georgian Bay; the Mail Road, from Barrie on Lake Simcoe to Meaford on Georgian Bay; and the Garafraxa Road, Ontario's first colonization road, from Shelburne to Owen Sound.

Once the roads were open, settlement took off. By 1860 all the townships had been surveyed and marked for concession roads and farm lots. Land-hungry settlers quickly gobbled up the lots and cut away the forest. Along the rivers and streams, mill sites grew into towns that provided basic services for area farmers.

Then the growth slowed. Although the 1870s and 1880s were the years of Ontario's railway boom, the railway builders found the escarpment to be an insurmountable obstacle. There was another difficulty, too. Many farmers moved away, discouraged by the steep, stony soils of the river valleys.

During the past decades, a new wave of development has swept over the crest of the escarpment. As sprawl has spread outward from Ontario's urban areas, and as better roads increased commuting distances, wealthy commuters grabbed scenic escarpment land for their country houses. Before this boom, gentlemen's agreements between the farmer-owners and the Bruce Trail Association had allowed the hiking to follow the escarpment crest from Tobermory to Queenston. But when city dwellers bought country lots from the original farm owners, many did not respect the agreements and hikers were rerouted onto dusty roads. The

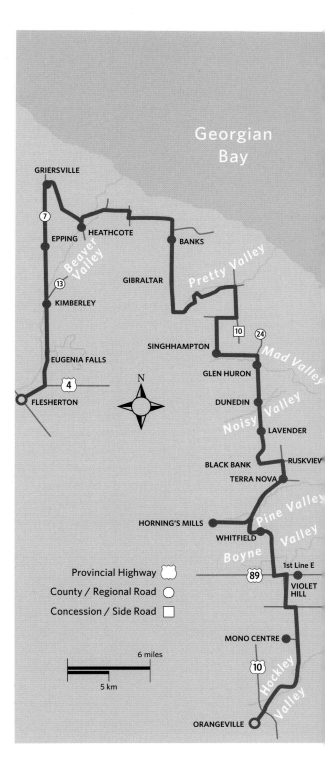

Ontario government then established the Niagara Escarpment Commission to protect the natural environment and to guarantee Bruce Trail hikers the best possible route. Yet the situation has a long way to go, and the escarpment landscape continues to fall to development.

Hockley Valley

Orangeville, the starting point of this trip, lies at the junction of Highways 9 and 10. Take some time in Orangeville to stroll its historic Broadway Avenue or amble down its side streets and gaze at the many "Tree Spirits" carved into the stumps of its old maple trees.

From Orangeville, follow Highway 10 north to the Hockley Road and turn right. The Hockley Valley is the southernmost of the great gorges you will pass through on the route. Measuring 15 km from head to mouth, it is one of the deeper valleys of the trip. Its beauty lies in tumbling streams and gently forested slopes.

The Hockley Road follows an ancient aboriginal trail, one used by the early settlers to reach their new farm lots. Today, the road is paved and heavily used, and it enters where the valley is a mere gully. As the valley widens and deepens, woodlands of maple and oak cling to the hillsides. On the valley floor a small creek called the Nottawasaga River begins its 100 km journey to Georgian Bay.

Five km from Highway 10, turn left onto the 3rd Line East. You will quickly cross the busy brook shaded by cedar forests. From the river the road twists and struggles up the steep valley side. After 1.8 km, it emerges onto the crest, and suddenly to your right is a panoramic vista. The view extends south across the wide forested valley and west toward the head. A few metres beyond, the road straightens out.

Mono Hills

"Mono" comes from the Scottish *monach*, meaning "hill," and that is what you will find along this section of the route. Within 3 km the escarpment falls away to the east, into a tumble of foothills, and then levels out into the farmlands. About 5 km from the lookout, the escarpment fractures into mesas or outliers, separated by a wide, shady gulch into which the road suddenly plunges.

At the 5.7 km mark you will meet County Road 8, the Mono Centre Road. For a short side trip, you can turn left and drive into the little village of Mono Centre. A former mill village, it lies nestled beneath the rim of a limestone mesa. With its former general store, the Burns United Church built in 1837, and a collection of 19th-century homes, it is a quiet shadow of its busy days. To return to your route, retrace County Road 8. After it bends left, look again for the 3rd Line East and turn left.

The next stretch of road passes the Mono Cliffs Provincial Park on the right and a wooded ridge on the left. After 4 km, you will come to the 25th Sideroad. Turn left here and drive for 2 km as the road winds up a gully between two rock mesas. Look for the next fork in the road, the 2nd Line, and follow it right. Here, about 1 km from the lip of the escarpment, your route passes a land of wealthy country estates. Then, after 2 more km, the road descends into the historic Sheldon Creek Valley.

Continue to the stop sign at Highway 89. A short drive to the right leads to Violet Hill, a little hamlet with preserved buildings that are well worth the side trip. Look for "Mrs. Mitchell's" and "Granny Taught Us How." The latter was an Orange Lodge built in 1898 and renovated into a craft shop. The former was the village school built in 1889 and is now a popular restaurant named after the last of its teachers.

Boyne River Valley

From Violet Hill retrace your steps west on Highway 89 for 2 km to the 1st Line East and turn right. You will soon begin to descend the wooded valley of the Boyne River. Although the river is just a trickle at this point, the valley floor is wide and swampy.

From the lip of the valley continue north for 3 km. Here, the terrain becomes level and the farms prosperous. Turn left at County Road 17. After 1.5 km, at the northwest corner of Centre Road, you will see a red church, Christ Church, built in the 1850s. It is all that remains of the once-bustling village of Whitfield. At its peak in the late 1880s, Whitfield contained stores, a blacksmith's shop and several homes.

Pine River Valley

Drive west from Whitfield and then turn right at Prince of Wales Road. Continue down a forested gully and into the valley of the Pine River, one of the widest and deepest on the trip. From the stop sign at River Road you can turn left and drive to the historic settlement of Horning's Mills. Today's 150 residents are fewer than half the number who lived here a hundred years ago, and the town's businesses have diminished from two dozen to a mere handful. The settlement began in the 1830s, when Lewis Horning opened a sawmill and, later, a gristmill. But the disappearance of the forest and advent of the railways that bypassed Horning's Mills doomed the village, and it suffered a decline from which it never recovered.

Return down the valley to the intersection with historic Hurontario Street (Centre Road), where you will pass the site of the former mill village of Kilgorie. After the road crosses the river, continue for 5 km and enter the hamlet of Terra Nova, another once busy mill town and now primarily a residential community. At the main intersection,

A classic view across Ontario's fertile Beaver Valley.

turn north onto 2nd Line East. Soon the road begins a long, steep climb from the valley, and after 3 km it reaches the crest of the north wall, providing the most extensive vista of the trip. Stop the car and enjoy the view. Below you, the homes of Terra Nova are tiny specks; 5 km away are the forested slopes of the south valley wall. At the intersection, the former general store (now a residence) marks the site of the ghost hamlet of Ruskview.

From the crossroad, drive west on County Road 21. After 2 km the road descends into the Black Bank Valley, a fissure in the bedrock that extends from the Pine Valley north to the Pretty River Valley. At the bottom of the little valley is the site of the former mill village of Black Bank.

As the road grinds up out of the valley, watch for a hidden intersection and then turn right onto Centre Road. Here, on the surviving northern portion of Hurontario Street, you will emerge onto a high, rolling plateau where healthy farms and cornfields stretch away on both sides. At 4 km from the intersection you will come to a hamlet

The quiet crossroad hamlet of Lavender was a busy village in pioneer times.

with the delightful name of Lavender. Although small, Lavender played an important role as a farm-service village and a stopping place on Hurontario Street. The former hotel on the northwest corner is now a private residence, as is the former store on the northeast corner.

Noisy River Valley

As you continue north for the next 1.5 km, the valley of the Noisy River reveals itself. From the lip, Hurontario Street winds to the valley bottom and enters the village of Dunedin. Here, where Hurontario Street crossed the Noisy River, Judah Baverman built the area's first sawmill, which became the focus for a busy village. Today, its population has shrunk to about 100 and its traditional businesses have vanished. A few of the old buildings still survive, mixing with newer houses. Halfway along the main street, at the stop sign, Simcoe County Road 9, an early settlement road known as the River Road merges in from the left. Turn right at the stop sign and drive to County

Road 18 and turn left onto the continuation of Hurontario Street, and follow it out of the valley.

North of Dunedin you will drive over rolling hills, where many of the original farms have been replaced by hobby farms and country estates, and after 3.5 km you will enter the Mad River Valley.

Mad River Valley

After 7 km, as the road descends into the valley of the Mad River, the first views of Georgian Bay appear far to the right. On the banks of the Mad River is the bustling modern mill village of Glen Huron, a village that today survives on its mills, as it has for 150 years. James Cooper built the valley's first mills in the 1840s, but he had already departed when the Hamilton brothers opened their gristmill in 1874. Hamilton's mill and company store operate to this day and continue a tradition that is as old as settlement in Ontario.

Pass the mill and drive up the hill out of the village. Continue for about 1.5 km to a stop sign at Highway 124. Turn left along the highway, and, after 2 km, you come to Devil's Glen Provincial Park. Perched on the side of the Mad Valley, which here is a narrow gorge, this park offers hiking, a viewing platform and access to the Bruce Trail.

Continue westward on Highway 124 for another 3.5 km to the mill village of Singhampton. Near the main intersection sits the popular Mylar and Loreta's Restaurant, a restored 19th-century hotel. It was built in 1865, as the Exchange Hotel, to provide room and board for stagecoach travellers. Not only has the attractive red-and-yellow brick exterior been cleaned, but the interior has been restored to a 19th-century style.

Pretty River Valley

From Singhampton's main intersection, drive north up County Road 31. After 5 km, turn right and drive another 2 km to the Nottawasaga 10th Concession. Turn left and follow the 10th for 6 km to Sideroad 33–34 and turn left again. Here is where it becomes the Pretty Valley Road, a looming rock wall hides the entrance to the valley. However, as you proceed west, the walls part and the road passes through a narrow defile into a wide pastoral valley. Surrounded by high, wooded hills, this is the aptly named Pretty Valley, nearly circular and about 3 km in diameter. More than a dozen farms are nestled on its floor, protected from the raging winds that can howl over the plateau above.

The scenic road winds through pastures and woods to the head of the valley, where it again seems blocked by a wall of rock. Stay on Pretty River Road for about 10 km and look for a narrow road that forks to the right. This is Reids Hill Road. Follow this road up the steep valley. As the valley drops away behind you, you emerge onto a high plateau known as the "Roof of Ontario"—southern Ontario's highest point of land.

The Roof of Ontario

From the wide expanse of Georgian Bay to the north, the winds sweep unhindered over this tabletop of land, bringing fierce storms in both winter and summer. And, from the lofty summits, you can gaze over the most extensive vistas in southern Ontario.

Just after you surmount the crest from the Pretty River Valley you will come to a stop sign at the 4th Line. Turn right. Along this stretch of road is a land of fractured rocks and abandoned farms. Drive 10 km to a crossroads and a hamlet called Banks. Turn right here, follow the road for 2 km as it descends a small cliff, and 1 km farther on you will come to the highest lookout in southern Ontario. Long ignored by local politicians and the Niagara Escarpment Commission, this lookout now has two parking areas and trails from which to view a patchwork of fields and, beyond them, the streets and port of Collingwood. As a backdrop there are the blue waters of Georgian Bay, its shoreline curving gently until it disappears on the horizon.

Before continuing your road trip, you may wish to explore southern Ontario's most extensive cave system. Privately owned, as they have been since 1934, the Scenic Caves are located another kilometre along the road you have been following. In these caves, linked by ladders and bridges, lie more than a half-dozen chambers bearing such descriptive names as Fat Man's Misery and the Ice Cave, where ice persists even during the summer. A tree canopy walk and zip line are recent additions to this popular attraction

Still pastoral, despite attempts to develop it, the Beaver Valley offers the best scenery on this backroad.

Old buildings have found new uses in the historic hamlet of Heathcote.

The Beaver Valley

To resume your journey, retrace your route to Banks. Turn right and again follow the 4th Line. This, the last segment of the trip, takes you into what many consider to be the most beautiful of Ontario's valleys, the Beaver Valley. Certainly it is one of the widest and highest, with grand views extending from its rocky walls and a rushing river winding across its wooded floor. Protected by its walls and moderated by the waters of nearby Georgian Bay, the valley's singular microclimate has produced extensive lush orchards that grow the now famous Northern Spy apple.

From Banks, the road continues north for 2.5 km and then bends sharply west to become Sideroad 21, following the escarpment. After another 1 km, a panorama of the Beaver Valley unfolds before you. Here, at its mouth, the valley is wide and gentle, quilted with orchards and pastures; 7 km away is the floor of the valley, and 11 km away the western wall. There is no single place here that can be called a lookout; rather, this is a vista that changes as you ease down the valley slope.

Here, you will pass rolling apple orchards—some of the trees old and gnarled, others young and spindly, but all in neat rows. Turn right at the 10th Line. This road will take you through more shady orchards to a stop sign at the 24th Sideroad. Continue straight ahead to the stop sign at County Road 13. This is the Beaver Valley Road, which runs the length of the valley. Turn left here and travel 2 km into the village of Heathcote.

This quiet residential community with three hotels and several businesses was once an

Opposite: Eugenia Falls slow to a trickle in the summer.

A strange-looking arch hidden in the forest at Eugenia Falls was a failed attempt at a hydro-electric power plant.

important stopping place on the Mail Road. You can still locate reminders of those busy days—an old church, a former Orange Lodge, and a carriage shop that now is an antique store.

From the main street of Heathcote, return north along County Road 13 for 0.3 km and turn left. This is the Old Mail Road, along which, during the 1840s, settlers trekked from Barrie to the newly opened lands of the valley and to the townships farther west. However, once the concession roads were opened, the Mail Road fell into disuse. The short section from Heathcote to Griersville is the only portion to survive.

From the turn, the road rises for 1 km to the Heathcote Lookout, where a historical plaque commemorates the road. From the lookout continue west for 0.3 km and fork right. For 7 km the road twists past cornfields, woodlots and the

farmsteads of early settlers, until it stops at Grey County Road 7 and the hamlet of Griersville. Turn left at Griersville and drive 8 km to the Epping Lookout.

One of the valley's best-developed lookouts, it provides the valley's most panoramic view. It is managed by the Conservation Authority and its extensive grounds include picnic tables and washrooms.

From the park, turn left onto County Road 7 and continue down the slope. Only a few metres away, at the first crossroads, is the former Mount Hope Methodist Church, which has stood here since 1887 and marks the site of the vanished hamlet of Epping. The road then descends steadily in a straight line down the valley wall until, after 7 km, it reaches the floor and tumbling Beaver River. A popular recreational canoe route, the river is also the scene of the zany River Rat Race. Each spring a flotilla of offbeat craft (anything but boats are allowed) bounce their way downstream, their navigators outlandishly attired.

The valley narrows here and its walls steepen to form a gorge and to provide some of Ontario's more popular ski slopes. In the valley bottom, County Road 7 stops at County Road 13. Here, a high, rocky cliff known locally as Mount Baldy looms above you. Turn right onto County Road 13 and you will shortly enter the former mill village of Kimberley, which still has many of its historic buildings and now caters to skiers. Even the old board-and-batten mill has become an antique shop.

Drive south from Kimberley on County Road 13. As the road climbs back up the east wall, the valley narrows until it is only 1 km wide, its walls almost sheer. After 2 km, a small viewpoint on the right offers you a last view down the valley before you leave it.

Eugenia Falls

About 6 km from Kimberley you enter the hamlet of Eugenia Falls, where small signs direct you to the Eugenia Falls Conservation Area. Here, again, the local conservation authority has been at work. Covering 23 hectares, this wooded park offers picnicking, hiking and a view of the 30-metre-high Eugenia Falls. You can see the gorge carved by the creek, and, on the opposite bank above the falls, a strange-looking limestone arch looking out of place in the hillside. This is the vestige of a failed attempt to create a power dam; the arch was to be the entrance to the underground flume. The gorge was the site of a "gold" rush in the 1850s, which prompted surveyors to lay out an extensive network of streets, anticipating a golden boomtown. But the "gold" turned out to be nothing more than iron pyrite, or "fool's gold," and the streets remained largely undeveloped. Now the lots are sprouting newer country homes.

This is a fitting place to end your tour of the escarpment, a location where one of the cuesta's features has been preserved for the public. It lends hope that this unique and attractive prehistoric ridge can be preserved for future generations and protected from insensitive development.

About 4 km from Eugenia Falls, County Road 13 ends at County Road 4, from which point Flesherton on Highway 10 lies about 4 km west.

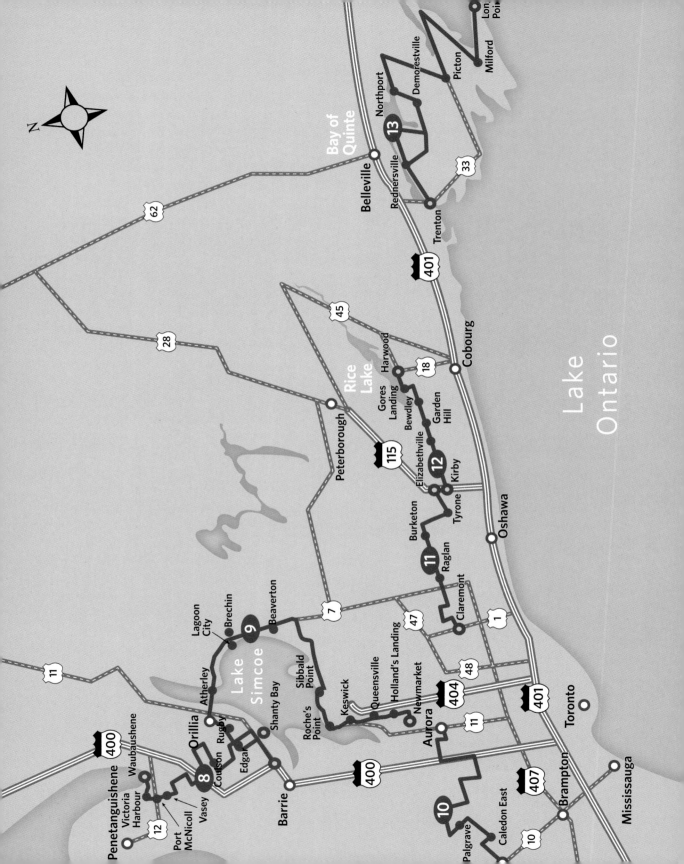

Section 2
Central Ontario

ROUTE 8 Those Surprising Simcoe County Highlands   80

ROUTE 9 The Lake Simcoe Steeple Chase   88

ROUTE 10 The Ridge Road West   96

ROUTE 11 The Ridge Road East   102

ROUTE 12 The Rice Lake Road   110

ROUTE 13 The Quinte Shore Road   118

8 Those Surprising Simcoe County Highlands

Carley Station was once a busy station village on the Canadian Pacific Railway.

Next time you venture north to Muskoka's cottage country, try and spend some time exploring the little-known yet often spectacular hill country of Simcoe County. This trip starts in the historic waterside mill town of Waubaushene on Highway 12 and zigzags south over 70 km of gravel concession roads through Simcoe's hills. Many of the views along the route are just as spectacular as those of the more famous Ottawa Valley or the Niagara Escarpment.

Summer offers bass and trout fishing in Georgian Bay at the north end of the route and in Lake Simcoe at the south end. The fall season brings out some of Ontario's best colours in the maple forests that shelter the winding roads. For admirers of country architecture, there are farmhouses of stone, brick and wood. And the forests and closed concession roads offer ideal hiking and skiing trails.

Simcoe County's first roads were military. During the War of 1812, two supply roads were built to move troops and equipment to the forts that guarded northern Lake Huron. The first was the Nine Mile Portage, a wagon road that linked Lake Simcoe with Willow Creek, a tributary flowing to Georgian Bay. The second was the Penetanguishene Road, which barged straight northward from a townsite called Kempenfeldt, also on Lake Simcoe, to the garrisons at Penetanguishene on Georgian Bay. Today the Penetanguishene Road has become Highway 93, and the Nine Mile Portage has vanished.

Following the War of 1812, the Penetanguishene Road was surveyed into farm lots, which were offered free to half-pay veterans of the war. After 1830 more settlers arrived to take up land in the back townships. A mixed group, they included Germans, Irish, Scots and fugitive American slaves, whose simple frame church still stands. Then, during the 1850s and 1860s, railways pierced the area and brought a new wave of growth, especially to the little ports that ringed the bay. A half-dozen ports soon boomed into busy sawmill towns. But when the roar of the mills and the puffing of the trains faded, so did most of the towns. Meanwhile, on the hillsides, many farmers found the steep, stony lands awkward and unproductive, and they moved away. In recent years, both areas have revived through tourism—the mill towns because of the popularity of Georgian Bay's waters and shores, and the hills for downhill skiing.

Waubaushene to Victoria Harbour

Beside the turnoff from Highway 400 onto Highway 12 sits what in 1860 was the largest of the mill towns, Waubaushene. Its industries and businesses, and many of its workers' cabins, have now vanished, and several new homes can be seen on the network of streets that overlook Georgian Bay.

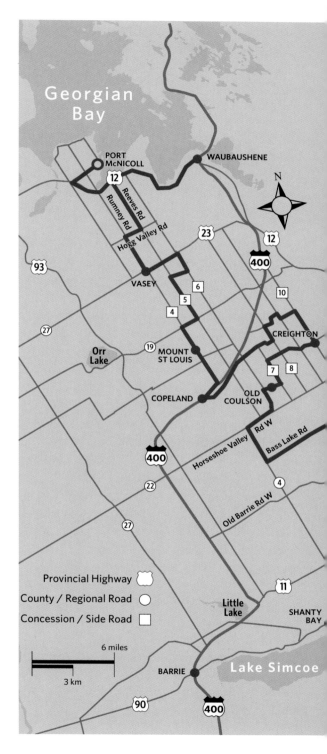

Georgian Bay

PORT McNICOLL

WAUBAUSHENE

12

N

Reeves Rd

Rumney Rd

Hogg Valley Rd

23

12

400

93

VASEY

6

5

4

10

27

Orr Lake

19 MOUNT ST LOUIS

CREIGHTON

7 8

COPELAND

OLD COULSON

Horseshoe Valley Rd W

Bass Lake Rd

400

22

4

Old Barrie Rd W

27

11

Provincial Highway

County / Regional Road

Concession / Side Road

Little Lake

SHANTY BAY

6 miles

3 km

BARRIE

Lake Simcoe

90

400

But a few reminders of the mill days linger on.

If you wish to look around Waubaushene, turn right at the directional arrow on Highway 12 and follow Pine Street up the hill. At the crest was once the commercial core, where Waubaushene Heritage and Maddison's Garden Centre occupy early buildings. As you continue along Pine Street, the red brick St. John's Roman Catholic Church comes into view. Continue down the hill to Hazel Street and turn right. On your left are Georgian Bay's waters and the board-and-batten gothic Memorial Church with its slender white steeple. The road bends to the right, where Government Dock Road leads to the shoreline before curving back to the Coldwater Road. Turn left here and you will find access to the Tay Shore Trail, which follows the scenic shoreline almost into Midland.

To continue your trip, follow Highway 12 for 8 km west of Waubaushene and look for the directions into the village of Victoria Harbour. To reach the historic centre, follow Park Street to Richard Street and keep left to Albert Street, where you turn right to reach William Street. This intersection marks the main part of town. To the north, newer development marks the harbour—once the site of the busy King and Fowlie mills.

Although the place is much smaller than it was then, it has retained many early features. Several of the commercial buildings and the post office at the main intersection date from the milling era. Look particularly at the facade of the restored wooden building on the northwest corner. Extending west on William Street for more than 2 km are similar two-storey houses once occupied by the mill workers. Most of these buildings have been renovated or are hidden beneath layers of aluminum siding.

Victoria Harbour to Vasey

William Street rejoins Highway 12. Follow the highway west to Triple Bay Road and drive to Port McNicoll and the new home of the historic CPR steamship the *SS Keewatin*. From Port McNicoll return to Highway 12. Go back east to Reeves Road (Tay Concession 5) and turn right. After 1.5 km you will see a historical marker pointing left down a side road to the site of St. Louis. Near this spot in 1649, the invading Iroquois tortured to death two Jesuits, Jean de Brébeuf, and Gabriel Lalemant. The Iroquois went on to sweep the Hurons and the Jesuits from Simcoe County and to become kings of the fur trade. This site, open only during the summer, is a memorial to the Jesuit martyrs.

Continue south on Reeves Road and be sure to keep your camera handy, for here the road climbs out of the valley of Hogg Creek and onto a high ridge. As you reach the summit, turn right onto Hogg Valley Road. After 1 km this road takes you back to the crest, and suddenly a vista of pastoral serenity unfolds at your feet, revealing in the flat valley a quiltwork of traditional farms.

Considering the size of the valley, the creek that meanders across its floor is surprisingly small. Most geologists believe that this little stream did not carve the valley by itself, but, rather, that it flows through a wide swath gouged out of the earth by glacial meltwaters 30,000 years ago. Because the valley runs at a 45-degree angle to the grid pattern of the roads, you must make one more zig into the valley before you zag back out of it.

Turn left onto Rumney Road, Concession 4, as soon as you reach the bottom of the valley, and grind up another steep grade for more than 1 km. At the crest you will emerge onto a wide, level agricultural plateau, the summit of one of the north Simcoe mesas, and a further 2 km will bring you to the hamlet of Vasey.

Once a busy farmers' town, Vasey contained all

The *SS Keewatin* has come home to Port McNicoll.

the services that the 19th-century farmer could want—a church, a school, a store, a blacksmith and an Orange Lodge. Later, with road improvements and the advent of fast cars, residents began to venture farther afield to shop, and Vasey became a quiet residential hamlet. Although the blacksmith's shop and Orange Lodge have disappeared, the red brick church still sees use.

Vasey to Copeland Forest

Drive east from Vasey for 2.7 km and turn right onto Newton Street (6th Line). After 2 km you will see the yawning valley of the Sturgeon River, which is even deeper and wider than the valley of the Hogg River. Its walls rise steeply, 100 metres from a flat valley floor that is nearly 2 km across.

The road you should follow turns right. Do not take the abandoned concession road that leads straight ahead. In laying out their roads, the early British army surveyors ignored the topography, and settlers often faced roads that ran into lakes or halted abruptly at cliffs. Although this road did once follow the survey line straight down the near-cliff of the valley wall, it soon proved useless and was abandoned. You should therefore turn west and follow the side road for 1.3 km to the next usable road, Line 5. Turn left and drive down a far gentler slope into the valley. The valley floor is wider here, and once more the river is a mere creek.

About 1 km from the creek, you will begin to leave the valley. The south walls may loom higher than the north, but its grade is gentler. As you reach the summit, you will be rewarded with wide views across the valley below. Turn right at the first intersection, which is Moonstone Road (County

Pioneers needed to move huge stones from their fields before they could farm the land.

Road 19) and descend the valley again until you reach still another crossroads, Line 4. Turn left here, leave the valley and climb the next ridge. More extensive views appear on the right. After 1 km, the road mounts the crest of the plateau and traverses a gentle landscape of pastures and farms with traditional farmhouses and barns.

A little more than 2 km from the crest, the road enters the quiet and historic hamlet of Mount St. Louis. Although it never had more than a school, a church, a hotel and a tavern, Mount St. Louis was a busy spot in pioneer times. The school and church still stand, though they no longer enjoy their original uses. Newer homes line the road beside them.

Mount St. Louis marks the intersection of two crossroads, but it was once noted for a more famous road that bisected the hamlet. This was the Gloucester Road, which bustled with traffic for a few years and then was abandoned. In the 1830s, the Gloucester Road guided pioneers from the Penetanguishene Road over the hills and through dark forests to Coldwater, 20 km east. Then, when the concession roads were opened, the old Gloucester Road was forgotten and left to the weeds and trees. If you look behind the homes on the northeast corner of the intersection, you will see a double line of maples marching at an angle across overgrown fields. They once shaded the Gloucester Road, and they are the only physical indication that the road ever existed.

South of Mount St. Louis you will begin to descend into the next valley, that of the Coldwater River. It is a two-stepped descent. From the lip of the first slope, you will garner your first glimpse of the Sand Hills. Steep and forested, they form a dark wavering line on the horizon and mark the south wall of the valley. At the floor of the first step, the terrain flattens out. About 1 km from Mount St. Louis, look on the right for a huge stone farmhouse. This massive building was constructed with stones gathered from the nearby fields and laboriously pieced together. It is one of the few such buildings to survive in Simcoe County.

Continuing along the road, you now begin to descend the second and last slope into the Coldwater River Valley. Before you lies the vast lowland of spruce and maple that was once the private forest from which Charles Copeland supplied his mills. In 1907 Jasper Martin had built a mill beside the newly constructed CPR line, and, to accommodate his 80 workers, he added the company town he called Martinville. Charles Copeland bought the operation in 1922 and his family continued operations until 1975, when fire destroyed the mill. So ended what was southern Ontario's last company mill town. Ontario's Ministry of Natural Resources took over the extensive tract and turned it into a forest management area.

As the road eases down the slope it crosses a bridge over the busy Highway 400 and stops at a T

Despite new growth, the historic intersection of Victoria Harbour retains its heritage buildings.

intersection. Parking for the Copeland Forest trails lies a few metres to the left.

Copeland Forest to the Sand Hills

From the Copeland Forest, your route follows the Ingram Road east to a stop sign that marks the intersection with Medonte Line 6. Here you can embark on a circle route through a farming community that has retained the houses, the barns and the traditions of the generations that preceded it.

Continue through the intersection and cross a small bridge over the Coldwater River, which again is only a trickle and could never have carved the wide valley through which it wanders. Nestled beside the river are rolling fields, white houses and red barns. Continue for 3 km to a T intersection and turn left; then follow the road for about 1.3 km

to Mount St. Louis Road, and turn right. Here the road winds past more rolling fields and farms. After 2 km turn right at a T intersection (Line 6), drive another half kilometre and continue on Mount St. Louis Road to the left. At the next crossroads, Line 10, 1.6 km farther on, turn right again.

The road now climbs steeply from the valley of the Coldwater River, offering views on the right which span the breadth of the valley. You'll see farms and forests, with the north valley wall looming up behind them. For 3 km the road traverses the plateau above the valley. Fences of cedar logs and mighty boulders show how the wily pioneers used the materials they had at hand. These boulders—some as tall as the men who struggled to move them—were the bane of the early ploughmen.

The road descends from the mesa into a little

The Sand Hills of Simcoe enclose a few pockets of good farmland.

gully, and here you will find the tiny hamlet of Creighton. This hamlet once had a store, a post office, a blacksmith's shop, and a couple of mills, but today only two houses remain, both of them made of brick and both standing at the crossroads. They have been altered little and are attractive survivors of agriculture's heyday in the closing years of the 19th century.

Turn right at the crossroads, Warminister Sideroad, and follow the gulch as it opens into the wide Coldwater River Valley. The views once more are grand. Back on the valley floor, your route takes you straight ahead through the next intersection and across an area of flat bottom lands that

are now luxuriant fields. Look on the right for the stone Carley School, with its bell tower still intact. Dating from the turn of the century, the school is still used as a community centre. At the next crossroads, you will see the former Carley store and an old home. Continue straight on until, after 1 km, you come to a railway crossing and a handful of old houses. This was once a busy railway settlement named Carley Station.

Travel on to the next intersection with the 7th Line and turn left. After 2 km, look for Mill Pond Road and turn right. This road leads into another of those little gulches that cross the valley floor. This one, however, had enough water power to fuel the little mill village of Coulson. It is still a pretty spot, and a few of the old village residences have been converted to modern houses. The road winds on through pasture lands, ending at Medonte Concession Road 6 (Line 6), where steep wooded slopes loom on the left. These are the foothills of the great Sand Hills. Turn left and continue until you come to County Road 22.

The Sand Hills

The Sand Hills were formed during the last ice age, when the retreating ice sheets halted and the raging meltwaters pushed sand, stones and boulders into great mounds. On this rugged ridge, early settlers purchased farm lots sight unseen. It was a decision most regretted, for the hills proved too steep and the sands too dry and bouldery for even the crudest farming. Most settlers left in disgust, and today the Sand Hills have reverted to forest.

Concession Road 6 ends at County Road 22. Turn right here and follow this paved road for 1 km to Oro Concession Road 5. Then turn left. This rugged road is not maintained and should be avoided during winter and early spring. In the heart of the Sand Hills, the forests part at intervals to reveal abandoned fields and overgrown foundations—reminders of the backbreaking attempts to wrest crops from this unyielding area. (If Concession 5 is unusable, go to Concession 4, farther west, as an alternative.)

After 3 km, the road intersects the Bass Lake Road. Turn left. This road is maintained and is passable year-round. It also marks the most rugged section of the trip. As it winds through a forest of pine and maple, it occasionally passes former pastures, long abandoned and overgrown. After 6 km, follow Oro 8th Line to the right for a few metres and then turn left to resume the Bass Lake Road. For the next 2.5 km the Sand Hills loom to the right. Below you on the left the fringe of productive farmland encroaches. Beyond lie the distant waters of Bass Lake. Although the lake is small and is becoming polluted, it remains popular with campers and cottagers.

At the next crossroads, that with the Oro 10th Line, turn right. This road takes you directly across the Sand Hills at one of their highest points. Here, the road climbs a steep, wooded gully and passes a couple of farms that have struggled to survive on one of the few pockets of better soil. Although the ridge is 20 km long, it varies only from 1 km to 2 km in width. By the time you reach the next intersection, the Old Barrie Road, you will be on the south slope of the ridge. Stretching before you and on to Lake Simcoe 8 km to the south, the terrain is flat and the farms productive. Your trip ends where the 10th Line reaches Highway 11. You may turn right only at this point to head west.

If you still have time, you can continue south from Highway 11 to County Road 20, Ridge Road, named for a ridge that was a lakeshore bluff from an earlier and higher Lake Simcoe. This is a former pioneer trail, now lined with country homes, and is an attractive way to finish your trip into Barrie. Be sure to pause in Shanty Bay to see St. Thomas Church, built in 1838 using mud.

9 The Lake Simcoe Steeple Chase

Ontario is blessed with almost countless attractive and historic rural churches. Like the one-room schoolhouses, they were an iconic element of the country landscape. But, unlike the look-alike schools, the churches offered a remarkable variety of architectural styles depending upon their age, denomination and the wealth of their congregations. This route tracks down the prettiest and most historic and even the most unusual country churches in Ontario, all the while following the scenic shoreline of Ontario's fabled Lake Simcoe.

The route starts off at the aged Yonge Street Quaker Meeting house in Newmarket and then circles the lake ending up at the St. Thomas Anglican Church in Shanty Bay, which, believe it or not, was once made of mud.

Newmarket; Quaker Meeting House

One of Yonge Street's oldest buildings, the Quaker Meeting House, dates back to 1811 and still functions as a religious gathering spot. It sits on spacious grounds on the west side of Yonge Street, a short distance north of Mulock Drive. The building was initiated by Thomas Doane and is the oldest church north of Toronto. After arriving from the United States in 1803, the Yonge Street Meeting of Friends, or Quakers, began to construct a meetinghouse on Yonge Street just west of the mill town of Newmarket. At the time, Yonge Street had been opened as a military portage to link Fort York with Lake Simcoe. Many of the early settlers along the road were Quakers. This board and batten wooden building, simple in its design, has remained a meeting place since that time.

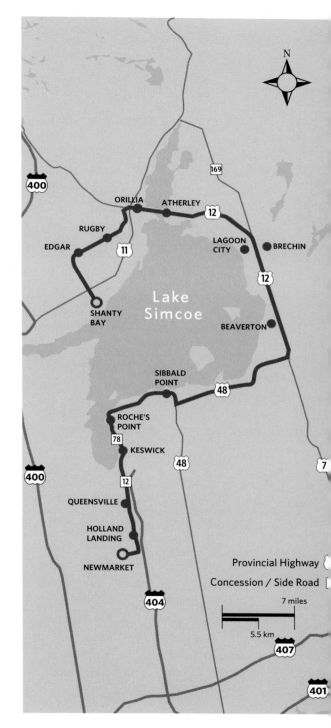

Opposite: The Yonge Street Quaker Meeting House has been in Newmarket since the early 19th century.

The unique Sharon Temple is now a museum and available for public use.

Newmarket to Sharon

From the Meeting House, continue north on Yonge Street. A short distance beyond Green Lane, at the site of the Newmarket Inn, take Road 51 to the right and follow it down the hill into the valley of the Holland River. As you approach the first set of traffic lights in Holland Landing you cross a bridge over the abandoned ruins of the Newmarket ghost canal. It was built in 1913 but because there was insufficient water in the river, it was never opened. Turn right onto Mount Albert Road and follow it out of Holland Landing to the traffic lights at Leslie Street where you turn right. A short

distance away is another traffic light where you turn right into the parking lot for the unusual and intriguing Sharon Temple.

Sharon Temple

This stunning structure was commissioned by David Willson, the founder of the Children of Peace, a breakaway sect of the Quakers in 1825 and was meant to resemble the Temple of Solomon. The sect faded away in the 1890s, at which time the York Pioneer and Historical Society rescued the weathered old building from destruction.

The white wooden building is four sided with central doors on each side to represent equality amongst the human race, and it's three-tiered akin to a wedding cake. Inside, a steep curved staircase (no longer accessible to the public) nicknamed "Jacob's Ladder" ascends to the musicians' gallery. The Children of Peace formed the first civilian band in Upper Canada. But after the group ceased to exist in the 1880s, the structure stood vacant until 1917 when the York Pioneer and Historical Society turned it into a museum. But beginning in the 1950s, many of the museum artefacts were moved to other locations, and the focus became on the history of the building itself. In 1991 the federal government declared the temple a national historic site, and the Sharon Temple Museum Society was formed to administer the building. The grounds also include the white study built by Willson and the 1819 farmhouse of Ebenezer Doan, as well as a log cabin and historic gatehouse.

Sharon to Roche's Point

Return to Leslie Street and drive north. This stretch of road leads you through the GTA's fast vanishing farmland, as the area around Queensville is slated to become a new city of 250,000 souls. Queensville itself remains a picturesque little crossroad hamlet with a historic former

Located at Roche's Point is one of Ontario's most picturesque churches.

general store, and a pair of houses constructed of fieldstone, a technique seldom found outside of York Region. (The general store in Baldwin on Highway 48 is another fine example of fieldstone construction.)

After crossing Ravenshoe Road, Leslie becomes the Queensway in the former cottage community of Keswick. After passing the usual array of chain stores and fast food restaurants, you encounter the Maskinonge River with its docks and marina. Then, when you hit the intersection of the Queensway and Metro Road, keep left on Metro Road. This takes you along the former "Metro" line, an interurban streetcar route that once carried Torontonians to the shores of Lake Simcoe. Stay on Metro Road until you reach Bouchier Street in the surprisingly historic hamlet of Roche's Point. Turn left here and go two blocks to Turner Street.

Roche's Point Anglican Church

When Upper Canada's Lieutenant Governor Sir Peregrine Maitland bought the point from James Roche in 1822, he envisioned it becoming Upper Canada's new provincial capital, as it occupied a strategically defensive point on Lake Simcoe should the dreaded Americans decide to attack from that direction. Instead, the area became a wealthy summer retreat in the 1860s, with grand homes such as Beechcroft and Lakehurst, homes that remain today. But it is the lovely little stone Anglican Christ Church that remains the best evidence of the hamlet's heyday.

This delightful stone church is considered to be one of Ontario's most picturesque. It was designed and built in 1867 by its first rector Walter Stennett. It is constructed of stone and features a delicate wooden steeple and gable over the entrance at the

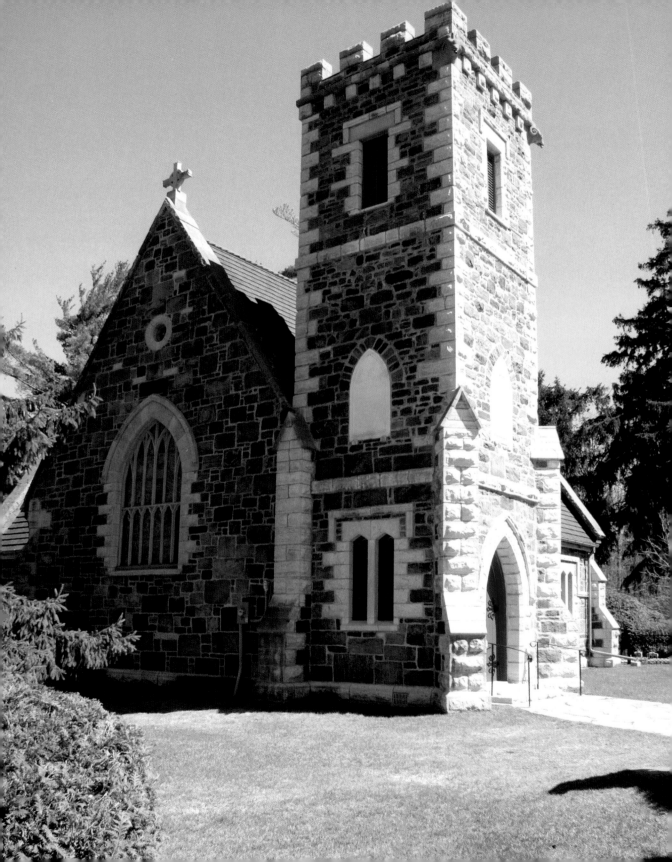

side of the building. It has been featured in numerous photographic publications as one the most beautiful country churches in Ontario. It stands beside Turner Street between Bouchier Street and Raines Street.

Roche's Point to Sibbald Point

Much of this part of the route follows the shore of the lake, passing closely packed cottages and the traditional resort town of Jackson's Point to yet another wonderful stone church, St. George's at Sibbald Point.

Return to Metro Road and turn left. Follow it until you see many old stone gates that lead to the grand lakeside homes (Varney Road). Turn left onto Lake Drive North and you will be at the shoreline, which you will follow right into Jackson's Point. Continue through the summertime shops of the community and then keep right onto Hedge Road, with its historic cedar hedges. This leads past The Briar's, a year-round resort that has remained in the Sibbald family for more than a century and a half. It is also a good place to pause for lunch. Hedge Road leads past some of the lake's oldest summer homes, some of which date to the land grants given to half-pay British army officers for their service in the War of 1812.

St. George's Anglican Church

As you see the road bending sharply to the right, look straight ahead to see the laneway to this church. Another stone stunner, the beautiful lakeside church was opened in 1877, replacing an earlier wooden building, on land donated by Susan Sibbald. Amid the graves in the churchyard are those of Stephen Leacock and Mazo De La Roche. Church doors often remain open for visitors to

Opposite: St. George's Anglican Church sits between Lake Simcoe and Sibbald Point Provincial Park.

enter and enjoy the historic interior of the building. Here, the east window above the communion table dates back to the original church and was hand painted in England in 1845 by the daughters of Ontario's first governor, John Simcoe. The west window depicts St. George slaying a dragon and is in memory of G.J. Brichta and Philip Brichta, father and son pilots killed in the First and Second World Wars, respectively. The altar, pulpit and reading desk were all carved by Reverend George Everest.

Sibbald Point to Beaverton

From the church follow Park Road south to Highway 48. This passes the entrance to Sibbald Point Provincial Park, a busy beach and campground that also contains the Eldon Hall mansion built by Susan Sibbald. Turn left onto Highway 48 and drive to Highway 12/Trans Canada Highway (roughly 30 km) where you turn left and travel to Simcoe Street (CR 15) on the outskirts of Beaverton, and the Old Stone Church National Historic Site (known as St. Andrew's).

St. Andrew's Presbyterian Church, Beaverton

Turn right at the traffic light onto Simcoe Street and travel the short distance to the church and its historic plaque. Built from 1840 to 1853, this simple stone church was declared a National Historic Site in 1991 because it is a "particularly gracious example of the few early vernacular stone churches surviving in Canada," according the Parks Canada description. It was built by a local stonemason, John Morrison, and replaced an earlier log structure. It retains much of its original woodwork and continues as an occasional place of worship. The simplicity of its style reflects the more conservative philosophy of the Presbyterians.

Beaverton to Orillia

Make your way back to Highway 12 towards the bustling City of Orillia. From Brechin, about half-way between, you may wish to take a side trip west from the traffic lights to Lagoon City, a community on Lake Simcoe built entirely upon a system of canals and known as "Ontario's Venice."

As you near Orillia, a large brick church looms high upon a hill to your right surrounded by farmland. This is St. Columbkille Catholic Church.

St. Columbkille Catholic Church, Uptergrove

The area was settled in the 1830s and 40s by Irish and Scottish Catholics. The current church was opened in 1905 and replaced an earlier frame structure. The church features a high vaulted ceiling, stained glass windows and side altars. The church is alleged to be haunted by a priest who is said to have failed to complete his desired schedule of sermons. A burial vault door is rumoured to creak open by itself, but parishoners strongly dispute this reputation.

Orillia

Before you cross the Highway 12 bridge at Atherley, turn left at the stop light for Creighton Street. A right into the laneway behind the Tim Horton's takes you to Queen Street, where a right turn leads a few metres to Bridge Street. If you stop here and follow the sidewalk, which leads under the bridge, you will come to a First Nations site of significance: the Mn'jikaning fishing weirs. It was here where Lake Simcoe flowed through The Narrows into Lake Couchiching, which various First Nations groups traditionally used to place their fishing weirs. A national historic site plaque outlines the importance of the location and of the "grandfather" rock that marks the spot. The weirs themselves are only visible at low water.

The aboriginal word for "place of the fishing weirs" is "Toronto," a name which early explorer Samuel de Champlain gave to Lake Simcoe. The portage from Lake Ontario to Lac Toronto became the "Toronto Carrying Place." When the French added a trading post on Lake Ontario near the start of the portage and called it Fort Toronto, the name stuck and thus, after Governor John Simcoe renamed Lac Toronto after his father, Toronto remained forever on the shores of Lake Ontario.

You may wish to drive through and visit downtown Orillia with its historic train station, main street and revitalized waterfront. Otherwise continue to follow Highway 12 to Highway 11. As you cross the bridge on Highway 11, keep left for Old Barrie Road.

Orillia to Shanty Bay

This 35 km scenic country road leads through the Sand Hills, a deposit of the last great glaciers with its rolling farmlands and forested hillsides. You will pass through hamlets with names like Rugby and Edgar before arriving at a lonely little wooden church at the intersection with the 3rd Line North.

Oro African Church

Beautiful for its stark simplicity, the Oro African Church was built in 1845 by the local community of black settlers, descendants of black militiamen who served Britain during the 1812 war. As early as 1783, Sir Guy Carleton, Commander in Chief of the British Army fighting the Americans, promised that black slaves who served the British army would be given land in Upper Canada. Eleven received such land between 1819 and 1826, with a further 30 families arriving a few years later. No descendants remain today, having intermarried or moved away. This is likely the oldest surviving African log church in North America and is a National Historical Site. Abandoned in the 1920s, it

Shanty Bay's Mud Church is the only one of its kind in North America.

is currently undergoing restoration by the Township of Oro-Medonte.

The Mud Church of Shanty Bay

From log to mud, follow the 3rd Line south, making a jog to the right to cross over Highway 11 and then right again at the stop sign to stay on the 3rd Line. Continue to the stop sign at Ridge Road where you turn right. Less than a kilometre brings you to a stop sign in Shanty Bay (2nd Line) where you turn left to reach St. Thomas Anglican Church, North America's only "mud" church.

This unusual building traces its roots to 1830 with the arrival of Edward O'Brien, founder of the Shanty Bay settlement on the north shore of Kempenfeldt Bay on Lake Simcoe. The church was completed in 1842 and was constructed using the rare technique of rammed earth: a doughy mixture of clay, straw and water. It was then set within a wooden frame and plastered over to protect it from the weather. It is the only such church building in North America. The church remains active and can be visited with permission from the adjacent church office, or by attending a worship service.

To return to Highway 11, and your way back home, retrace your steps to the 3rd Line and head north to the interchange with the highway.

10 The Ridge Road West

The views extend in several directions from Mount Wolfe.

Within the shadow of Toronto's skyscrapers there is a series of roads that wind along a ridge of billowing fields, through hardwood forests and past stone houses and churches that date back more than a century and a half. Here is a country landscape that has still mostly defied the sprawl of look-alike houses and fast-food drive-ins that mark the Greater Toronto Area's urban fringe.

The route starts at the intersection of Yonge Street and Bloomington Road, 2 km south of Aurora and about 30 km north of downtown Toronto. It zigzags westward along a series of country roads for about 50 km and ends at Highway 10 just 20 km south of Orangeville.

Most of the land along it is private, and the opportunities to hike or picnic are few. Snack bars, grocery stores and gas stations are located along the main cross streets, such as Yonge Street, Airport Road and Highway 10.

Next to the Niagara Escarpment, central Ontario's most prominent landscape feature is the great Oak Ridges Moraine. About 20,000 years ago the waters from melting glaciers carried sand, gravel, boulders and even great chunks of the glacier itself into a long fissure in the ice, creating this ridge of rugged hills that stretches from Orangeville to Trenton.

Between the ridge and the lake lies a level clay plain that has provided some of the best farmland in Canada. Here, early settlers cleared their farms, gradually extending northward from Lake Ontario until they struck the great Oak Ridge. Its steep hills defied road-building, and only a few winding trails penetrated low saddles in the hills. Not until the 1830s did the pioneers penetrate the ridge. At first the tall pines gave rise to a prosperous sawmill industry. But because the high country cradled the headwaters of the rivers that flow into Lake Ontario, the streams were small and mill sites few. As a result, the villages were scattered and served only the immediate needs of the pioneers. Moreover, farming was poor. Boulders and stones plagued the steep hillsides, and the sandy subsoils retained little water. Many of the farmers left, weary and defeated.

During the 1930s, under a system of county forests managed by the Ontario government, the worst lands were replanted in pine. Later, during the 1960s and 1970s, much of the remaining land was sold to developers or to wealthy commuters. Nevertheless, the area retains a landscape of spacious grasslands, dark forests and spectacular views.

Aurora to Eversley

Follow Yonge Street north from Toronto, or take Bloomington Road west from Highway 404 to the intersection with Yonge Street. Continue west from Yonge Street. At the southwest corner of

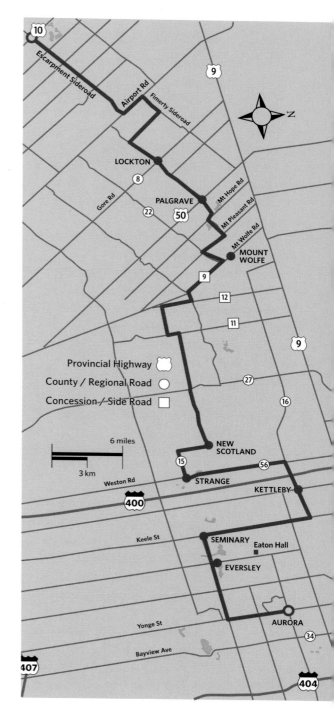

Bathurst Street, 2 km west, stands a large fieldstone farmhouse. It hugs the roadside and dates back to the earliest days of settlement. Thoughtful owners have preserved it in its original condition.

Continue west for a further 2 km and you will come to Eversley and its old stone church. Begun in 1834 as a crossroads hamlet, Eversley takes its name from a village in Hampshire, England. On the northeast corner of the intersection is the one-time general store, now a private residence. The blacksmith's shop, which stood on the southeast corner, has long vanished. However, just 0.7 km south stands the most remarkable building on this route, the Eversley Church.

Early pioneers yearned for a place to worship. They gathered up the stones from their fields and laid them together to build the Eversley Presbyterian Church. The year was 1838. Services were held there until 1958, when the stone church was closed. Concern over whether this handsome structure would survive was lifted in 1960 when Lady Eaton, who had owned a large estate to the north, purchased the building so that it could be preserved. It stands today amid its pioneer headstones, with a plaque in front to recount its story.

Eversley to Kettleby

Near Eversley, two kettle lakes appear on two large estates, both of which are open to the public. Geologists will tell you that a kettle lake is a pond in a depression that formed during the glacial retreat when a huge chunk of ice was trapped in the sands of the ridge and gradually melted to leave a large hole.

The first of these lakes is at Eaton Hall. From the Eversley Church, drive north 2 km, turn left into the grounds of Seneca College, King Campus, and follow the lane to the right, leading you to Eaton Hall. Built in 1919 by Sir John Eaton of department store fame, this estate was a popular summer retreat for the Eaton family. The last to use it was Lady Eaton. On her death in 1971 it became the property of Seneca College. Extensive grounds are spread over rolling hills and covered by an attractive forest of pine and hardwood. In its midst is the turreted stone Eaton Hall, which overlooks the lake and is used by the college to host conventions.

The second estate in the area is the Marylake Shrine, home of the Augustinian Seminary. From Eaton Hall return to Eversley and turn right onto Sideroad 15. At the next crossroads, you will come to an arching stone gate. But it is a gate that never closes, for the grounds are freely open to the public—provided no one disturbs the order's sanctuaries. Drive straight ahead, past the gates to the laneway on the right and follow the lane as it winds through a tunnel of spruces. Where the woods give way to pasture (the group raises Herefords) you will see a massive red brick barn. Then the lane forks: the right branch leads to the stone religious retreat house, a private area; the left takes you to the modern seminary and church. Here again, the Eaton touch is felt: the organ in the shrine once rested in Eaton Hall. The site itself is the original farm and summer home of Sir Henry Pellatt, builder of Toronto's Casa Loma. Beyond the buildings is a placid pond called Mary Lake. Although the grounds are open, this is not a park. You may stroll and photograph, but you should not picnic.

Most of the side roads that lead west from the seminary have been blocked by Highway 400. The most attractive place to cross the highway is through the old village of Kettleby, which you can reach by driving 7 km north from the seminary gates. (Kettleby lies 1 km west of Keele Street on Kettleby Road.) Unlike other north-leading roads, Keele Street is lightly travelled. The road begins to rollercoaster as it enters the steep hills that typify the ridge. Although new country homes now dominate the old pastures, watch for the old farm-houses, many of them dating back to the 1840s and 1850s.

Kettleby

Kettleby has changed little since its early days. Many of its original buildings line the treed main street, though several have found new uses. The Methodist church built in 1873 has become an antique store. However, the stone Anglican church (erected in 1891) still opens for worship each Sunday. The general store is now the Kettleby Italian bakery, while across from it are two handsome early houses, Brunswick Hall and Curtis House.

From the store the road winds down the hill and into the little valley that once hummed with gristmills and a distillery. It is now a grassy meadow.

Kettleby to Palgrave

Continue west across Highway 400 and, at Weston Road, turn left. A busy artery, it leads you quickly to the next portion of the ridge backroad. When you have gone 7 km on Weston Road, watch for the 15th Sideroad and turn right. Because the great ridge blocked most roadbuilders, only Weston Road brings you to its southern face in this area. Continue on the 15th Sideroad to the 7th Concession Road, where you will encounter the southerly thrust of the ridge and a landscape of rugged hills that have attracted still more country estates.

Turn right onto the 7th Sideroad. It leads you

A solid gate invites entry to the Augustinian seminary grounds.

northward to the ridge that deflects it westward onto the 16th Sideroad.

Just beyond the bend you will pass a once active pioneer community named New Scotland. Settled in the 1830s by Archibald Kelly and a colony of Scottish immigrants, this community contained a sawmill, a blacksmith's shop, an Orange lodge and a school. Today these buildings have been replaced by spacious country estates. The only relic of the early Scottish community survives in the name of the small kettle lake at the foot of the peak, Kelly's Lake.

For the next 10 km the 16th Sideroad doglegs back and forth at intersections, through scenic sand hills and little gullies, until it ends abruptly at King Concession Road 12. Turn right here and travel 2 km to the next intersection, that with Sideroad 17. Turn left and follow it less than 1 km to Mount Wolfe Road, then turn right. For 3 km the road grinds up a steep hillside and then enters the heart of the ridge, the Albion Hills. Here the summit of Mount Wolfe overlooks a quiltwork of farms and country homes and, on the distant southern horizon, the towers of Mississauga. Although the slopes of the mountain are steep, the summit, which is home to a community of farmers, is level. On the northwest corner of the first intersection stands a well-preserved complex of traditional red barns. Turn left onto Old Church Road and drive 1.5 km across the plateau and down the side of the mountain to Mount Pleasant Road, where you turn right and remount the hill. This is the west end of Mount Wolfe, and the views from here extend both south and west. It was on its peak that the Mount Wolfe post office and church once stood. However, all that remain are the headstones preserved in a common foundation.

Continue north and descend the mountain for the last time through a hardwood forest dotted with country estates. Turn left onto Hunsden Sideroad and drive through rolling farmland to a T intersection. Turn right here onto Mount Hope Road, and then after 1 km turn left onto Pine Avenue, which leads into Palgrave, the Albion Hills' only village.

Palgrave

Although they are surrounded by estate subdivisions, some of Palgrave's historic buildings survive. The village was originally known as Buckstown and was first gathered around Robert Campbell's gristmill. It remained small until the Hamilton & Northwestern Railway was built through town. Then it boomed. In its heyday it contained several hotels and stores and a number of small industries. Today the industries are gone, as is the station and the rail line itself, though Campbell's millpond remains. Period houses and churches line the narrow back streets, while at the corner of Pine Street and Highway 50 Palgrave's old hotel with its three gables has remained much as it was along with two neighbouring structures. A short distance south on Highway 50 you will find the Albion Hills Conservation Area. With its fields, swimming hole and access to the Bruce Trail, it provides an opportunity to leave the car and explore the beauties of the ridge on foot.

Palgrave to Highway 10

Today Highway 50 follows Palgrave's main street south, crossing the abandoned railway line, now converted to a scenic rail trail, to the Patterson Sideroad 25, where you turn right. Once free of the jungles of estate subdivisions, the ridge becomes a range of smaller wooded hills. Near the first crossroad, you will cross the two branches of the Humber River; 3 km farther on, at the Gore Road, sits the former village of Lockton, which now retains only its store and a log house. Continue west for 2 km to the next intersection,

The Caledon Rail Trail, shown here in Inglewood with the Credit Valley Flyer tour train, crosses the main street of Palgrave.

the Centreville Road. The road here winds around wooded hillsides and through dark gullies to the open farmland of the Centreville Road. Turn right, drive 3.5 km to Finnerty Sideroad and turn left. Here the road resumes its winding way through a landscape of hills, forests, fields and new country homes. After 3 km it stops once more, this time at the busy Airport Road.

Busy even in pioneer days, when it was known as the 6th Line, this is the same Airport Road that, 40 km south, carries six lanes of traffic past Pearson International Airport. Here it carries country commuters. Turn left and drive south 2 km to the Escarpment Sideroad and turn right.

The last leg of the Ridge Road, it surges over the peaks of the rugged Caledon Hills. To the south the views extend across pastures and woodlots and culminate in the distant Metro skyline. For 9 more km you wind past fields, some overgrown, some replanted in pine, a few still grazed by slow-moving cattle. The great ridge ends abruptly at the Niagara Escarpment. So high is the ridge that at this point it has buried even that great rocky cuesta.

It is here at Highway 10 that the Ridge Road drive ends. To the left lies Brampton and, less than an hour away, Toronto. Orangeville is a short drive north, to the right.

11 The Ridge Road East

Mirroring the Ridge Road West, this scenic route wanders through the rugged Oak Ridge hill country east of Toronto. To get to your starting point, drive east from Toronto on Highway 401, exit north onto Brock Road and follow it 15 km to Claremont. The tour follows a series of gravel concession roads and side roads easterly for about 50 km to Highway 35/115 at a point 3 km north of Kirby (the hamlet where Backroads Route 9, the Rice Lake Road, begins).

In contrast to the Ridge Road West, there are fewer estate homes on this trip and more of the simple settlers' farmsteads and churches. And although the views are less spectacular, the hills are more rugged, the gulches deeper and darker. So difficult is some of the terrain that many early roads have been abandoned.

Again, this is a tour for the recreational driver who wants a country getaway.

The eastern Ridge Road passes the historic general store in Claremont.

The story of this area closely parallels that of the Ridge Road West. Although the lakeshore area was bustling with farms by 1810, the steep hills discouraged the movement of pioneers inland until after 1830. By then the government had constructed a few crude roads over low spots in the hills. But being a headwater area, the region had few mill sites, and many of those that did attract mills dried up shortly after the forest was cleared. As a result the landscape is one of abandoned farms, rough pastures and small villages and hamlets that have long lost their functions and have largely disappeared (though in recent years some have become dormitory communities for commuters to such cities as Oshawa, Whitby and even Toronto).

Claremont

There are two Claremonts: Old Claremont: the original crossroads village; and Claremont Siding, which came into existence after 1884, when the Ontario & Quebec Railway, now the Canadian Pacific Railway, was built through the settlement.

As Brock Road approaches Claremont, it leaves its original route and bypasses the village. Continue past Durham Road 5 to the north end of the bypass. Turn left twice to Claremont Siding. At the crossing the station is long gone, a victim of the CPR's heritage policy, though one of its original feed mills still stands. Across the track, forlorn yet solid, a brick carriage factory hugs the roadside. Along the side streets and the road to Old Claremont are the large homes of the early railway days.

The settlement of Old Claremont lies 1 km from the crossing and contains this route's most interesting building. Here, where the Brock Road intersected an important side road, now Regional Road 5, an early settler named Noble built a general store. Known at first as Noble's Corners, the community had little more than a couple of

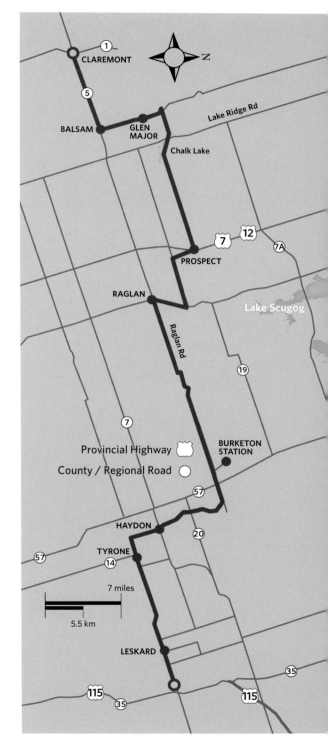

stores and a hotel. But when the railway arrived to the north, the back streets of Old Claremont filled with houses and more businesses moved to the village. Many still stand on these narrow roads and today mix with newer homes.

As Claremont gradually became a dormitory town to Oshawa, its residents paid less attention to their own stores. Now most shops are shuttered or serving a different purpose. Three of the four corners of the Old Claremont crossroads have been stripped of their original buildings, but the fourth boasts the most ambitious country general store in central Ontario. In 2009 this 1847 historic store burned and was replaced in 2011 with a larger replica.

Claremont to Glen Major

Drive east from the store on Durham Road 5. Here several old village buildings line the street. Two blocks from the store is the 1865 brick Baptist church. Since leaving Brock Road you have made three left turns, bringing you back to Brock Road, also called Durham Road 1.

From Durham Road 1, continue east on Durham Road 5 and drive across the south face of the ridge for 5.2 km to a historic crossroads hamlet called Balsam.

Halfway to Balsam, two bridges cross the tumbling headwaters of Duffin Creek, which was once the power source for countless mills. The creek is now the focus for a string of conservation areas. Conceived originally to provide flood-control measures, these extensive conservation areas fill a growing need for public recreation areas that neither the province nor the municipalities are prepared to fill. The Claremont Conservation Area lies just 2 km south of Durham Road 5 on Westney Road, and the Greenwood Conservation Area is just 3 km beyond that. Both offer hiking trails, picnic areas and playing fields.

To reach Balsam, stay on Durham Road 5. This village had its origins in 1869, when J. Palmer opened a crossroads general store (including a post office) to serve the needs of area settlers. Soon the intersection added a second store, a temperance hall and a blacksmith's shop. But it failed to grow beyond that. Palmer's store closed after a few decades, though it still stands on the northeast corner of the crossroads. Graham's yellow brick store, which opened in the 1890s, is on the southeast corner.

At Balsam, turn north onto Balsam Road and follow it to one of the more scenic portions of this trip. For about 1 km you stay on the flatlands below the hills. But after you cross the railway tracks, the scenery changes dramatically. As you enter the valley of Duffin Creek, the wooded hills steepen and close in on the road, forcing it onto the contours of the valley wall. About 3 km from Balsam, a string of simple homes cling to the steep slope and peer into the gulch. This is the picturesque valley village of Glen Major.

Glen Major

Although Duffin Creek at this point is little more than a brook, its source a mere 1 km upstream, it became the focus for a busy 19th-century mill town. Because of the steepness of the hills, this area was not settled until 1840, long after the plains below. Among the first to settle here were the Sharrards, who dammed the waters of Duffin Creek to power a sawmill and a gristmill. The bustling settlement became known as Sharrards Mills. In the 1870s, E. Major acquired the Sharrards' properties and ran three sawmills and a gristmill. The settlement's name was changed to Glen Major, and the community added a church

Opposite: The Oak Ridges Moraine is home to many diverse species of plants and animals.

The little white church at Glen Major has been called one of Ontario's prettiest.

and school. But when the forests vanished, so did the mills. The ponds have survived and are now maintained by a private fishing club. Although they lie close to the road, you have no access to them. Beyond them is the village's feature attraction, at least for photographers. Built in 1873, the white board-and-batten Methodist church at the north end of the village, its simple pioneer architecture framed by a hillside of maples, is an image that earned it a place in *Steeple Chase*, a photo book on Ontario's most attractive churches.

Glen Major to Burketon Station

North of Glen Major the road winds out of the narrow, steepening gully onto a plateau. Watch for

the road sign that announces Chalk Lake Road and turn right. For 2 km the road runs through pastures and fields and past the new country homes that are sprouting on them. Then it plunges into the valley of Lynde Creek.

From the stop sign at Durham Road 23, continue straight on. Through the trees on the right you will see the sparkling waters of Chalk Lake. Ringed by steep hills, Chalk Lake's waters fill a pothole that was left by a stray piece of melting glacier 20,000 years ago. For several years it has remained an enclave of large summer homes and country estates, shielded from prying eyes by the thick hardwood forest that cloaks the hillside.

East of Chalk Lake the road returns to the crest

of the ridge. Continue for 7 km to the intersection of Highways 7 and 12. Over this section of road, the rugged knolls gradually diminish, and at the intersection they have levelled off to become prosperous farmland. Highway 7/12 was an early settlement road laid out by the government in 1825 and called the Centre Road. In 1852 a private company acquired the route and planked it from Whitby to Orillia. But in 1876 the company went bankrupt and the road was absorbed into the county system. The intersection was once the site of a little hamlet called Prospect, but all you will see of the community today is a new country home.

Drive east through Prospect on Scugog Line 2 and immediately turn right onto Diamond Sideroad. After 1 km, the road plunges into a gully. As you rise onto the next crest, you return to the heart of the ridge and to a view that extends south to Lake Ontario. After 1.5 km, turn left at a T intersection onto Coates Road West. Here the road follows the crest of the ridge over its peaks, through its gullies and past its simple farm homes. The most striking of these homes lies less than 0.5 km from the turn—it is the first house on the left. The board-and-batten building retains small window panels, gable fretwork and a graceful door.

A stop sign 4.5 km from the house marks busy Durham Road 2 (Simcoe Street North). However, pause in the Purple Woods Conservation Area on the southeast corner. Here the ridge is at its narrowest and gives you views that extend both south to Lake Ontario and north to Lake Scugog.

Drive south on Simcoe Street to the historic hamlet of Raglan and turn left onto Raglan Road. Here the White Feather Country Store offers light lunches and a popular bakery. Here the hummocky hills are lined with neat rows of pine. So infertile were these sands that they failed to regenerate even grassland and, by the 1930s, had become a dusty desert. Then, under the guidance of provincial public servant and leading conservationist A.H. Richardson, and in conjunction with several counties, the province began to replant the blowing sands with pine. Today, this system provides not only a place for recreation but also a source of pulpwood.

Stay on Raglan Road as it bends left. At the next intersection it becomes Concession Road 10. Turn right to bypass another section of abandoned roads. Follow this route eastward to the stop sign at Old Scugog Road. Though the hills are lower, the terrain remains rugged, the soils sandy. Fewer than a half-dozen farms survive along the once busy concession road.

About 1 km north of the intersection, on the Old Scugog Road, is a little railway village named Burketon Station, which is now a quiet residential community. Although a few freight trains rush through on the Canadian Pacific line, they no longer stop at Burketon. The station was identical to the other two-storey frame stations that the Ontario & Quebec Railway constructed. And, like the others, the CPR has demolished it. Like many early railway towns, Burketon Station's homes are modest, typical of railway homes of the 19th century.

Burketon Station to Haydon

Continue east from the Old Scugog Road 1 km to Durham Road 57. Proceed through the intersection for almost 1 km and watch for the Grasshopper Park Road leading to the right. For 2.5 km this quiet trail winds through a gully that erosion carved into the ridge. Beside the road a tiny creek bubbles beneath the hillsides, which are forested and steep, here and there widening into pasture. More than a century ago, when the ridge was covered in pine, this little valley buzzed with a string of sawmills. But all are gone now, and the route is strictly residential.

Although only a small kettle lake, Chalk Lake exudes a wilderness aura.

After about 2.5 km, you will come to a stop sign. Continue straight on until the road emerges from the valley onto a plain of farmlands and estate homes, and ends at the village of Haydon.

Haydon was the only mill site on the upper creek to develop into a village, and it quickly acquired the usual stores, shops and institutions. The old wooden church still survives, as does the school, which is now a private home. Among the buildings that line village's streets you will yet see a few original frame cabins built by the village's first inhabitants.

Haydon to Leskard

At the stop sign in Haydon turn left onto Concession Road 8. Turn right onto Middle Road and drive for 2 km to see a remarkable sight on your right; in the front lawn of the Model A Acres B&B sit replica model A cars and vintage wartime aircraft made from recycled materials.

At the stop sign, turn left onto Concession Road 7 to the living pioneer village of Tyrone, where the modest main street mirrors the past with its stone blacksmith's shop, vacant general store, and 1846 Tyrone Mill. Remarkably, the mill still cuts timber and grinds grain using the water of the adjacent creek. (And don't forget to stop in for fresh doughnuts and apple cider in season.)

The Tyrone Mill began grinding grain with water power in 1846, and the mill still does.

Continue east from Tyrone for 6 km to the old village of Leskard. Now a commuter town, it was once a near ghost town. Leskard began promisingly in 1842, when Ichabod Richmond started a sawmill and a gristmill. In 1854 James Banks laid out a town plan and Leskard quickly became a bustling regional centre. But like many a mill town, it quickly lost its industries and for years several of its buildings stood vacant. However, the recent rush on country real estate has turned it into a dormitory village for such cities as Oshawa and Whitby. The general store on the southeast corner of the junction, the red brick Methodist church (c. 1885) and the school are all now private houses.

Highway 35/115 lies 3.5 km east of Leskard, and here you may end your trip. Alternatively, you can add a final scenic loop. For another 6 km the road rollercoasters eastward over the ridgetop, past fields and picturesque weathered barns. Then it bends south to stop at Durham Road 9, the route of the Rice Lake Road in the following chapter. Highway 35/115 lies 6 km to the right, and Highway 401 is 20 km to the south from that point.

12 The Rice Lake Road

An attractive country church set in the gentle hills near Rice Lake.

Beginning in the tiny hamlet of Kirby on Highway 35/115, 20 km north of Highway 401, this gentle rural route follows paved country roads through the one-time counties of Durham and Northumberland, running east-ward 50 km to Rice Lake. Along the way are ample picnic sites, general stores, gas stations and fast-food outlets. Be sure to bring: your camera (there are some lovely views of lakes and old buildings), your sketch pad and your love of Ontario's rural traditions.

Although this route is close to Toronto and runs through part of prosperous central Ontario, it lies inland from the lakeshore and has escaped the fingers of urban sprawl that have stabbed out from the metropolis. Instead, here are gently rolling hills where several rivers have carved quiet valleys as they rush south to the lake; and here are the wooded shores of Rice Lake. To reach your starting point, exit Highway 401 to Highway 35/115 and follow it north to Durham Road 9 and the crossroads hamlet of Kirby.

Settlers carved their farms on Lake Ontario's shore as early as the 1790s, but four decades would pass before the frontier moved inland. By the 1830s, many of the interior lands had been opened and settlements had sprung up at key crossroads and at water power sites on the numerous streams. As long as there were forests, the sawmills prospered. Then, as the woods disappeared, the wheat years took over. But American tariffs ruined the grain trade, and by 1900 Ontario farmers had turned to dairy and beef farming. Today, this inland area remains one of family farms, quiet country villages and rural traditions.

Kirby to Kendal

Kirby began its life during the 1850s, after the opening of the Kendal Road, and it soon became a busy crossroads hamlet. Unfortunately, highway widenings have left little of Kirby. On the west side of the highway is the 100-year-old brick former Methodist church, and beside it a house built in 1858. On the northeast is a school that has been converted into a museum.

From the exit at Kirby drive east along Durham Road 9, which was once known as the Kendal Road. It developed as a municipal toll road and opened around 1850. The first 6 km roll over gentle hills and past lush fields and a few new country homes. Then the road descends into the valley of the Ganaraska River and to the village of Kendal.

Although Kendal contains a number of newer homes, several early houses and shops still line its shady streets, preserving the appearance it must have had in its palmy days. Kendal was laid out not on the main road, but slightly to the south of it, for it was here that in 1848 Theron Dicky built his sawmill and later added a gristmill. Only 20 years later the village contained two sawmills, four shingle mills, two hotels, two churches and four stores.

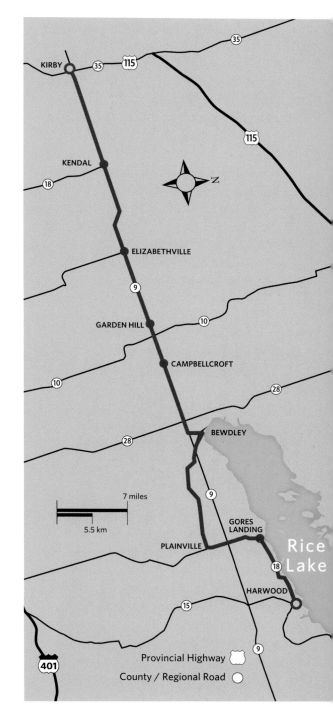

The first road to the right is Church Street, and it contains the white frame United church, built in 1870, and the one-time Orange Lodge. Turn left and drive past attractive homes to Durham Road 18.

Turn left and drive back to Durham Road 9, which is also posted as the Ganaraska Road. At the 10 km mark from Kirby, look for the turn left to the Ganaraska Forest Centre. The farms that were carved onto the sandy ridge that parallels the route have been replaced by forests. From this centre you can follow hiking or cross-country ski trails through the area. The centre is 5 km north of Durham Road 9. This is also the point at which you enter Northumberland County from what was Durham Region, but the road remains number 9.

At 15 km from Kirby you enter the hamlet of Elizabethville, first settled in the 1830s, and a small stopover village at the intersection of the Kendal Road with the Decker Hollow Road. Today the Decker Hollow Road is closed and the village of Decker Hollow has vanished, as have many of Elizabethville's original buildings.

Drive east from Elizabethville and, after 3 km, watch for the sign to the Richardson Lookout. This lookout was named after the father of Ontario's conservation movement, Arthur H. Richardson. It was he who devised the notion that municipalities sharing river watersheds should pool their resources with the province to prevent flooding, to encourage improved farming techniques and to replant forests on infertile soils. A beneficial by-product has been the development of conservation areas, and small recreation parks have been established beside reservoirs and at flood control dams and old mill dams. In parks where an old mill still stands, the conservation areas have sometimes mushroomed into "pioneer villages," with nearby buildings of historical interest being moved to the park to create a living museum. And all thanks to Richardson.

From the Richardson Lookout, look north. There the irregular peaks of the great Oak Ridge indent the horizon. This 150 km mound of sand and gravel was laid down during the last ice age, 50,000 years ago, by the swirling meltwaters from two huge glaciers. The Ganaraska River pours off the ridge into the plain below you, where it has carved its gentle valley. Here lies a landscape of green fields, barns and houses.

Return to County Road 9 and continue east. For 3 km the road descends the hill into the valley of the Ganaraska River. Beside the bridge over the river are a millpond and the village of Garden Hill, once one of the busiest villages on the Kendal Road. It began in the 1830s, when one Mr. Kirkpatrick arrived and built a mill on the river. By 1880 Garden Hill had five sawmills, two gristmills, and the largest woollen mill on the river. Its population stood at 450.

Although the mills are now gone, there remain a few interesting vestiges of Garden Hill's glory days. The general store dates back to the start of the 20th century and, unlike most of its contemporaries, still retains its wooden porch. There is the old brick church and several early houses. Take a short spin around the single residential block. Little wider than a laneway and lined with trees and simple homes, the street appears much as it did during the town's heyday. Beside the pond, the conservation authority has developed one of its picnic and swimming parks.

Garden Hill to Bewdley

Continue east from Garden Hill. This swampy lowland is the flood plain of the Ganaraska Valley, where several little tributaries seem to meander without purpose. If you had been travelling this road over a century ago, you would have been

Opposite: A view of Rice Lake.

The Garden Hill General Store carries on an Ontario tradition that is generations old.

stopped 1 km east of Garden Hill and asked for a toll. The tollgate was at the intersection with one of the earliest roads to penetrate the interior from the lake, the Port Hope–Millbrook Road. Here, too, was an early mill settlement called Waterford, but, like the tollgate, Waterford has disappeared.

After 2 km, look on the right for a large white building with a porch, originally a general store and post office. Opposite this building is a white frame hall. This building was the centre of Campbellcroft, a village that began with Thomas Campbell's mill but did not take off until the late 1850s, when the first steam engine of the newly opened Midland Railway putt-putted across the road. The place was renamed Garden Hill Station and became an important shipping centre. Lumber and grain were loaded into freight cars for the 15 km journey down to Port Hope and thence for export to the United States or England. Apart from the old store and hall, few buildings remain from these busy times, and the village has reverted to its original name.

The next 5 km continue through the lowland, past a string of farms and country homes. From the traffic lights at Highway 28, which links Port Hope and Peterborough, travel another 1 km and turn left at Rice Lake Drive. This is the old Port Hope–Peterborough stage road, and one of its stopover towns was Bewdley.

Bewdley

Bewdley sits at the west end of Rice Lake, one of Ontario's most beautiful lakes. Pastures and woodlands that are gentle and green roll down to the shore, and islands dot the placid waters. As the name Rice Lake implies, waving fields of wild rice once surrounded the lake's low shores. They sustained both the Native population and the pioneers. But the builders of the Trent Canal dammed the lake and drowned the rice fields.

Long and narrow, Rice Lake stretches 30 km west to east but is only 5 km across. It is fed by the Otonabee River from the north and drains east into the Trent River. Being near Ontario's urban heartland, it has become a popular destination for cottagers and boaters, but not for campers and picnickers. Ontario's park planners have fallen behind, providing only a few sizable parks on this especially suitable lake.

Like the lake itself, Bewdley is a resort area, with few indications that it was once a busy port of call for the Rice Lake steamers. Today the wharves have been replaced by an attractive lakeside park, while the pioneer Halfway House has become Rhino's Roadhouse.

Bewdley to Gores Landing

Leave Bewdley driving south, on the road on which you entered it. After just a quarter kilometre beyond the marina, take Cavan Road to the left. Here you encounter an early pioneer road, this one linking Bewdley with Plainville. Follow it for 2 km to the intersection with County Road 9. Cross through the intersection and stay on the old pioneer road, now called Oak Ridges Drive.

As in its early days, the road bends and twists around the hills and valleys. Now paved and widened, it passes handsome family farms with their farmhouses of brick or clapboard. Here the landscape changes as you enter the land of the "whalebacks." These hills, so named for their resemblance to the smooth, elongated back of a whale, were moulded when the great glaciers re-advanced over their earlier deposits of sand and gravel. Geologists call them drumlins.

About 5 km from County Road 9 you will

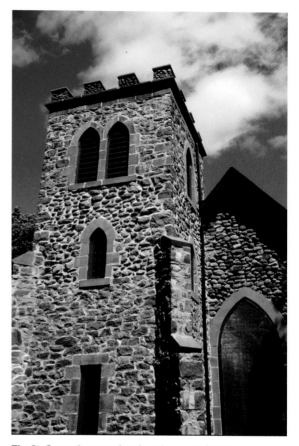

The St. George's stone church at Gores Landing is one of the most historic and picturesque along the Rice Lake Road.

encounter the Plainville United Church, which was built in 1903 as a Methodist church. Its tall steeple soars above its red brick frame in the midst of gentle farmland. About 1 km beyond it are the few houses and the feed mill of Plainville itself.

At the T intersection in Plainville, turn left onto County Road 18, cross County Road 9 and continue to the shores of Rice Lake. Here, with its century-old summer estate homes, is Gores Landing. This village began in the 1820s as a landing at the end of the Cobourg–Rice Lake Road. Stagecoaches from Cobourg and Port Hope turned passengers over to steamers such as the *Forester*, which puffed across the lake and up the Otonabee River to a fledgling mill town that would become Peterborough. Among its early travellers were Peter Robinson's Irish colonists fleeing the potato famines at home to seek the promise of Canada's wilds.

With the building in 1854 of a railway to nearby Harwood, Gores Landing lost its importance and settled down as a resort community of summer homes—a role that was reinforced during the 1950s, when the great Toronto cottage boom gobbled up the Rice Lake shoreline.

As you enter the village, follow the left fork and continue on Kelly Road. From this road you can see the length of the lake. Dotted across its waters are small forested islands, the crests of partly submerged whalebacks. By the water, where the high road meets the low road, are the large summer mansions of an earlier wealthy class. Built of clapboard and painted white, many are two- and three-storey houses overlooking wide green lawns. From a small park where the two roads meet, Church Hill Road leads left. Along this remnant of a former shore road is St. George's Church, a small stone building that is one of the most photographed churches in the Rice Lake area and, incredibly, once threatened with demolition.

Gores Landing to Harwood

As you continue east from Gores Landing, you come to the historic Victoria Inn. It was constructed in 1902 by renowned Canadian artist Gerald S. Hayward, who named it The Willows. It yet retains its iconic tower and landscaping and today offers comfortable rooms and fine dining.

Continue along the shore road, County Road 18. For the next 4 km, between Gores Landing and Harwood, the road hugs the scenic shore but never allows you access. Crammed into even the narrowest beaches are cottages and campgrounds.

Harwood began as a railway town but did not remain one for long. In 1852 a group of Cobourg merchants formed the Cobourg and Peterborough Railway. Across the shallow lake they built a 5 km trestle and causeway, much of it only a few metres above the water. On December 29, 1854, the first train rumbled across it. But after only six years the spring ice movements on the lake had so weakened the trestle that it was deemed unsafe and abandoned. Shortly afterward, it collapsed. Harwood's life as a railway town collapsed with it.

Like Gores Landing, Harwood is now a resort community, but a few vestiges have survived from

A beautiful sunset on Rice Lake.

the days of the railway: its main street, named Railway Street; and the remains of the causeway itself, a broken finger of fill that extends several hundred metres into the lake. You can park at a small public beach to explore the remains of the causeway. But use caution because the path is narrow and the footing tricky.

Return along Railway Street, the alignment of the old railway, to County Road 18. At this corner is the Harwood convenience store in a building that also dates from the days of rail.

There are two ways to return home. If you are bound for Ottawa or points east, stay on County Road 18 east until you reach Highway 45, where the Alderville First Nations has erected a stunning war monument. A short distance north leads you to Roseneath, with its historic carousel. Continue north on 45 to reach Highway 7 and thence Ottawa. If you are returning to the Toronto area, turn right onto Highway 45, which takes you to Highway 401, in the vicinity of Cobourg.

13 The Quinte Shore Road

The cliffs of Prince Edward County soar above the Bay of Quinte, rising in places to heights of 100 metres above its waters. This route guides you on a shoreline drive along the crest of these cliffs. It starts 150 km east of Toronto at the northwest corner of Prince Edward County and follows 120 km of paved county roads to Point Traverse, the county's southeast corner. Most villages on the route contain gas stations and general stores, and some have a snack bar. Midway, Picton offers opportunities for shopping and licensed dining. If you prefer a picnic lunch, there are frequent roadside and waterside parks, at some of which you can swim or fish.

Prince Edward is both a county and an island, for it is separated from the Ontario mainland by a narrow Z-shaped body of water called the Bay of Quinte. A tilted limestone plateau, where long limestone peninsulas jab into Lake Ontario, the island's north and east shores form rugged grey cliffs, while its west and south shores slope gently under the lapping waters of the lake.

The Quinte Shore Road offers something for almost everyone. If you are a photographer or artist, you will stop for the red cupola-roofed barns, reminiscent of New England, or the stone farmhouses; if a sailor, you will linger at a fishing cove or at one of the lighthouses that are among the oldest on the Great Lakes. If your penchant is 19th-century architecture, you can stroll past the century-old mansions and workers' homes of Picton. And if, like most, you are a pleasure driver, you will find on this route all the fields, orchards and clifftop vistas that you could want.

More than 100 years have passed since the Murray Canal was chopped across the neck of Prince Edward County, making it an "island."

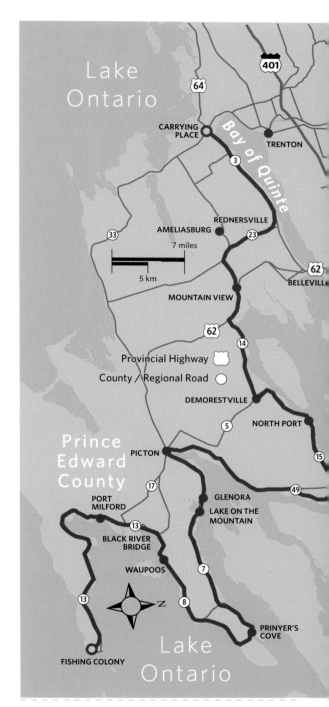

Opposite: A view of Quinte's cliff-lined shore.

f you trace your roots to United Empire Loyalist stock, you may find them here, for Prince Edward is one of Ontario's oldest settlements. In 1783 when American persecution of British supporters peaked, John Weese fled the hostility of New York State to the peaceful shores of Prince Edward County. Others followed him, and within a decade Prince Edward's shores and coves were well populated. During the peace that followed the War of 1812, the county farmers began to ship barley to American breweries across the lake. Barley ports popped up in every cove that could shelter a schooner. Later, as steamers replaced the schooners, and as the barley trade died, the little ports dwindled. Farmers turned to cheesemaking, and soon the county could claim 28 cheese factories. But this industry also declined, and now only one factory, Black River Cheese, remains. However, the flat fields and moderate climate ensured Prince Edward of agricultural prosperity, and it soon led Ontario in vegetable growing and canning. It has now evolved into a major wine destination with more than a dozen wineries, many of which offer wine-tasting and meals.

Carrying Place

The trip begins at Carrying Place, in a small treed park beside the Murray Canal. To reach it, exit from Highway 401 south onto Wooler Road, about 150 km east of Toronto. At Highway 33, 5 km south, turn right and drive another 2 km to the park. Here you can watch sleek schooners or antennae-laden cruisers edging their way past the swing bridge. Here, too, you will realize that Prince Edward was not always an island. Until 1889 a swampy neck of land connected Prince Edward with the mainland. A popular portage for Native peoples, the location was called Carrying Place. Then in 1889, when Great Lakes shipping was at a peak, Thomas Murray eliminated the long,

perilous outer voyage by chopping a canal through the portage.

Carrying Place is also the site of the long-lost Fort Kente. In 1668 responding to the pleas of local Cayuga, the Sulpician priests Claude Trouve and Francois de Fenelon built a mission fort. It prospered only briefly, and by 1680 the dispersal of the Indian population and soaring costs forced the mission to close. Its exact location remains a mystery.

Carrying Place to Rednersville

Drive south from the park until you come to County Road 3. Turn left and follow it to Rednersville. The area is now popular commuter country for Belleville and Trenton workers, and modern sprawl surrounds the old farmhouses and infiltrates the apple orchards. From the road you will enjoy frequent views of the Bay of Quinte and of the spires and apartment towers of Trenton on the opposite shores.

After winding past limestone rock outcrops, orchards and barns, you arrive at the ancient port of Rednersville. The village was founded by Loyalist Henry Redner, and during the 1850s, it went on to prosper as a barley port. There are two outstanding buildings here that predate even that period. One, Henry Redner's home, is a solid stone house set back from the road on the south side, just west of the intersection. The other is his store at the southeastern corner of the intersection. In operation since 1803, it became Ontario's oldest general store and is now an antique store. The brick facade replaced the stone face following a fire in 1860.

Rednersville to Demorestville

A short distance east of the store, turn right and follow County Road 23 for 6 km to County Road 19. Turn right and continue another 1.5 km into

An abandoned cannery at Waupoos.

Ameliasburg. This was once a busy village, but its shops are now silent. The tall stone United church has been converted into a museum and houses pioneer farm and household utensils, as well as a large collection of old area maps and photographs. On the grounds, the curators have reconstructed a log cabin and also a blacksmith's shop, where you can watch blacksmithing as it was done a hundred years ago.

Leave the village east on County Road 19, then turn left onto County Road 2 and travel 3 km toward Highway 62 and the picturesque community of Mountain View. Here the road begins to follow the brink of one of the county's limestone escarpments, lined by a woodland of maples and cedars. Tucked under the cliff is Mountain View. To take a short side trip to its twin-spired church follow Highway 62, a few metres to the left.

From Mountain View continue east on Highway 62 and drive 4 km to County Road 14 and turn left. Once again the road edges up to the brink of the cliff, where opportunities to glimpse Muscote Bay are limited to a few gaps in the roadside vegetation. After following the rim for about 5 km, the road inches inland and, 4.5 km farther along, enters the village of Demorestville.

Demorestville

In Demorestville a handful of homes, old and new, mingle on a small grid of streets. This hamlet is a mere ghost of what it was a century and a half ago, when it was the county's grandest village. It all began in 1800, when William Demorest dammed the waters of Fish Creek and built a mill. By 1824 the busy new town contained four taverns and six stores and had nearly 2,000 residents. However,

Demorestville was once Prince Edward County's busiest town.

the growth of the barley trade and the coming of the railway to the rival town of Picton turned the inland town into a backwater, and it soon declined. Although many of the empty lots now sprout new homes, you can still spot the old streets, a few now just dirt tracks that vanish into the fields. The general store is now the National Hope Studio Gallery. Beside it stand the gothic-style town hall and the historic stone United church.

Demorestville to Picton

From the stop sign on County Road 5, follow County Road 15 north down the cliff and along the low Quinte shore and, after 6.5 km, into the former port of Northport.

This historic hamlet still retains its narrow streets and old houses that lead to the shore. Some 14 km from Demorestville, the Highway 49 bridge looms into view. Turn left onto County Road 35 and drive under the bridge. Here, at Prince Edward County's northeastern shoulder, the road bends south and for 6 km follows a 100 metre clifftop to Highway 49. Turn left here and follow the highway south toward Picton.

After 10 km on Highway 49, watch for a historical marker to the White Chapel. This two-storey clapboard church was built by William Moore in 1809 and has been fully preserved. It holds an annual service each June and is Ontario's oldest Methodist meeting hall still in use.

Past the White Chapel, Highway 49 enters Picton and joins Highway 33, which is Main Street West in downtown Picton. The town has provided parking spaces behind the stores on Main Street West, so you can park here and enjoy Picton's attractions on foot. Pick up your walking tour map

The historic Glenora mill sits right below the mysterious Lake on the Mountain.

at the tourist office at Ferguson and Main Streets, four blocks west.

A Walking Tour of Picton

This short tour of Picton takes in about 12 city blocks and takes about an hour. From the intersection of Highways 49 and 33 (Main Street and Bridge Street), walk north on Main to see Picton's most prized mansions, the slender Italianate form of the McMullen mansion (built in 1850) and the Georgian mass of the Striker mansion (1868). Taking Union Street east from Bridge and then following Church Street will bring you to the museum and archives, housed in a stone church built by Rev. William MacCaulley in 1823.

As you return on Union and Bridge Streets, walk left on May Street just before you come to Main. It parallels Main Street and contains vintage homes of workers. Along Main Street West, in the downtown area, look for the North American Hotel (1835); the Allison Block; and the Regent Theatre, built as a vaudeville showhouse in 1931 and now restored.

Picton to Lake on the Mountain

Leave Picton on Highway 33 east (Bridge Street). Soon you will encounter vistas across Picton Harbour and, on the far shore, the sprawling hulk of the Essroc Cement Company, with its limestone crushers, its quarries and its conveyors. After driving 9 km from Picton, turn right onto County Road 7 and follow the signs to Lake on the Mountain Provincial Park. Designed for picnickers and offering expansive views, this park includes the county's highest lookout point and one of the province's most mysterious lakes.

The historic Duck Island lighthouse has been preserved on a museum ground.

The lake site is on a lip of cliff 100 metres above Lake Ontario, and for many years its depth and source puzzled geologists. In the 1970s divers at last determined its depth to be more than 50 metres and its source as underwater springs. The lake's origin remains a mystery, although theories suggest that it is the result of the collapse of an underground cavern.

Beside the park lie the remains of a village. In 1796 Loyalist Peter Van Alstine built a mill on the cliff and started a village named Mountain Mills. In 1813 he built a second mill below the cliff and there created the village of Glenora. His historic store stands adjacent to the picnic grounds.

Although Van Alstine's first mill was demolished more than a hundred years ago, his second mill survives. To see the three-storey stone structure, return to Highway 33 and turn right to Glenora (which today is the terminal for the Ontario Ministry of Transport ferry to the mainland). The large stone building beside the dock is a Ministry of Natural Resources fish hatchery and provides tours during working hours. Beyond it is Van Alstine's mill, now a private residence.

Lake on the Mountain to South Bay

Return to County Road 7 and follow it east from Lake on the Mountain along the north shore of Cressy Point. From the clifftop, the road offers views across Adolphus Reach to the Lennox and Addington County shore. There the incongruous bulk of a Hydro thermal-generating plant squats on a coastline that is otherwise pastoral and green.

Gradually the cliffs subside, reaching water level at Prinyer's Cove. In 1784 the cove witnessed the landing of one of Ontario's first parties of Loyalist refugees, led by Colonel Archibald MacDonald. A busy shipping and fishing centre during barley days, the cove is now a retirement and cottage community.

Prinyer's Cove signals the end of the Bay of Quinte. Here its waters swirl into the vastness of Lake Ontario. The long, thin, fingerlike peninsula, which is called Cressy Point, is the county's most easterly point of land. County Road 8 cuts sharply south near the head of the peninsula to the south shore. Keep right here and follow the low shore. While the lake stretches away to the south, on the shore are the farms and orchards that were started by the Loyalists. Along this road you will come to Rose House Museum, with rooms decorated and furnished in the style of the mid-19th century, when the house was built.

Continue west from the museum and descend the mesa, past more orchards and white wooden farmhouses, the shoreline interspersed with cottages. The Waupoos Marina, with its former canning factory, marks the village of Waupoos, a one-time fishing village. The nearby Waupoos winery is one of the county's oldest. One and a half km from the marina turn left onto County Road 13. For 4 km the route teases the lip of the cliff and, from the Rutherford-Stevens Lookout Point, offers views over the waters of South Bay. It then descends through a dark forest of maples and oaks into the Black River Valley. The village of Black River Bridge was another of Prince Edward County's once busy ports and is home of the last of its 28 cheese factories.

Continue on County Road 13 for another 5.5 km. If the squat stone lighthouse on the left side seems far from the water, it is. The second-oldest Canadian lighthouse on the Great Lakes, it guided ships around the distant Duck Islands from 1838 to 1965. It was then moved, stone by stone, to the South Bay Mariners' Museum. A modest frame building beside the lighthouse houses relics of the glory days of Great Lakes' shipping. Anchors, bells, oars and lamps date from the days of sail and steam, some salvaged from wrecks that occurred within its very sight.

South Bay to Point Traverse

This is the last segment of the Quinte Shore Backroad and it follows the shore of Long Point to the county's southeast tip. From the museum, County Road 13 continues south around the head of South Bay to follow the Long Point shore easterly, passing through a scattered string village also called South Bay. Look for the sign to the Little Bluff Conservation Area. The view from the clifftop extends from the lip of Long Point to the east, to the far shore of South Bay.

East of the park the road hugs the shore as the cliffs subside to just a few metres. Pavement soon gives way to gravel as County Road 13 enters the Prince Edward Point National Wildlife Area acquired in 1979 by the Canadian Wildlife Service.

Here the road bends south to follow the windswept headland of the point. Below the 10 metre cliffs lies a beach of boulders washed smooth by the clear lake waters. The road ends at Prince Edward Point, where the still waters of a tiny unexpected cove reflect the forms of a pair of fishing tugs and government boats. From a public wharf on the north side of the inlet, you can fish or watch the occasional yacht glide in from the open lake. You can then follow the road as it becomes a dirt track winding its way around the cove and ends at the historic wooden lighthouse. Here, in a setting that is silent and idyllic, your trip along the Quinte Shore Road ends. But other county attractions include the mountainous sand dunes of Sandbanks Provincial Park and the unusual "Birdhouse City" in the Macaulay Mountain Conservation Area.

To return home, follow County Road 33 west from Picton through such historic villages as Wellington and Consecon and along the scenic shore of the lake.

Overleaf: Picton's charming waterfront.

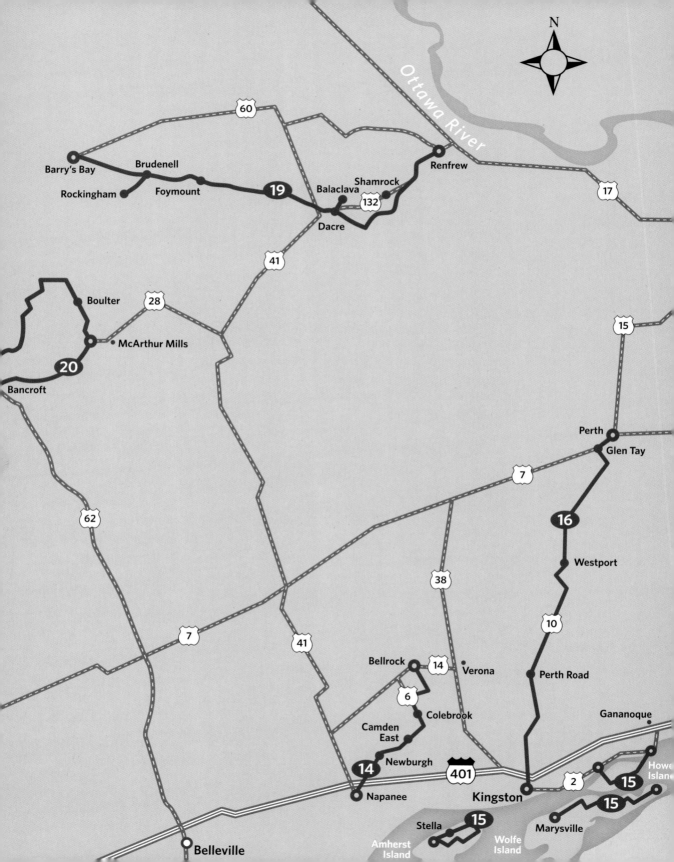

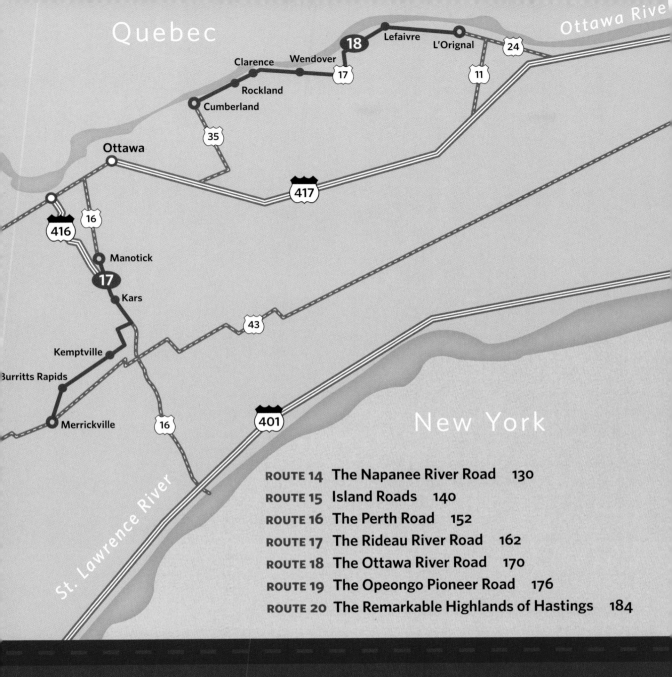

Quebec

Ottawa River

18 Lefaivre
Wendover
Clarence
Rockland
Cumberland
35
17
L'Orignal
24
11

Ottawa

417

16
416

Manotick
17
Kars

43

Kemptville

Burritts Rapids
16
401
New York

Merrickville

St. Lawrence River

ROUTE 14 The Napanee River Road 130
ROUTE 15 Island Roads 140
ROUTE 16 The Perth Road 152
ROUTE 17 The Rideau River Road 162
ROUTE 18 The Ottawa River Road 170
ROUTE 19 The Opeongo Pioneer Road 176
ROUTE 20 The Remarkable Highlands of Hastings 184

Section 3
Eastern Ontario

14 The Napanee River Road

Much of Ontario's early settlement was determined by its rivers. This route probes the fertile valley of the Napanee River, which, with its string of unusual old mill villages, marks one of the thrusts of pioneering into what was then a dark and mysterious back country.

The trip begins at the Lake Ontario town of Napanee, 200 km east of Toronto, and follows the river valley 45 km north eastward. To arrive at your starting point, exit from Highway 401 at exit 579 and follow Highway 41 south into Napanee. While most of the villages you will visit contain gas stations and general stores, only Napanee has a selection of restaurants, so either snack beforehand or pack a lunch to enjoy in one of several parks.

The historic Grand Trunk railway was built over the falls that attracted Napanee's original mills.

This route contains much for you to see and do. For the photographer, stone houses, country stores and old mills provide ample subject material, while the angler can pause to cast a line in the rushing river or one of the tranquil millponds.

The gentle slopes of Lake Ontario's back shores are cut by many rivers. In a day when roads were seldom negotiable, if they existed at all, the rivers were the highways, giving early settlers their first opportunities to move inland from the communities along the lakeshore. The rivers also provided much-needed power sites for the vital sawmills and gristmills.

Yet settlement along the Napanee progressed slowly. In fact, five decades passed before the pioneers finally overcame the obstacles of rapids and windfalls and completed the settlement of the valley. While the many rapids and falls provided power sites for the early sawmills, not until the river road opened did the first settlers trudge up the fertile valley. Soon busy farms lined the concessions and the mill sites boomed into farm service towns.

Gradually the era of the mill passed and the towns declined. Today, though most of the old mills are gone, the early townscapes and farms-capes have left their imprint.

Napanee

The outskirts of Napanee now sprawl outward to meet Highway 401. But 200 years ago there were no highways, and Napanee was little more than a sawmill settlement. At the falls on the river, Robert Clarke, Napanee's founder, built a sawmill, along with a store and a number of houses. Mill manager James Clarke gave the settlement its first name, Clarkeville, and in 1787 he built the first gristmill between Toronto and Kingston. But Clarkeville remained small until 1812, when Allan MacPherson took over the mills and built a large store and, later, a school. By then the surrounding area was bustling with pioneer farms, and the village began to grow. In 1831 Sam Benson surveyed a townsite, and Napanee began to take the form it has today.

Drive to the stoplights at Highway 2, Dundas

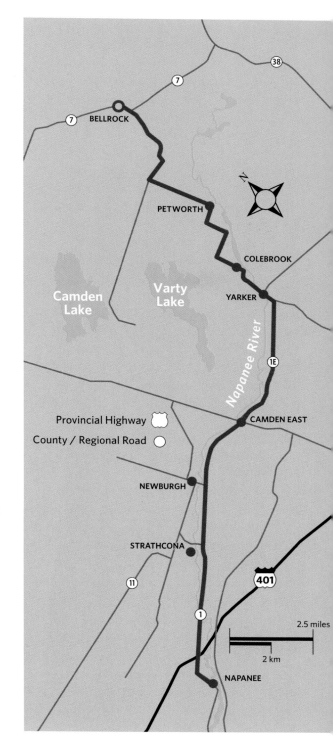

Street, in the heart of Napanee, and turn left. This takes you through the business district, with commercial buildings that date back more than a century. It is a streetscape that has largely been spared from fires and much of the needless demolitions and insensitive alterations that have decimated so many Ontario towns of Napanee's size. One block north of the main street on John Street is the market square, anchored by its slender-columned town hall. Built in 1856, the hall has recently been restored and painted; it is one of the oldest in eastern Ontario.

Across the street and half a block north looms the massive red sandstone building, the Napanee post office, which was built in 1888. If you go north on John Street and then right, or east, onto Thomas Street, you will come to the Lennox and Addington County courthouse, which was built in 1864 when Napanee was proclaimed the county seat. Its cupola and pillars dominate what is otherwise a shady residential street. Behind the courthouse, and predating it by several years, is the former jail, now a museum, where you can still see the cells.

By following Dundas Street east from the downtown area and passing under the railway bridge, you will come to Clarke's old mill site, set in an appealing little riverside park. Here, at the falls in the river where Napanee began, you can enjoy a picnic before setting out on your backroads drive.

From the park retrace your steps along Dundas Street to the bridge. Watch for Camden Road and turn right. Turn right again onto Elizabeth Street and park by the historical plaque in front of a large white house. This is the mansion once owned by Napanee's co-founder, Allan MacPherson, and built around 1825. Having stayed in the MacPherson family until 1896, the house has been refurbished by the Napanee Historical Society. It provides you with a glimpse into upper-class life in early 19th-century Ontario.

Napanee to Newburgh

Leave Napanee on Camden Road, which swings right and becomes Newburgh Road (County Road 1). After crossing Highway 401 and the Napanee River, it follows the former pioneer road up the Napanee River Valley, leading through gentle farmscapes to a string of historic mill villages.

The Greek style pillars distinguish the Napanee town hall.

The first of these is Strathcona, about 8 km from Napanee.

Strathcona owes its existence to John Thompson, who, in Windsor in 1864, perfected the modern pulp-making process. Moving to the Napanee Valley in the 1870s, he established paper mills near Camden and Newburgh, and also at Strathcona, then a tiny sawmill village known as Napanee Mills. Not only is the mill at Strathcona one of the only two in the valley to survive, but it is the only one that grew. Today, its 250 employees each day produce 130 tons of heavy paper for boxes.

Strathcona's buildings line a pair of parallel

Newburgh's main street never fully recovered from a fire that destroyed most of its buildings more than a century ago.

streets that strike westward from County Road 1 and continue up the opposite side of the river. Turn left onto County Road 16. As you cross the bridge you will see the sprawling bulk of the Strathcona mill on your right, the original section now so engulfed by additions that it is barely distinguishable. Turn right onto Finlay Street. In addition to the workers' houses, there are two outstanding stone structures—the former Methodist church, built in 1875, and the handsome two-storey public library. They face each other across the road about half a kilometre from the bridge. To resume your journey, return to County Road 1.

As you continue up the valley you will pass stone farmhouses with their wide pastures that drop gently toward the valley floor, and, after 3 km, you will come to Newburgh. At the green directional arrow turn left and drive down the valley wall into the unusual village.

Newburgh

In contrast to Napanee and even to Strathcona, Newburgh exudes an air of quiet, a memory of days past. The streets are deserted for the most part. But it wasn't always that way.

In 1824 when David Perry built a sawmill on a waterfall in the woods, he didn't foresee a bustling mill town that would challenge Napanee for the county seat. By 1832 settlers were coming in growing numbers and soon there were factories, mills, stores and hotels in this thriving community that was known throughout the area, somewhat ingloriously, as Rogues' Hollow. Then, in the 1870s, there came John Thompson and his paper mills, and the town entered its glory days. But its

Newburgh's historic academy has survived in its pastoral setting.

booming growth was shattered when in 1887 a raging fire razed 84 buildings. By then Napanee was the county seat and the area's leading town. Most of Newburgh's destroyed industries either relocated in Napanee or were not rebuilt. More fires in 1902 and 1908 reduced the town still further, to a mere shell of its former self.

As you descend the hill to the first bridge, you will find a clutch of fine stone buildings, the only part of the main street spared by the many infernos. Here, a one-time hotel, stone stores and handsome old homes are a "must" for the photographer and historian. Cross the bridge and turn right to the conservation area that has been developed on Thompson's mill site. Here you can enjoy a lunch or stroll beside the swirling river. About half a kilometre upstream you will see the town's

original railway station, a two-storey structure built by the pioneer Bay of Quinte Railway.

To see Newburgh's most celebrated building, continue north on the main street to the hardware store and turn left onto Academy St. Drive half a kilometre to the top of the hill, where you will confront a massive stone building topped by an octagonal cupola. This, the Newburgh Academy, is the oldest such institution in Ontario to survive in its original form. Started in 1839 by three local residents, it grew to become one of the province's leading teachers' colleges. The present building replaced the original in 1853, and, despite a fire in 1887, it retains its original appearance. Thanks to a fund raised by local residents and former students, the college has been restored and preserved.

This stone store is Camden East's landmark.

Newburgh to Camden East

Retrace your trail to County Road 1. Northeast of
Newburgh the valley walls retreat still farther and
the pastures roll toward the river. After 3 km, you
will enter the village of Camden East.

To describe Camden East as a "picture postcard"
is not an exaggeration, for that is what it once was:
a subject of artist Manly MacDonald for Coutts
Hallmark Christmas cards.

Camden East got off to an early start, considering the difficult transportation problems that the
settlers faced. By 1850 the village could claim mills,
factories, stores, hotels and even a distillery. When
the Bay of Quinte Railway arrived in 1871, Camden
East's prosperity seemed assured. But rather than
enhancing the town's trading position, the railway
weakened it by putting the town in Napanee's
shadow. The most striking building in town, and

one of the most remarkable on this backroad tour,
is the massive grey stone hulk of a former hotel
and store on the northwest corner of the main
intersection.

Camden East to Yarker

As you continue east from the village, you drive
by pastoral landscapes of fields and barns, as well
as the river. After a little more than 6 km, County
Road 1 comes to County Road 6, which bends
steeply to the left and descends into the village of
Yarker.

Yarker is a relative newcomer to the Napanee
Valley. It began in 1840 when David Vader built
a sawmill, and it received a boost nine years later
when George Miller established a gristmill. The
falls at one time dropped 10 metres straight down,
but so consistently did the log drives wear away

Two disused railway bridges at Yarker.

the soft limestone riverbed that the brink of the falls now lies 15 metres back of the base.

As Yarker grew, it attracted an array of mills and businesses and, in 1871 the Bay of Quinte Railway, which wound its way northward to Bannockburn. Four decades later, when the Canadian Northern Railway pushed the line on toward Ottawa, the village found itself on the railway's busy main line.

Although the village has slipped from its population peak of 600 to just around 400, it has retained its winding streets and many of its older buildings. The best grouping is near the corner of Water and Bridge Streets, where the former hotel that was a church stands a block from the oddly attractive Waterfall Tea Room built as M. Wright's store in 1902.

Cross the bridge and bear right on Vanluven Street, County Road 6.

Yarker to Bellrock

As you leave the village, you pass beneath a former railway bridge that now carries the Cataraqui Rail Trail along the roadbed of the Canadian National Railway. As you proceed to Colebrook the wooded valley wall closes in from the left, while the river swirls by the road on the right.

Attracted by the landscape, country dwellers have lined the river to Colebrook with new country houses, and the two villages have become nearly one. However, you will find the heart of Colebrook beside the bridge over the river. Like Yarker and its sister river towns, Colebrook began as a sawmill village. But when the Bay of Quinte Railway passed it by, the village stagnated; what little it had was destroyed in 1877 by a fire that gutted two sawmills, three stores and five homes. Few were rebuilt, and the gaps remain.

A small park by the river has replaced the mills and provides a picnic spot. Below the dam you can still see the foundation of the gristmill, the victim of a fire in 1961. (The original mill, spared by the 1877 fire, burned in 1939.) One of the village's oldest homes, and certainly its grandest, is a stone building that sits south of the bridge and faces the river.

Leave Colebrook north on County Road 6 and look for the Petworth Road sign on the right. Follow it for a little over 3 km to the least successful of the Napanee River mill towns, the ghost town of Petworth. Petworth started with a sawmill and then grew with the settlement of the area's farmlands. A stone gristmill was added in 1845, and at its peak Petworth possessed two hotels, several stores, an Orange hall, a cheese factory, a blacksmith and a carding mill. Following Petworth's demise, most of its buildings stood empty until, one by one, they succumbed to fire or were replaced by country homes. You may still see a portion of the stone foundation of the old mill. From the intersection just west of the river, drive north on German Road 3 km to a T intersection at Huffman Road and turn right. The route is narrow, passing barns and farm homes that date back more than a century.

Suddenly the road plunges into the Portland Swamp. Dense woods rise overhead as the Napanee River divides into a myriad of small tributaries that wind aimlessly through the bush. Although the swamp is over 10 km long, your crossing is less than 2 km. The road then rises from the swamp to meet County Road 7 and the unusual little village of Bellrock.

Bellrock

Bellrock rose on the fortunes of the Rathbun Lumber Company. One of the logging giants of the 1800s, Rathbun logged the area and drove or shipped the logs to its mills at Deseronto on the Bay of Quinte. Bellrock grew not only into a supply centre for the Rathbuns but also into a milling centre in its own right. In addition to hotels, stores, a blacksmith's and a cheese factory, the village also had two sawmills, one gristmill and a carding mill, all powered by the rushing falls on the Napanee River. And one still survives. By the river stands a sawmill built in the 1920s. Under the same roof were a shingle mill and a gristmill. Once operated by the local conservation authority, the building is now vacant.

This finale to the trip is appropriate, for mills such as these created the towns on the Napanee River and brought prosperity to the valley.

To return to Kingston or points east, travel east on County Road 7 to Highway 38, which leads south to Kingston and Highway 401. If you are returning to the Ottawa area, take Highway 38 north to Highway 7 and east to the nation's capital. For returning Torontonians, travel west on County Road 7, which becomes County Road 14 on entering Lennox and Addington County. After 20 km you will come to Highway 41, which you take south to Highway 401.

Opposite: Water power once drove the saws at the Bellrock sawmill.

15 Island Roads

If you really want a break from life in the fast lane, try following some backroads that you cannot drive to. You need to take a ferry to get to the backroads of Lake Ontario's largest island communities—Wolfe, Amherst and Howe Islands. A side trip to the smaller Simcoe Island also awaits you on this route.

These low limestone outcroppings crowding the outlet of Lake Ontario and the beginning of the St. Lawrence River are linked to the mainland near Kingston by frequent ferries. While Wolfe Island provides a full range of services for any traveller, Howe and Amherst have only small stores and few gas pumps.

Allow half a day to visit each island. You can base yourself in Kingston, which has the best collection of early 19th-century stone buildings west of Montreal.

This is a trip for the traveller who likes tranquility. On these islands you may stop in the middle of the road to take in a view without fear of an impatient horn behind you. Just as there is little traffic, there has been less pressure to demolish old farmhouses and stores. So if you love the simple architecture of the 19th century, you can find it here, often little changed. On these island backroads you can take in both history and scenery, all at your own pace.

Opposite: A few of the many Thousand Islands in the St. Lawrence River.

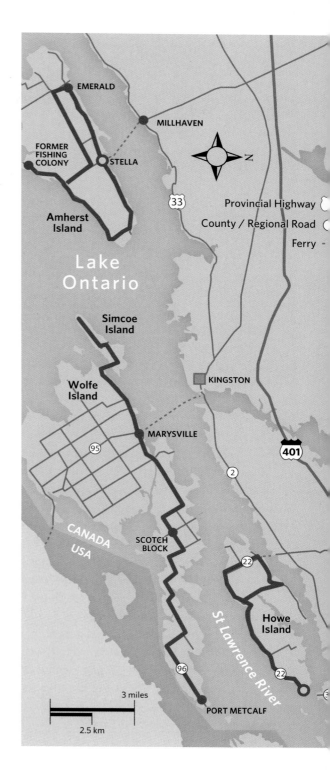

141

Island backroads are traffic-free.

Wolfe, Howe and Amherst Islands were originally within the Seigneury of Cataraqui, which was once held by the Sieur de La Salle. After the British conquest of Canada in 1760, the islands passed to the British, though settlement did not begin until half a century later.

As the 19th century progressed, all three islands developed rapidly. The once-brooding forests were stripped clean and replaced by busy farms. Any cove that could shelter a schooner soon sprouted a wharf to ship wheat, barley or timber. Wolfe Island's population peaked at 3,600 in 1860, while the populations of Amherst and Howe peaked at 850 and 400, respectively. Each island was incorporated as a separate municipality.

With the turn of the century, urbanization reduced farm populations everywhere, and the populations of Lake Ontario's island communities plummeted to less than half their peak totals. Today, the pace of island life remains leisurely. Traffic is light and the islanders have time to chat, even with a backroader from the mainland.

Howe Island

Howe Island is a flat limestone plateau about 9 km long and 4 km wide. Its roads follow the shore, offering views of the historic farmsteads and the sparkling waters of the St. Lawrence River.

To get to the island, leave Kingston on Highway 2 and travel east 15 km to Howe Island Ferry Road. Turn right and follow the signs to the dock. Here the 15-car cable ferry *Frontenac-Howe Islander* shuttles back and forth nonstop during busy periods and on request when traffic is light. It takes only ten minutes to complete the crossing.

Ontario's island roads enjoy tranquil wave-washed shorelines.

Howe Island has only four main roads, two that hug the north and south shores, and two that connect them. From the dock travel south and turn left at North Shore Road, the first crossroad. This road was built to link the waterfront farms, and it winds through rolling pastures and past once busy farmsteads. After a little more than 1 km, look on the right for St. Patrick's School, which was built in 1894 and is now owned by the volunteer fire department. It is the only survivor of the island's three public schools. Although it has lost its bell tower, it appears today as its pupils might remember it.

Shortly after passing the school, you will come to a fork in the road. Keep left and pass more handsome century-old farms. As you skirt and then descend the steep limestone cliff that forms the north shore of the island, you will be treated to pleasant views of the mainland. Here the island's northern coast is interrupted by an inlet called variously Johnson Bay and Big Bay, and the farm road ends. Return all the way to the ferry road and turn left onto County Road 22.

After 2 km, you will come to the south shore. Here, at a T intersection, turn left. As the road winds in and out of the little coves, you can look across the St. Lawrence River to the Wolfe Island shore. Beside the water is a line of new cottages and country homes, occupied by Kingston commuters and seasonal occupants.

After 1 km look for a pair of renovated log cabins, one on the left beside the road and the other on the right close to the water. These are original settlers' cabins, and they are the oldest homes on the island. Over the next 2 km you will pass, almost imperceptibly, more than a dozen former

farm lots. Although they are not very wide, they are nearly 1 km deep and represent an old water-front survey technique that, in the days before roads, insured that every settler had access to water. Of the 40 or so original farms, there are now fewer than a half-dozen.

Halfway along the south shore drive, you will encounter the island's most imposing building, St. Philomena's Roman Catholic Church. Built in 1858, it is the only island structure that was built with local limestone. Continue driving east, and, after 2 km, you will come to the island's oldest store. No longer in business, it was operated by the Goodfriend family for more than a century. The final 2 km bring you to the end of the Howe Island drive and the three-car township ferry back to the mainland.

Wolfe Island

Shaped like a long-handled dipper, Wolfe Island is the largest of the islands and the closest to Kingston, the richest agriculturally, and the most populous. It is connected by ferry not only to Kingston, but also to Cape Vincent in New York State. Although Wolfe Island is busier than Amherst or Howe, it contains quiet coves and unhurried farm lanes. Among its more interesting features are its photogenic stone halls, houses and hotels, many of which predate Confederation itself. Two side trips—to Simcoe Island and to Garden Island—can be taken from Wolfe.

The 55-car *Wolfe Islander III* leaves Kingston from the dock at the corner of Ontario and Barrack Streets. It makes 20 crossings a day during the navigation season, but you should expect to wait your turn on a holiday weekend. Even on a regular summer weekend, it is wise to arrive early.

Despite its small size, Howe Island's church is a grand building.

The crossing takes 20 minutes, and time passes too quickly.

As the ferry glides toward Wolfe Island's wooded shore, the buildings of Marysville, the island's only village, appear through the trees. On arrival, follow the ramp to the stop sign at Marysville's main street. Here most of the ferry traffic turns right to follow County Road 95 to island homes or the Cape Vincent ferry. The forest of wind turbines that rises above the flat landscape evokes an "other-worldly" feel to the pastoral island.

From the dock you should turn left onto County Road 96 and head toward the less populated "panhandle," the island's long peninsula that juts into the St. Lawrence River.

After a little more than 1 km, the road crosses what appears to be a weedy ditch. Incredibly, this was once a ship canal. In 1857 in an attempt to attract barge and schooner traffic, the Wolfe Island Railway and Canal Company sliced a 2 km canal through the island's narrowest point, eliminating the longer passage around the tip of the peninsula. But steamers had already begun to replace barges and schooners, and in 1870 the company abandoned the narrow canal. It never did build a railway.

Continue east on County Road 96, the main road, as it zigzags through the maze of old farm concession roads that crisscross the panhandle. After 3 km, follow the sharp bend to the right and then, after another 2 km, another sharp bend to the left. At the next crossroads you enter what was known as the Scotch Block Settlement, where a band of hopeful Scottish immigrants moved during the 19th century. The road passes an area of shallow soils, where farms and homesteads were abandoned. Another 4 km of twists and turns lead to the Scotch Block's Christ Church. Built in 1862 with local limestone, the church has seen steady worship

Amherst Island is known for its dry-stone walls.

ever since. From the church, continue east for 7 km to Port Metcalfe. Here the panhandle narrows to a width of only one or two farm lots. You can still see many of the original shoreline farms that were built when the water was the only highway. Port Metcalfe is the end of the road. You will need to retrace your route to return to Marysville.

Marysville

At some point during your visit to Wolfe Island, walk around Marysville. The town started as a landing in 1802, though very few settlers arrived before the 1820s. The original wharf stood three blocks to the east of the present ferry dock, approximately where the Wolfe Island marina now sits. On the south side of the street, across from the old wharf, is the renovated General Wolfe Hotel. Built in 1860, it has served Marysville for

a century and a half. Today, it offers nine guestrooms and a 130-seat dining room.

Walk west along Main Street and at the southeast corner of Main and Division Streets you will see a small limestone building. This is Wolfe Island's original town hall, built in 1850, just nine years after the island was incorporated as a separate municipality. It is one of Ontario's oldest and most attractive township halls. At the next corner is a red brick store, built in 1878 by Edward Baker and in the same family for more than a century. One block farther on is the village's oldest building—and one of the oldest buildings on the island. In 1832 Archibald Hitchcock built a wharf and a stone hotel, which he called the Hitchcock House. Two-and-a-half storeys high, it was constructed of local stone; the frame addition on the back came later.

The interesting old town hall on Wolfe Island.

Simcoe Island

If you want to leave the traffic behind altogether and enjoy a short drive to view an historic lighthouse, then tiny Simcoe Island is ideal, for it has only 3 km of road. From the ferry dock in Marysville, follow County Road 96 west for 4 km until you reach the ferry landing. The two-car ferry has a schedule that coincides with the *Wolfe Islander* (for car drivers, so cyclists might miss the departure). On the island, follow the only road west. Although it's a narrow gravel road, it is in good condition. The lighthouse is at the end of the road. Constructed of local limestone about a century ago, it no longer guides vessels through the shoal-strewn waters. Because it is owned by the Canadian Goast Guard, there is no access to it, but it is easily viewed from the road.

Garden Island

Garden Island is unique. For three-quarters of a century, this tiny island housed a busy shipbuilding community and was home to nearly 700 people.

The shipyards were begun in 1835 by an American named Dileno Dexter Calvin, and they continued to be run by that family until 1926. During this period the family launched 25 ships, ranging from barges to ocean vessels. The wharf and shipyards were clustered at the eastern end of the island, while the workers' simple frame homes lined a road that ran down the middle. By 1866 the population had grown large enough to have its own school, church and post office—and even its own municipal council. But when the shipyards closed, the population dwindled. Some people remained, and they proudly preserved many original structures.

There is no public access to this private domain.

Still standing are the office (with its cupola), the former post office, and the mansions of the owners: the White House of Ira Brock; and the Green House, home of the Calvins themselves. And still on the now grassy main street are some of the simpler workers' houses.

Garden Island is a museum piece, the only example of a 19th-century shipbuilding centre to survive in such remarkable condition. However, because no public authority assumes responsibility for it, its accessibility to heritage enthusiasts depends utterly on the invitation of its occupants.

Amherst Island

The ferry for Amherst Island leaves from Millhaven, 18 km west of Kingston on Highway 33. You will be unlikely to find a lineup here, for Amherst Island, about half the size of Wolfe Island, is the most tranquil of the three main islands and has the fewest cottages and commuters.

The new *Frontenac II* glides away from the dock every hour on the half-hour and has a capacity for 33 cars. Half an hour later, the engines rumble into reverse and the gangway clangs onto the dock of the island's main village of Stella.

The roads of Amherst Island wind along windswept coastlines and cross lush farmlands. Happily, the lack of development pressure has left a legacy of farmsteads and churches. So light is the traffic that even driving for its own sake becomes a pleasure. Whether you explore the village of Stella before or after your drive, be sure to set aside a little time for that purpose.

From the ferry dock, drive a few metres to the intersection and turn left. Stella is a small treasure trove of heritage buildings including the general store and house on the main corner, the old blacksmith shop, and a gothic wooden church. Stella's Cafe offers meals for the hungry.

The island is noted for its dry-stone walls erected by early Irish immigrants. Thirteen of the walls are now designated as heritage sites and are described as "one of the most significant concentrations anywhere in Canada."

The road now mounts a low mesa, offering views

Amherst Island's only link with mainland Ontario is its ferry.

The net racks are dry now as the former fishing colony on Amherst Island has largely moved on.

over the North Channel to the treed mainland. A large stone house on the left, the Poplar Dell B&B, is one of the island's oldest estates. After 2 km the road bends right, leading you 1.5 km to the south shore where the road edges so close to the low limestone shore that, during a southerly blow, waves spray across the roadway. On the landward side you will pass a string of old family farms, most of them originating a century ago or more.

When you reach Stella Road on your right, continue straight ahead on Long Point Road, which leads to Emeric Point—the site of the island's last fishing operation. Most of the old fishermen's cabins are now seasonal dwellings. From this point you can return to Stella Road and turn left toward Stella.

After 1.5 km, you will come to a handsome gothic church set against a backdrop of maples. This is St. Paul's Anglican Church, built in 1884, its grey limestone blocks having been wrenched from a quarry at Kingston Penitentiary by sweating convicts. Continue past the church for less than 1 km and then turn left to follow the 2nd Concession, one of only two interior farm roads on the island. Here the fields have been stripped of their forest cover and the farmers carry on in much the same way as those in earlier generations.

When you reach Emerald Road, 3 km later, turn right. A farther 1.5 km will bring you into the tiny one-time port of Emerald. Once a busy shipping village, it died with the grain trade. From Emerald you can see across the north channel to the low shoreline of Bath, now dominated by the chimneys of a generating station.

Once you have returned to the mainland and joined the rush of traffic home, you will soon realize why the Howe Islanders, the Wolfe Islanders and the Amherst Islanders are in no hurry to trade the "inconveniences" of island life for life in the fast lane.

Overleaf: Sailing is popular off the shores of Wolfe Island.

16 The Perth Road

Two of Ontario's best-preserved stone towns, Kingston and Perth, are linked by one of its most historic backroads. This 80 km paved road grinds over granite ridges and swoops into villages nestled in valleys. Along the way are barns, churches, general stores, a railway station and a ghost town. There are water holes to fish in and parks to picnic in. So pack well for this trip, taking fishing rod, camera and a picnic lunch.

Perth's turning basin was severed from the main Rideau Canal when short-sighted county politicians built a bridge too low for vessels to pass under.

The Perth Road began as a settlement road. Although both Kingston and Perth were growing towns by 1820, and in full bloom by 1850, the land between them lay empty and neglected. The opening of the Rideau Canal in 1832 brought settlers to the shores of the Rideau lakes, and there Westport grew. The government then hired the Kingston and Perth Road Company to survey and cut a road northward from Kingston to Perth, finally opening the interior. By 1854 however, the road had progressed only 20 km, and in 1860 a series of lawsuits forced the company to relinquish its contract. The government came to the rescue and completed the road.

Kingston to Perth Road Village

Before leaving Kingston, allow time to visit its numerous historic sites and to sample its small but growing contingent of fine restaurants. Leave Kingston north on Division Street. Or, if you are exiting directly from Highway 401, do so at Exit 617 (Division Street) and turn left at the stoplights at the bottom of the ramp and onto the Perth Road.

The first portion of the route passes through a flat limestone plain, where early stone farmhouses mingle with the rural sprawl that emanates from Kingston. Soon after starting your trip you will see on your left, about 2 km north of Highway 401, the entrance to the Little Cataraqui Creek Conservation Area. This park is a nature reserve with nearly 20 km of hiking trails.

Continue north for 8 km. Here you will pass the large old farmhouses and the fertile countryside that gave birth to a prosperous farming community and the village of Inverary.

About 5 km north of Inverary, a striking transition occurs. As the road descends a steep hill it suddenly leaves behind the flat limestone plain and enters the rugged granite landscape that typifies the Canadian Shield. Rocky knobs jut from the

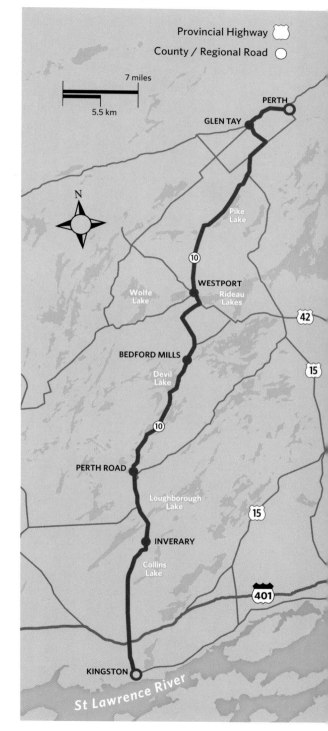

earth as forest replaces the pastures and cornfields. The line of demarcation is the linear Loughborough (pronounced locally "Lober") Lake. This lake is so narrow where you cross it that you may easily mistake it for a river. Beside the bridge a public boat ramp provides you with a place to cast for a few bass or perch. From the bridge continue north, where you will pass the last pocket of good farmland on the southern portion of the road. Another 5 km bring you to the village of Perth Road.

If this had not been the site of the Perth Road's first tollgate, there would probably not have been a village here at all. County Road 10 now bypasses the quiet little place, and to reach it you will need to turn off at the directional arrow. With its old houses, churches and former store, Perth Road village has altered little over the years. At the village intersection is the former Perth Road general store, a red brick building that 100 years ago was the Jabez Stoness Hotel.

Perth Road Village to Bedford Mills

As you leave the village you cross the now-abandoned right-of-way of the Canadian Northern Railway. Built in 1912 to connect Toronto with Ottawa, the line was abandoned and the track is now part of the Cataraqui Trail.

Continue along County Road 10. As you drive the next 25 km section of the route, with its bare rocks and weedy ponds, you will understand why many settlers shunned the area. The few who tried have left a legacy of overgrown clearings and sagging barns, many of which you can see to this day. However, the maze of lakes has attracted summer cottagers and restored some prosperity; yet, aside from a pair of boat ramps, there is no public access to the lakes.

Bedford Mills

After more than 15 km from Perth Road village, watch for Bedford Mills Road, and follow it left. This pretty lane was the original Perth Road alignment up to Bedford Mills. From a high granite ridge, Buttermilk Falls cascades into a back bay of Loon Lake. Here, in the 1830s, Benjamin Tett built a sawmill. Not only was there water power to drive the mill, but Loon Lake led directly into the Rideau Canal. When the long-awaited Perth Road finally arrived and settlers moved in, Tett added a store and a gristmill to serve the new community. Bedford Mills boomed and, at its peak, could claim a powerhouse, a church, numerous private dwellings, and a cheese factory. But after the turn of the century most of the buildings shut down and many of the residents moved away. The place is now a ghost town.

You will probably want to spend some time photographing the site. The mill is a private residence, but its location beside both the road and the pond makes it an ideal photo subject. Avoid trespassing. Near the mill stands the one-time powerhouse, its flume still visible in the falls. St. Stephen's Church still stands, though services are held only in the summer. Beside the church is the plaque that summarizes the history of the quiet little mill village.

Bedford Mills to Westport

Continue along the gravel road for a short distance until it returns to County Road 10, then turn left. The road soon leaves the rocky highlands and once more enters an area of fertile farmlands, those that surround the Rideau Lakes. In this geological basin a pocket of silty and fertile soils has sustained a prosperous farming community. The

Opposite: The gristmill at Bedford Mills is one of this ghost town's few surviving structures.

Glen Tay's mill survives as a residence.

road passes near fields and pastures as it leads toward the historic town of Westport, with its slender steeple and white frame houses, all set against a picturesque background of field, forest and lake. Stop at the T intersection with Highway 42 and turn left. After 1 km, County Road 10 bends right onto Rideau Street, and enters Westport.

Westport

The village began life as Manhard's Mills. Its location at the head of Upper Rideau Lake boomed with the Rideau Canal and, later, the Brockville & Westport Railway. But when commercial traffic on the canal stopped, the town slid from boom to bust. The upsurge of cottaging and boating in the past five decades has injected new life into the old town and made it a popular recreational spot.

Despite its new prosperity, Westport has retained many of its historic buildings and streetscapes.

Most of the town's early buildings are on Rideau Street, and on Church and Main Streets. Follow Spring Street to the shore to see the refurbished waterfront and the town's historic natural spring. The town has several restaurants if you wish to stop here for lunch, or you may prefer to picnic in the conservation area just north of Westport. The Cove Country Inn at Main and Bedford occupies what was the original 1875 home of mill owner William Fredenberg. After lunch, stroll along the refurbished waterfront with its pedestrian bridges and landscaped grounds. Look for the gazebo that covers the town's original spring.

Leave town travelling north on County Road 10. This road grinds up the steep side of Westport Mountain—a granite cliff that soars 100 metres above the lake and the town and extends along the lake for 20 km. The view over the town is spectacular, its church spires poking through the trees, while lakes and fields stretch into the distance. Continue to the summit and to the Foley Mountain Conservation Area, where you can enjoy both the view and your picnic lunch. To help you work up an appetite, the area has 13 km of hiking trails.

Westport to Perth

Leave the conservation area and continue north on County Road 10. For 15 km the route winds through granite hills, where pioneer bush farmlands have been replaced with country estates. Soon the road again emerges onto a flat plain. Here the soil is deep and fertile, the farms large and prosperous. About 7 km farther on, look for the side road to Glen Tay, where you will find another of the area's photogenic stone mills. Built in the 1860s and now a private home, it looms above the rushing Tay River against a backdrop of rocky riverbank and cedar woods.

Drive east from Glen Tay on either Christie Lake Road or Highway 7 into the remarkable stone town of Perth.

Perth

Allow plenty of time to stroll this town of old stone buildings. Perth has been spared the high-rise intrusions and senseless demolition of many of Ontario's downtowns. Much of the credit belongs to concerned citizens, farsighted planners and the Heritage Canada Foundation. While the town council has designated most of the downtown a heritage district, the foundation has provided the funding to preserve and promote that heritage, all of which has made Perth one of Ontario's most historic and photogenic towns.

It is also one of its oldest. Along with Richmond, 40 km to the east, Perth was surveyed

in 1816. Its town lots were to be awarded to the officers and men of the Glengarry regiments who had served in the Peninsular War and the War of 1812. Mills were built on the swift Tay River, and stores appeared on the main street. In 1834, when the Tay Canal provided a link with the Rideau Canal, Perth experienced a boom in growth, and when the Ontario & Quebec Railway rumbled into town, new factories and mills propelled Perth's population toward 3,000.

Its unrivalled stone heritage must be credited to the builders of the Rideau Canal. To construct the stone locks and lock buildings, canal mastermind Colonel John By lured a bevy of Scottish stonemasons to Canada. When the canal was completed, many of these men settled in local towns, and there they applied the trade they knew best. During the boom years, these skilled builders erected—particularly in Kingston and Perth—some of Ontario's finest stone structures.

Perth must be enjoyed on foot. The short tour that follows covers only Perth's core. Detailed walking-tour brochures are available in the town hall, and that is the best place to start your tour.

The town hall, with its domed clock tower, was built in 1863, of cut stone, and it combines the Georgian and Federal styles of architecture that were popular at the time. From the town hall, walk north up Gore Street through the commercial core, where many blocks date back 150 years. All are of stone, peak roofed and some with front gables. A few paces north, by the stone bridge over the Little Tay River, you will find a clutch of Perth's oldest stone stores, many built in the 1840s, and a riverside restaurant.

Continue north another block and a half to the mansion built in 1840 for Roderick Matheson. This house was saved from demolition in 1966 by a group of concerned citizens, and, with the help of an Ontario Heritage Foundation grant, it became

The Big Ben Statue at Glen Stewart Park.

corner stands the former Perth Hotel, built in 1838 and Perth's second oldest.

Continue east on Foster to Drummond Street and turn right. Before you lies one of the town's oldest residential streets, an avenue of stone houses, large and small, and most predating 1850. On the northeast corner stands what once was the Merchants Bank of Canada, built in 1850. A block south, on the southeast corner of Herriott Street, is one of Perth's first stone houses. It dates from 1835. Walk south to the turning basin of the Tay Canal, a side canal to the Rideau. Here a new market facility provides a watery foreground for a photograph of the town hall and the other early buildings on the opposite side of the canal. The canal is little used because, in a moment of short-sightedness, the county council built a new road bridge over the canal a short distance east. The bridge sits too close to the water for large boats to pass beneath.

Cross the bridge and walk up the hill to the corner of Harvey Street, the site of two of Perth's more interesting buildings. On the southeast corner is St. James Anglican Church, built in a high-steepled gothic

a museum. You can tour the grand rooms, which have been furnished in the style of the period.

Carry on along Gore Street another half-block to Foster Street. On the southeast corner stands the beautiful stone block housing stores that have been in business since the 1850s. On the northeast

Opposite: Perth's Town Hall was granted National Historic Site status in 2001.

Perth's main street.

style in 1881. Beside it sits the courthouse, erected in 1842. On the courthouse lawn are two 200-year-old cannons that have seen action in three wars. On the northeast corner is another of Perth's most celebrated houses, Summit House, built in 1823 for James Boulton, Perth's first lawyer. It was modelled after Toronto's famous Grange, now a part of the Art Gallery of Ontario.

A right turn takes you back to Gore Street and what is perhaps Perth's most famous house, the McMartin House dating from 1839.

From Harvey Street, walk south one block to Craig Street. One block west on Craig sits the legendary Inge-Va. Set back from the road beneath a canopy of willows and maples, with its stone walls and delicate fretwork, it has been described as Ontario's most beautiful house.

It was also the site of Ontario's last fatal duel.

In 1833 two young law students, John Wilson and Robert Lyon, confronted each other with duelling pistols. When the smoke cleared from the early morning air, Lyon lay mortally wounded.

Perth contains much more to see. But if you are ready to rest your feet, you can do so in the neatly landscaped Stewart Park behind the town hall. And if you want a meal Perth has a variety of restaurants, many in the old stone buildings that make Perth one of Ontario's most historic towns.

At the corner of Herriott and Wilson Streets, a restaurant occupies the Code's Mill across from Stewart Park and a statue of Canada's legendary race horse Big Ben, and his rider Ian Miller.

Opposite: A riverside setting in downtown Perth.

17 The Rideau River Road

This short route, just 45 km long, follows the Rideau Canal between two early mill towns, Manotick and Merrickville. Most of the villages on this route are exceptionally rich in historic buildings, so be prepared to do some walking.

Actors in period costumes perform a gun salute during the opening day of the Watson's Mill Museum in Manotick.

I n the 1820s, when memories of war with the United States were still fresh, a British army engineer named Colonel John By built the Rideau Canal between Ottawa and Kingston. Its purpose was military, to provide a transportation route for troops and supplies, safe from the American border. The canal was a remarkable engineering feat. Rapids had to be dammed and bedrock blasted. Stonemasons had to haul great stone blocks through roadless backwoods and fit them precisely into locks and lock buildings. When By finished the canal in 1832, it was considered an engineering marvel, and it remains a marvel to this day.

Even before the canal was completed, the many waterfalls and rapids had spawned mill villages. When the canal became a busy commercial highway, the little villages grew into towns. They thrived until the 1870s and 1880s, when the railways heralded another transportation era. Then canal traffic dwindled and the towns stagnated—ironically one reason for the wealth of early, unaltered buildings.

The canal left another, even more enduring legacy. The Scottish stonemasons who hewed the canal's great limestone blocks settled in the Rideau Valley, where they applied their trade to the construction boom. There they built many of the limestone houses, mills and stores that you still find between Kingston and Ottawa. They are among the most photographed, painted and praised of Ontario's 19th-century buildings.

In 1975 Parks Canada recognized the unique heritage role of the Rideau Canal and its buildings and declared the entire system a historic park. Locks, lockmasters' houses and the protective blockhouses have been thoughtfully preserved, as have the century-old techniques of operating the locks and swing bridges by hand. Later UNESCO designated the Rideau Canal and Kingston Fortifications as a World Heritage Site.

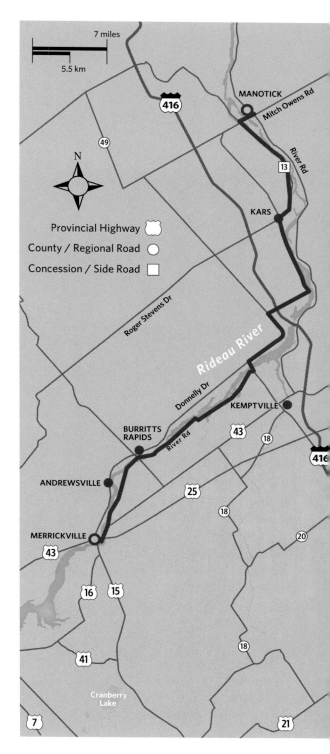

People gather at Watson's Mill, a historic gristmill established in 1860, for the annual Manotick Harvest Festival.

Manotick

The start of your trip, Manotick, lies 15 km south of Ottawa. Follow Riverside Drive, south from Ottawa until it becomes River Road. Watch for the signs to Manotick, cross the Rideau River and enter the old part of the village. A left turn down the first side street will bring you into Dickinson Square, the historic heart of Manotick. Park by the stone mill.

Dickinson Square is bounded by three historic buildings: the F.E. Ayers building, the Dickinson House and the Watson mill. The Ayers Building, a handsome flat-top brick structure, was built in 1902 and originally housed the Union Bank. Its arching doors and windows still retain the facade that greeted its early customers.

The yellow frame Dickinson House was constructed in 1867. Over its life it has been a store, a post office and the home of Moss Kent Dickinson, who was a mayor of Ottawa and one of the Watson Mill's first owners. The Rideau Valley Conservation Authority bought the house in 1972 and restored it, right down to the pioneer herb garden.

The star attraction of Dickinson Square is the Watson (or Long Island) mill. Built by Scottish stonemasons between 1857 and 1860, this five-storey stone mill was the centre of an industrial complex that included a sawmill, a carding mill and a bung mill. It has been described as one of Canada's best remaining examples of a 19th-century gristmill. It is now a living museum.

From Dickinson Square stroll west along shady Mill Street. Beside Dickinson House stands Waddel House, a turn-of-the-century sister to the Ayers Building. It housed the town tailor. Halfway along Mill Street, look for the Miller's Oven tea shop. Built in 1870, this mansard-roofed frame shop was originally a village store and a popular gathering spot for the townsfolk.

If you wish to know more about Dickinson Square's many historic buildings, visit the Manotick website at www.manotick.ca.

Manotick to Kars

Follow Mill Street to Main Street, which becomes Rideau Valley Drive, and turn left. Here are Manotick's more modern amenities, including restaurants and gas stations. As you leave the village you will see how the banks of the Rideau have attracted Ottawa commuters, who have converted the shore into an expensive Ottawa suburb. Five km from Manotick, Rideau Valley Drive bends right to follow Roger Stevens Drive to an intersection. Turn left and continue on Rideau Valley Drive to enter the 150-year-old hamlet of Kars.

Kars

With its parklike river bank, its narrow streets, and its 19th-century homes and shops, Kars beckons you to amble, to photograph and, perhaps, to picnic or cast a line from the wharf. Drive through the village and turn left onto Wellington Street, a road that leads to the water.

Kars traces its origins back to 1829, the year James Lindsay arrived and, a little to the south of the present dock, built a wharf to ship lumber. Three years later the Rideau Canal brought a commercial boom, and Lindsay's wharf became a busy spot. North of the wharf, a six-street town plot was laid out and named Wellington. It became the focus for the homes, shops and churches that collected at the site. But in 1854, when the railway shunned Kars, the community's growth faltered, and to this day the village has changed little.

From the wharf, walk back along Wellington

Street two blocks to Lord Nelson Street. These waterside blocks retain their narrow streets and their canopy of trees. At the northeast corner of Wellington and Lord Nelson Streets is Adam Eastman's old home. Built in 1854 by one of the settlement's first mill owners, this white frame house still has its original windows with their irregular panes. Walk north on Lord Nelson two blocks to Anne and turn left to Rideau River Drive, the main street. Just north of the corner is St. John's Anglican Church, a white clapboard building that was constructed by John Eastman in 1850. It is Kars's oldest church. Continue your walk south on Rideau back to the corner of Wellington Street. The house on the southeast corner is the former Zena Ault Hotel, a boisterous spot during the boom days. Return along Wellington to your car.

Kars to Burritts Rapids

Continue south on Rideau Valley Drive. Half a kilometre from Kars, look for a stone farmhouse. This is James Lindsay's original home, built in 1829. South of Kars, the shoreline is flat. Even so, it has attracted cottagers and commuters, whose homes mingle with old farmhouses and barns. At 7 km from Kars you will come to Baxter Conservation Area, where you can picnic or even swim (if the algae growth is low enough).

From the park, Rideau Valley Drive continues west as Dulworth Road across Highway 416. Turn left onto 4th Line and then onto Regional Road 44 (or Marilyn Wilson), where you fork left over the river to the south bank. Here your route leads to the right onto River Road. If forestry or hiking interests you, drive instead straight south from River Road to the Ferguson Forest Centre. This 300 hectare tree garden offers hiking and gives tours during the year.

Then, back at the bridge, drive west on River Road 12 to County Road 23. Turn right and drive

Burritts Rapids' attractive frame Christ Church.

across the bridge for one of the highlights of the trip, the village of Burritts Rapids.

Burritts Rapids

Beside the road you will find Burritts Rapids lock 17. As part of Parks Canada's preservation efforts, the locks are operated by hand, as they have been since 1832. But the village predates even the canal.

In 1793 two Loyalist brothers, Stephen and Daniel Burritt, fled from Arlington, Vermont, and made their way up the Rideau River to a set of rapids, which they felt could power their mills. By the time the Rideau Canal opened, nearly 40 years later, Burritts Rapids was a flourishing mill village. But the railways bypassed the village, businesses fled and, for years, many buildings stood empty. Today, most are residences maintained by owners who care for the past.

From the lock continue to Grenville Street and turn right to cross the swing bridge and continue north up Grenville Street. Here the tight rows of wooden 19th-century homes and former businesses present a century-old streetscape. At Centre Street you will find the old hotel and old village homes. Venture down the side streets and you will find a row of simple frame cabins, a large white frame house with an elaborately fretted wraparound porch that architects call gothic revival, and a 150-year-old Methodist church that is now a private home. Then continue north to the next bridge. In a small park beside the river is a plaque commemorating the founding of the village. Beside it is a former store that now contains a community centre.

At the head of Grenville Street, set back from the road in a large churchyard, is Christ Church,

The Jakes Block is a downtown Merrickville landmark.

one of eastern Ontario's most photographed churches. It was built in 1831. A square crenellated tower soars above its white frame body, and in its gable is an unusual circular window. The cemetery surrounding the church contains headstones that date back more than a century and a half.

Burritts Rapids to Merrickville

From Burritts Rapids return to the south side of the river and continue west on River Road, County Road 23. This quiet road winds along the Rideau's swampy shores past century-old riverside farms and several handsome houses, some of brick but many of them built by the Scottish stonemasons who laboured for John By to build the Rideau Canal. But one in particular is strikingly different. At 2 km from Burritts Rapids the road bends left and then back to the right. At this second bend, watch for the house set back on the left. While its storey-and-a-half style is typical, its alternating pattern of red and yellow bricks is found among only a few old houses and is unique to this area.

Here the river's banks are steeper, its flow swifter. Over the next 6 km the river plunges so steeply that the canal builders had to construct four separate sets of locks. Just past the house is the entrance to the Poonamalie Locks, and half a kilometre beyond that are the Nicholson Locks, with a bridge and side road to Andrewsville.

Founded in the 1830s by Rufus Andrews, Andrewsville grew into a busy mill village with a store, a cheese factory and a population of 150. The mill is gone and fewer than a half-dozen original houses remain, with a few new cottages and homes between them.

Return across the bridge to your route and turn right onto Provincial Highway 43, which takes you into Merrickville, the finale of your trip.

Merrickville

On this particular trip the best comes last, for Merrickville's buildings, many of stone, have changed little in more than a century. Like Burritts Rapids, the town began with a Loyalist fleeing the oppression in post-Revolutionary America. William Merrick arrived in 1793 and built a sawmill at the rapids. The steep drop in the river required John By to build three sets of locks and one of his protective blockhouses. When the canal opened, Merrickvllle boomed. In 1848 Merrick's son Stephen built extensive woollen mills and a gristmill. When the railway entered town, Merrickville boomed again. Most of its present buildings date from one of these two boom periods.

The flashing light marks the corner of Main and St. Lawrence Streets and is the centre of town. Either turn left and park by the stores on St. Lawrence or continue straight ahead, past the blockhouse, and park by the river.

Merrickville is another town that is best enjoyed on foot. Start with the blockhouse. Built in 1832, it is the largest of John By's blockhouses. Like the others, it never saw military duty, and today it is a museum of military and pioneer paraphernalia.

Walk north from the blockhouse across the bridge to an island in the river, the site of Merrick's woollen mills. On one side of the island are By's locks, on the other the tumbling rapids that powered Merrick's mills. The mills operated uninterrupted from 1848 to 1954 and were slated for preservation, but a raging fire destroyed them, and Parks Canada was left with only a few limestone walls to stabilize. Cross the second bridge and walk

up the road to the driveway to William Merrick's grand mansion. Set behind stately maples, it was built with local limestone and has stood as the town's finest home since 1821.

Return across the two bridges to the town's commercial core. At the southeast corner of St. Lawrence and Main is another of Merrickville's outstanding buildings, the Jakes Block, which was built by Eleazer Whitmarsh sometime in the late 1860s. Its stone walls rise three storeys, its

A boat in the Merrickville Locks.

corner a graceful curve. What makes it particularly appealing is the fact that its facade has never been altered and still displays the arching doors and windows of Whitmarsh's early design. It is now the Baldachin Inn and Restaurant. The Block is architecturally balanced by another three-storey stone structure opposite it.

Inevitably, Merrickville has been discovered. How could it not? After nearing death in recent years, the business district has been revived with boutiques and cafés, especially in and near the Jakes Block.

There are many reasons to linger in the region. West of Merrickville, on Highway 43, is Smiths Falls with its extensive railway museum, and the two-storey outhouse at the Bates House Museum.

But if home beckons, then Highway 7 lies just a few kilometres to the north, and Highway 401 to the south.

18 The Ottawa River Road

Although ski-slope roofs and silvery steeples are common in rural Quebec, they are not seen as often in Ontario. Yet many lurk along the Ottawa River Road, proudly proclaiming their French-Canadian origins. Mansard roofs crown village homes, and church steeples punch the sky. It is Ontario's French-Canadian heartland: the Ottawa River Road.

It is also a riverside drive. The road begins at Cumberland, east of Ottawa, and winds easterly along the Ottawa River shore, following paved county roads for most of its 70 km length. It ends at L'Orignal, near the Quebec border. The trip

Views across the Ottawa River follow most of this route.

offers breathtaking views to the mountains deep in Quebec on the opposite shore, which you can reach on any of several small ferries that shuttle across the river.

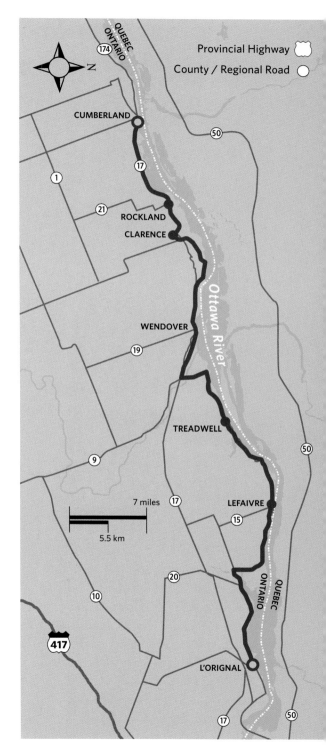

ost of the route that you follow was orig-inally known as the Montreal-Bytown Road. Completed around 1840, it was the first road to open up the south shore of the Ottawa River and to link the little steamer villages that huddled on the banks.

Settlement in the region began with an Ameri-can called Abijah Dunning, who in 1801 purchased an extensive tract of land around Cumberland. Meanwhile 70 km downstream, another American, Nathaniel Treadwell, was creating L'Orignal. At first there was little settlement between the two towns. The shore was swampy, thickly wooded and remote from Ontario's early roads. Most settlers shunned the area in favour of the lighter, more accessible soils of the Lake Ontario shorelines. Then in 1848, Pierre Lefaivre left the crowded confines of Saint-Benoit in Quebec and made his way up the Ottawa, where he bought a portion of land from the Treadwell family. His son Hercule encouraged others to move from Saint-Benoit and settlement began in earnest. By 1867 half a dozen little wharf villages had sprung up along the shore.

Cumberland to Rockland

Cumberland lies on Regional Road 174, a former railway roadbed, about 35 km east of Ottawa. As you enter the village from the west, you will see the sign for Hillmillar Street. To the right behind some landscaping, the two-storey house is the former Canadian Northern Railway station. Left leads to the ferry, which plies the water to Masson in Quebec. Turn right onto Rue Cameron and drive two blocks to the Old Montreal Road, Cumber-land's former main intersection. Sadly, the historic crossroads buildings are gone now, some burned, others demolished.

From the intersection drive east on Old Montreal Road to one building that has survived, the Heritage Restaurant. Built of stone in 1885, it was the home of the town's first doctor, James Ferguson, who occupied the building until 1920. Note its wraparound wooden two-storey porch, one of the few still existing in the area. A little farther along the road is the Cumberland Heritage Museum, where the curators have assembled a wide variety of 19th-century buildings, including the Grand Trunk Railway station from the nearby town of Vars.

Your route continues east on the Old Montreal Road where it crosses Becketts Creek, the site of an early sawmill, and rejoins Highway 174, which becomes County Road 17 as it enters the County of Prescott & Russell. Stay on the highway for 3 km and then watch for a directional sign to Rockland. Turn right onto Rue Laurier and follow it in this historic town.

With a population of 11,000, Rockland is the largest town on this route. It was no more than a small wharf village until 1889 when the merchants lured the Canada Atlantic Railway to their community. This brought a prosperity that is reflected in Rockland's magnificent stone cathedral

Rockland offers the widest range of facilities on the trip. You can snatch a fast snack or linger over a licensed lunch. If you wish to picnic, follow Rue Edouard to the site of the wharf and the riverside park.

Rockland to South Nation River

East of Rockland, Rue Laurier rejoins County Road 17. Follow it for 1.5 km to Clarence, and at County Road 8 turn left onto "Old Highway 17." When the Montreal Road was opened, this string village replaced the original wharfside settlement 2 km away. Although several newer homes have been constructed, there is a small stone Baptist church dating from 1825. A little more than 1 km beyond the church, Sophie Street to the left leads to the Clarence Island wharf, where two ferries still link Clarence with the busy mill town of Thurso on the Quebec side.

Continue east along the old Highway 17. For the next 12 km the road meanders along the river bank. Modern homes and summer cottages now mingle with the older, French-Canadian farmhouses and barns. Along this stretch of road you will enter Wendover, which was originally a wharf settlement. Another of the French-Canadian string villages, it stretches 3 km along the road, yet has few back streets. In the historic centre of the village, Rue Quai leads to the site of the old wharf. Here the Ottawa River widens and flows sluggishly around long, swampy islands and over shallow weed beds. As with many Franco-Ontarian villages, the grandest building is the stone Roman Catholic church.

From Wendover your route continues east on Old Highway 17 (Rue Principale). After 2 km the road bends inland to follow the bank of the South Nation River, a sluggish muddy river that flows slowly through eastern Ontario before emptying into the Ottawa. This leads you back once again to Highway 17. At the stop sign, turn left and cross the bridge. Look north to see the line of concrete abutments from the long-abandoned Canadian Northern Railway bridge. South of the road is a small park called Jessup's Falls Conservation Area. With its stand of pines it offers a shady picnic site.

South Nation River to Lefaivre

The next 15 km follow a peaceful shoreline that draws you deeper into Little Quebec. From the conservation area, turn north onto Plantagenet Road 21. After 2 km, keep right at a T intersection marking Concession Road 1 and follow the south bank of the Ottawa. Below you in the river are the twin islands of Grande Presqu'ile and Petite Presqu'ile, while on the horizon are the peaks of the Gatineau Hills. The farm buildings on this road are close together, set on long, narrow lots

The concrete supports for the railway bridge still stand in the South Nation River.

that stretch about 2 km from the river. This was a common pattern of French settlement when the river was the only highway, for it ensured that the early settlers all had access to the vital water route.

Continue for 4 km to Treadwell, a cluster of buildings at a crossroads. Like the other villages, Treadwell originated as a wharf settlement and saw little activity until the road opened up the interior. The small frame church with its slender silver steeple was built in 1923. At the church, jog left and then right to follow County Road 24 (Concession Road 1) east from Treadwell. Here the road winds along the river bank, descending through wooded gullies and past old farmhouses and barns, many of which date from the early days of settlement and are now surrounded by newer country homes. On the opposite bank of the Ottawa, the Gatineau Hills loom ever higher.

After 6 km the road climbs a wooded ridge and emerges to a panorama of farm, river and mountain. A further 3 km brings you to a string of houses. This is the village of Lefaivre, the heart of Pierre Lefaivre's historic colony.

Lefaivre

During its early years Lefaivre grew slowly, because its low and swampy back shore discouraged settlers. The village remained little more than a shipping point until the 1850s, when Lefaivre's colonists began to stream in from the crowded parishes of rural Quebec, giving this area the appearance and culture it has retained to this day.

Lefaivre is arguably the most "French" of the villages along the shore as silver ski-slope roofs and a tall church steeple dominate the string village. At the main intersection are the historic hotel and traditional shops.

Beside the school, less than 1 km beyond the main intersection, Du Quai Street leads down the river bank to a quiet riverside park. The wharf here has been out of use since 1923, but only half a kilometre away, from a more modern wharf, a six-car ferry shuttles across to Fassett, near Montebello, Quebec. There the CPR acquired its magnificent Chateau Montebello, described by many as the world's largest log castle.

Lefaivre to L'Orignal

Continue east from Lefaivre on Concession Road 1. It was along this section that, in the 1850s, Lefaivre's colonists carved out their farms. As the land was handed down from fathers to sons, the farms were severed lengthwise so that each lot had access to the river, creating no fewer than 25 strip farms on a section of road only 5 km long.

Five km from Lefaivre the road, now Bay Road, turns sharply inland, leaving behind the river and the farms. For 2 km it crosses a flat plain, pockmarked by small, swampy depressions, and then abruptly halts at a T intersection. Turn left here at County Road 24, which is a continuation of Bay Road. At a swampy arm of the Ottawa called Baie des Atocas, the route rejoins the river and continues along the bank 8 km to L'Orignal. As you approach this quiet and historic town, you will see its large steel foundry looming above the plain.

L'Orignal

Now a dormitory town of the larger and less interesting Hawkesbury, L'Orignal contains two of the more intriguing buildings in eastern Ontario—a cottage called Riverest, and Ontario's oldest county courthouse. Drive across the bridge and turn left onto King Street, where you can park if you wish to take a short walking tour.

It was on the banks of the creek by the bridge that, in the heady 1800s, Nathaniel Treadwell's sawmills belched steam and smoke into the sky, while mountains of lumber awaited the next schooner. L'Orignal was one of the busiest ports on the river and a major reason for the construction of the Montreal Bytown Road. Today it is a quiet residential village of 2,000 people, most of whom are French Canadian. However, L'Orignal contains surprisingly few examples of French architecture.

At King and Water Streets is the historic Stirling Bank building. Continue on King to Court Street, where the Ontario Court of Justice occupies the former "Hotel de Ville," or town hall. This intersection is the focus of L'Orignal's small downtown core. Even the stout turreted houses on King Street smack more of Victorian England than of the French town L'Orignal subsequently became. So, clearly, do the street names.

Continue east on King Street to Wharf Street. At the foot of the street, you will find the cottage called Riverest nestled behind stately elms and pines. It was built in 1833 by John Marston, using local rubblestone. With its wraparound porch, it is considered by architects to be the best remaining example of Ontario's few Regency cottages. The road ends at the large federal dock, where you can view the mountains of Quebec across the wide river.

Return to the downtown area and walk south from King Street on Court Street. Brooding over the village from the head of the street—its roof a red that nearly glows—is the L'Orignal courthouse. Although several sections were later added, the original portion was built in 1825, making this building the oldest county courthouse in Ontario. Attached to the courthouse to the east is the historic county jail happily now minus its usual occupants. At the corner of Court and King Streets is St. Andrew's Church, constructed in 1836 as a Church of Scotland. It became a United church and is one of eastern Ontario's oldest churches.

L'Orignal's courthouse is Ontario's oldest.

Ontario's countryside harbours many cultural groups. Few, however, have left their distinctive imprint so indelibly on the landscape as have the Franco-Ontarians of the lower Ottawa River. It is just too bad that countryside sprawl is eating away that precious heritage.

19 The Opeongo Pioneer Road

Deep in the Black Donald Mountains of Renfrew County lies a pioneer landscape of log cabins and barns, of snaking rail fences and simple churches. Through it winds the Opeongo Road. This route begins at the town of Renfrew, 320 km northeast of Toronto and 130 km west of Ottawa, and it follows the old pioneer trail for 110 km to Barry's Bay. Fill your lunch bag and your gas tank in Renfrew, as you will find few facilities along this route.

From the heights of the Opeongo Road, the views extend across the Ottawa Valley to Quebec.

n 1854 Peter Vankoughnet, chief commissioner for Crown Lands, announced that the unsettled wilds of central Ontario would be thrown open for settlement. Two dozen settlement roads would breach the timbered highlands, and the land along them would be free.

The Opeongo Road, which was surveyed in 1855, was among the first of these colonization roads. Despite its deplorable condition, in its first nine years the road attracted 300 settlers. Villages sprang up at water-power sites, at stopping places and major road junctions. But the rush soon subsided. The harsh climate, the infertile soils and rumours of starvation sent prospective settlers searching for friendlier regions.

Reflecting on the road scheme's collapse, a Renfrew journalist wrote in 1900: "Immigrants who came in considerable numbers were disappointed … Those who had means mostly fled the country … those who were poorer had to stay and make the best of it." Those who did stay could scarcely afford major improvements, and so the agricultural landscape today retains the log cabins and barns of the pioneers who settled it in its early days.

Renfrew

Although the Opeongo Road as surveyed began at Farrell's Landing on the Ottawa River, this tour starts at the McDougall Mill Museum in the town of Renfrew. The mill was built of stone fired locally by John McDougall in 1857. Inside, the museum houses a collection of 19th-century clothing, furniture, early farm tools and local artifacts. It is open daily during the summer and has picnic tables located beside the scenic gorge of the Bonnechere River.

From the mill, follow Stewart and Bridge Streets south to Raglan Street and through the main business district. Many of these solid commercial

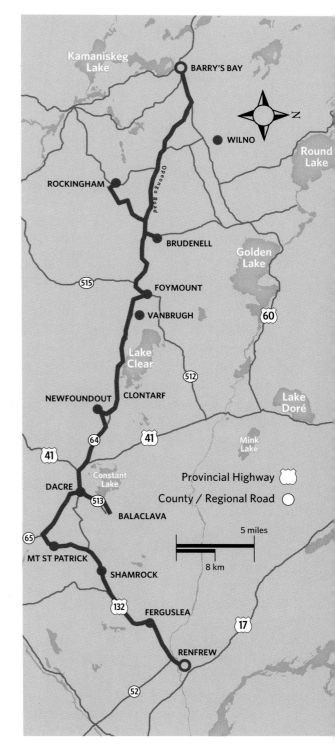

blocks were built in the late 19th century by wealthy lumbermen. One was Robert Carswell, whose baronial estate still stands on the Opeongo Road on the outskirts of town. You will recognize it by its high brick gables and treed grounds.

Renfrew to Dacre

Follow Opeongo Road west from Raglan Street for 6 km to Highway 132 and turn left. After less than 1 km turn left again onto the Opeongo Road, which diverges from Highway 132 here, and drive 2 km to Ferguslea. Founded before the Opeongo Road opened, Ferguslea became a busy stopping place for the roads' settlers. Today its hotels are gone, and the historic hamlet has newer country houses and only a handful of early homes.

Continue through Ferguslea to rejoin Highway 132, and turn left. From this junction to its intersection with Highway 41, about 20 km west, highway widening has buried and bypassed the winding old road, but the landscape is little changed. The terrain is still rugged, the swamps numerous. The few farms along here were small, and today the log barns and weathered houses peer from fields that are overgrown and forgotten.

About 10 km from Ferguslea, just past the junction of Highway 132 and Gorra Hill Road, a small collection of buildings marks the site of another former road village, one with the very Irish name of Shamrock. It too predates the road, settled by a band of Irish who fled Ireland during the deadly potato famines of the 1840s.

About 3 km past Shamrock, turn left onto the Mount St. Patrick Road for a side trip to an interesting church. After about 5 km, the twisting road brings you to Mount St. Patrick. This was the location of the agency for the Opeongo Road, where hopeful settlers would meet the road agent and select their free lots. Today, it is known for its high-steepled stone Roman Catholic church, built in 1869. It has long been a pilgrimage destination because of its "Holy Well." Irish legends hold that certain springs, or "holy wells," have spiritual powers.

Continue west through Mount St. Patrick and drive to Flat Road and turn right. Here the broad, flat lowland of the Ottawa Valley halts abruptly at the looming form of the Black Donald Mountains—a great granite ridge with peaks that soar more than 300 metres above the lowlands. For 9 km the road winds past the foot of these peaks (now the popular Mount St. Patrick ski area) and through a valley of forests and old farms until it comes back to the Opeongo Road itself and the village of Dacre.

Dacre

Dacre was once the largest place on the Opeongo, the junction of roads that lead north to Eganville and south to Calabogie, with hotels on all four corners. Sadly, many of its historic hotels and houses have been demolished. But enough remains to give you the feel of a true pioneer landscape. An even more interesting pioneer landscape awaits you about 3 km north, the ghost town of Balaclava. Here, gathered about a weedy millpond at the outlet from Constant Lake, stood a sawmill, a blacksmith's shop and a store, all of which have changed little since the pioneer days. Today only the store and mill remain, decidedly on their last legs.

The rambling wooden mill was originally built by Duncan Ferguson in 1885 and continued to be driven by the water of the creek right up to the late 1960s. Its frame, burner and machinery all remain in place. Sadly, no agency has been able to preserve this unique piece of early Ontario for future generations, and its future is uncertain.

Dacre to Brudenell

Return to Dacre and continue west on Highway 132. After 2.5 km you will come to an intersection with Highway 41. Turn right and, after 1.5 km, turn left to return to the Opeongo Road.

The Opeongo here is no longer a provincial highway, but rather a municipal road, which, although it has been straightened and asphalted, still retains enough of its pioneer curves and bumps to take you back to the days of pioneer travel. For 10 km it winds along the foot of the lofty Black Donald Mountains. Bordering the road are dense woodlots and rugged pastures. And there, in the small clearings, one sees pioneer farms with their string barns, a style unique to this region. Unfortunately, many of the log cabins that stood along the road have been bought by land developers and removed to distant sites to become cottages or ski chalets. The Catholic church you pass is all that survives of the pioneer community of Esmonde.

At the first crossroads, on the north side, you will see a rare example of a pioneer homestead. Four attached log barns enclose the small barnyard.

The trail on the south of the road leads you to some real ghosts. High in the mountains lies an abandoned settlement. As the lands along the Opeongo filled, branch roads were pushed into high mountain gulches. There, the soils were at their worst, and many of these side settlements were forsaken. One went by the optimistic name of Newfoundout. If you wish to make a side trip to look at it, turn left from the Opeongo Road at the Davidson farm onto what's left of the road. After 5 km you will see, amid the overgrown fields that have now almost reverted to forest, the collapsing shells of half a dozen log cabins and barns. The rugged terrain defeated the settlement's pioneers. This side trip takes you up the steep mountainside, so it is best attempted in a 4-wheel-drive vehicle or on foot.

The church at Rockingham remains a focus for the community.

Continuing on the Opeongo, the road wanders along the foot of the mountains and into a pocket of relatively productive soil. Here a rural settlement known as Clontarf sprang up and still offers a good collection of period buildings including the St. Clement's Lutheran Church; pioneer farmsteads that still retain their log cabins, barns and outbuildings; and a large white house that was known as Plaunt's Stopping Place, one of the best known of the Opeongo's hotels.

Now the road begins its long climb to the summit of McDonald's Mountain. As you grind slowly up the hill, the roadside drops away. Below you shimmer the waters of Lake Clear. Beyond

Lonely log barns litter the fields of Newfoundout.

the lake the fields and forests of the Ottawa Valley roll into the distance until they reach the Gatineau Hills of Quebec, 70 km away. Geologists will tell you that the Ottawa Valley is a huge block of rock that cracked away from the adjacent rock and sank. The Gatineaus and the Black Donalds are the rocks that held firm. The land between them is still sinking today. You may hear your Ottawa friends tell of occasional earthquakes. This is the reason.

For the next 10 km, the road rollercoasters over the lofty peaks. Even here, pioneers tried to wrest their fortunes from the rocky ground. Again, many of the log buildings still stand.

Just past the school you come to a T intersection with Highway 512. Turn left and, after 1 km you will come to a startlingly modern town, Foymount. Built after the Second World War, this was a radar base and townsite. Modern homes, apartments,

and even a recreational hall and library were built on curving, suburban-like streets. But the base has long since closed, and its radar domes dismantled. Efforts to revive the site have been only partially successful and many of the apartments and buildings sit empty, the lawns overgrown.

From Foymount, continue west on Highway 512 as the Opeongo Road swings back from the crest of the mountains to wind over the highland plateau. Although lofty rock outcroppings still peer down, the pockets of soil between them are wider and deeper; the fields are larger and the farms more numerous. Then, 10 km from Foymount, you will come to the town of Brudenell, almost a ghost town.

Opposite: The residents of Wilno proudly celebrate their Polish heritage.

Barry's Bay's Booth Line railway station and water tank have both been preserved.

Brudenell

Like Dacre, Brudenell marked the junction of two colonization roads, the Opeongo and the Peterson, and was one of the larger villages on either road. Most of its stores, hotels and houses are gone now. The only vestiges of its pioneer legacy are the former Costello Hotel on the south side of the road, and the nearby former store.

At Brudenell, Highway 512 follows the Peterson Road north. But your route continues straight along the Opeongo. A few kilometres beyond the intersection is Our Lady of the Angels Roman Catholic Church, built using red stone. Beyond the church and on the left, the Letterkenny Road leads to Rockingham, another interesting old pioneer site.

Side Trip to Rockingham

If you wish to make a side trip to this pioneer village, follow the Letterkenny Road for 4 km and then turn right onto the Rockingham Road. After a further 2 km the road descends into the gully of Rockingham Creek.

Rockingham sits nestled in this wooded hollow, its rustic pioneer buildings little changed and its simple wooden church the oldest on the trip. Rockingham dates from 1859, when John Watson led a band of English colonists to a mill site on the Peterson Road. The village grew quickly and soon added a gristmill, a sawmill, several stores, taverns and hotels, and St. Leonard's Church. Many of these structures remain, including the church. It was one of the few built using a board-and-batten style. Fortunately, it survives thanks to the efforts of the Friends of St. Leonard's Church. Continue south on Letterkenny Road to a point about 2 km north of the hamlet of Quadville, where local legend claims that a large abandoned and overgrown log cabin in the bush many have been the secret retreat of mobster Al Capone.

Brudenell to Barry's Bay

Return to the Opeongo Road and continue west, where the road enters its most truly pioneer state. For the next 10 km the terrain is rugged, the farms few. Some of the old farmsteads retain their early log barns, a few their log homes. A short distance past Hopefield Road, County Road 66 leads north. Continue straight ahead to remain on the Opeongo. Here, too, the road becomes narrower, the curves and hills steeper. But all too soon the Opeongo emerges from its pioneer past and stops at Highway 60. Only 3 km to the left lies Barry's Bay, a lakeside lumber town and the heart of Canada's first Polish community.

Since Barry's Bay had more locational advantages than the other towns of the Opeongo Road, it grew larger and stayed that way. Its position on Kamaniskeg Lake meant that logs could be boated in from much of the extensive Madawaska River watershed, an area particularly rich in pine. When John Rudolphus Booth, Canada's premier 19th-century lumber magnate, added his railway in the 1890s, it boomed even larger.

During this period, the Poles began to arrive. Between 1864 and 1895, more than 300 Poles migrated to Canada to settle the Opeongo Road and nearby lands. But the harsh conditions caused many of them to give up farming, and they moved to Barry's Bay and to Wilno, a nearby village, where they engaged in lumbering. Wilno is named after a town in Poland and, although smaller than Barry's Bay, remains the cultural focus of the Polish community. The village, with its twin-spired cathedral, stands 8 km east on Highway 60. Stop into the Wilno Tavern for some genuine Polish cuisine such as sledzie (pickled herring), golabki (cabbage rolls) or pierogies.

Many buildings in Barry's Bay date from its lumber days. Look in particular for the Balmoral Hotel, an early lumberman's hotel and now a popular family restaurant. Opposite the hotel, the Barry's Bay railway station is now a museum. This building is the oldest Booth station still standing, a rare find especially with its rare wooden water tank still standing nearby.

After your long drive through pioneer country, you will appreciate the town's other features. Set at the junction of two modern provincial highways, 60 and 62, Barry's Bay caters to the travelling public and has a selection of stores, restaurants and picnic facilities.

To return home, Highway 60 leads east toward Ottawa or west through Algonquin Park to Highway 11. Highway 62 leads south to the Belleville area. But you won't be in a rush to leave, for the ghosts of the Opeongo pioneers will beckon you to linger.

20 The Remarkable Highlands of Hastings

Between Toronto and Ottawa, in the northern part of a county called Hastings, there is a remote region of mountain scenery that is unmatched elsewhere in southern Ontario. This backroads trip takes you through the area on a circular route that begins in Bancroft and follows a series of mountain roads for about 80 km. The beauty of the hills is a naturalist's delight, while the many pioneer homes, barns and general stores offer much for the photographer and historian alike.

This is a tour that will appeal to the rockhounds as well, since the hills around Bancroft have become internationally known for their minerals and their gemstones. Each summer, during Bancroft's Gemboree, rockhounds arrive from throughout North America to scour them.

Although the route has no facilities other than general stores (and even they are few), you will never be more than half an hour's drive from Bancroft, where there are restaurants, motels and a full range of services. If you are coming from the Toronto area, you can reach Bancroft via Highways 401, 35/115 and 28. From Ottawa follow Highway 7 to Highway 62, which leads north to Bancroft.

Although two good provincial highways bisect the area, the Highlands of Hastings retains the feel of its pioneering roots. Bancroft has only 3,800 residents, and its nearest neighbour of comparable size, Madoc, is more than 70 km away. The highlands themselves are a high rugged plateau deep in the Canadian Shield, surrounded by the canyons of the Madawaska, Mississippi and York Rivers.

Opposite: The view from the lookout near Bancroft encompasses the valley of the York River.

Although the area was not railway country, Bancroft has preserved its historic station.

Settlement came late to north Hastings, and with good reason. Although loggers had swept up the Madawaska Valley and decimated much of the area's forests during the early decades of the 19th century, settlers had been discouraged by the poor access, the swamps and the forbidding rocky highlands. Finally in the 1850s and 1860s, the government held out the twin carrots of new roads and free land, and pioneer farmers at last began to arrive.

The first of the colonization roads, the Hastings, was built northward from Madoc in 1855 and finished by about 1860. Soon, other branch roads were opened, including the Mississippi Road to the old Perth settlement in the east; the Monck Road to the west; and across the north, the Peterson Road.

The site that would be Bancroft had an advantage from the very beginning. Not only was it the junction of the Hastings and the Monck colonization roads, but it possessed excellent water power—a steep falls on the York River. As Bancroft boomed as a lumber town, the hills began to fill with settlers. But when the trees disappeared, so did the lumbermen. However, the area had one more natural resource that would help retain its prosperity—its minerals. In the rocks lay a remarkable variety of minerals. While they lacked the glamour of gold and silver, the minerals served a variety of industrial uses. There was feldspar, mica and corundum, the hardest mineral then known, and, of course, uranium. Although the mines are closed now, the abundance of collectible minerals and the beauty of the highlands have brought new life through tourism and an active arts community.

Opposite: Egan Chutes Provincial Park.

Bancroft

Bancroft began in 1879, when the Bronson Lumber company moved its headquarters to the falls on the York River. Mills, churches and hotels quickly sprang up by the mills and around the intersection of the two settlement roads. Then in 1900, the Central Ontario Railway rumbled into town, followed in 1903 by the Irondale, Bancroft and Ottawa Railway.

Although many of the original stores have been replaced or been covered with plastic and plate glass, Bancroft retains a frontier appearance. One of the town's most attractive and historic buildings is the Bancroft Hotel, built in 1899, which now houses TO's Pub and Thomas Oliver's Restaurant. On Railway Street, one block north, is the preserved COR railway station, repainted from CNR red to its original colours of red and white. It has housed an art gallery, a mineral museum and community services. You will also find on the site a log cabin built for the Bronson Company in 1853 and moved to town as a Centennial project in 1967.

Bancroft to New Hermon

Before leaving Bancroft, obtain a rockhound's guide from the Chamber of Commerce listing 30 of the more interesting rock-collecting sites. Then leave Bancroft east on Highway 28, which closely follows the route of the Mississippi Colonization Road. After 3 km, look for the Princess Sodalite Mine. A rare, decorative blue stone, sodalite is found in only a few locations throughout the world. This once busy mine is now a rock shop with a "rock farm" that has nearly 100 specimens of minerals.

Rockhounds' Side Trip #1

Continue east for another 4 km to the York River and the Egan Chutes Provincial Park. Although the park is not signed, dirt roads lead north from each side of the bridge over the river. In the old quarries along these trails lie samples of chondronite, spinal and wollastonite, and possibly even small quantities of sodalite. The Chamber of Commerce booklet gives you the details. Trails lead farther along the river to the falls themselves.

Your main route continues east along Highway 28. As you emerge from the York River Valley, you will see the foothills of the Black Donald Mountains looming ahead. A drive of 8 km brings you into these foothills and to the junction of the Fort Stewart Road (originally known as the New Carlow Road), which was built to link the Peterson Colonization Road in the north with the Mississippi Road. At its original junction with the old Mississippi Road (a little to the south of today's Highway 28) was the village of Hermon, which has long since vanished. But its successor, New Hermon, still exists, only a couple of kilometres north. Drive north from Highway 28, and almost immediately you will come to New Hermon's homes.

New Hermon to New Carlow

Keep right at the fork in New Hermon and continue north on Fort Stewart Road as it twists its way into the hills, passing scattered clearings of pioneer farms. After 5 km it, arrives at the breezy summit of a high plateau and the hamlet of Fort Stewart. This settlement was an early stopping place on the road, and its hotels provided rest and nourishment for weary stagecoach travellers. The Stewart part of its name derives from an early hotelkeeper; the "Fort," from the height of land the hamlet occupies. Although the hotels are gone, the village still contains several early buildings.

From Fort Stewart, continue north for 1 km to a T intersection at Whytes Road. Turn right, and, after half a kilometre, you will come to a view worth lingering over. Here, the plateau plunges 100 metres into the valley of the Little Mississippi

Ontario has some surprisingly mountainous scenery hidden along this backroad.

River, while beyond the valley the forested peaks of the Black Donald Mountains roll toward the horizon.

Turn left at the intersection and continue on Boulter Road, which follows the top of the plateau for 5 km. The northern peak of the plateau is crowned by the village of Boulter, which was named after an early county warden. Boulter began as a roadside stopping place for travellers and developed into a farm service village. North of Boulter, the scenery shifts dramatically once more. As the York River Valley opens at your feet, the road glides down the slope of the plateau and into a swampy lowland. Here it crosses over the York River, which meanders northeastward to the mighty Madawaska.

About 1.5 km north of the bridge, look for Park Road to the left. This short lane leads to Fosters Lake, one of the few lakes that are tucked into these highlands, and to one of the area's few municipal roads with a beach and picnic ground. If you have packed a lunch, this is the place to have it, for there are no other lakeside parks on this route.

Near this turnoff, look for Highway 517 leading northeast. This offers you a side trip to Craigmont, once one of the world's leading corundum producers and now a ghost town (only a few overgrown foundations and village streets remain) and rockhound site. It is about 6 km along and down the Craigmont Road to the east.

As you continue north from the park, your route bends westward to complete half of the circle.

Rockhounds' Side Trip #2

Rockhounds should, after 2 km, look for a dirt road on the right. It leads to the site of the once busy Burgess mines, another corundum operation. After 1.1 km, it will bring you to a hunting

The road passes through the rugged rural hamlet of New Carlow.

lodge located roughly on the site of the old village. On the hill behind it, in the old pits, you may find some crystals of corundum. But be sure to take a pick and hammer, for corundum is one of the world's hardest minerals. Park well beyond the lodge and remember that the owners' facilities are off limits to rockhounds.

Back on the Boulter Road, after 3 km you will come to a T intersection. Here is the picturesque hamlet of New Carlow, which was once a busy crossroads village. Its store, school and shops are closed now, but many of the buildings still cluster about the intersection and dot the wooded hillside over Papineau Creek.

New Carlow to Musclow
Turn left onto New Carlow Road and cross the bridge over Papineau Creek. The road now climbs out of the valley and onto another mountaintop plateau. Here, again, the level and relatively fertile soils have sustained a small farming community. At the second intersection the road bends right and descends into a dark, swampy valley, then mounts yet another plateau, which has the curious name of Monteagle Valley (Monteagle being an English lord). Here you come to a T intersection with East Road Loop, where you should turn left. As you drive south from the intersection, look to the left for views across the valley of the York River to the plateaus and mountains through which you have just travelled. Here the landscape changes once more as the road twists through the rugged foothills and descends through a chain of ravines to the flat sand plains that lie north of Bancroft.

At 4 km from your last turn, the road meets another T intersection. Turn left here onto the

Musclow-Greenview Road. Throughout this area, the mountainsides have been dissected by the rivers and creeks that are slowly eroding their way into the plateau.

Rockhounds' Side Trip #3

Shortly after the turn, look for the MacDonald Mine Road leading to the right. Drive for 3.6 km to an open area on the right. A 200 metre walk will bring you to the old mine site where you can rummage in the piles for feldspar, quartz and pyrite (fool's gold). (At the time of writing, summer of 2012, the site was unavailable to visitors.)

Your original route stays on the Musclow-Greenview Road and brings you to the historic hamlet of Musclow, which took its name from a pioneer family. Musclow began life as a busy service village at a once important road junction, but it ceased to serve this purpose when the road that led east to Fort Stewart was closed. Still, a few of the old village buildings yet guard the intersection. Many of the old pioneer farmsteads in this area provide prime subject material for the landscape photographer.

Keep right in the village corner and follow the Musclow-Greenview Road west for another 6 km. This road descends from the plateau through forested ravines and emerges onto a wide sandy plain. Here, at Highway 62, the mountain road ends. You have come almost full circle and are 7 km north of Bancroft.

This side trip leads to a high lookout. Turn left onto Highway 62 from the Musclow-Greenview Road, drive for 3.5 km and then follow the signs to the Eagle's Nest Park. From this vantage point, the wide valley of the York River opens at your feet. The cliff itself is an outlier of the plateau from which you have just descended. Looking north, you can easily discern the high plateau wall as it winds its way along the York Valley.

A view of the MacDonald Mine.

As you can see along Highway 62, many of Ontario's historic landscapes have vanished, buried by the relentless demand for roadside commercial sprawl, and even here there are big box stores. However the distance from the heaviest urban growth has saved much of the region's heritage, at least for the time being.

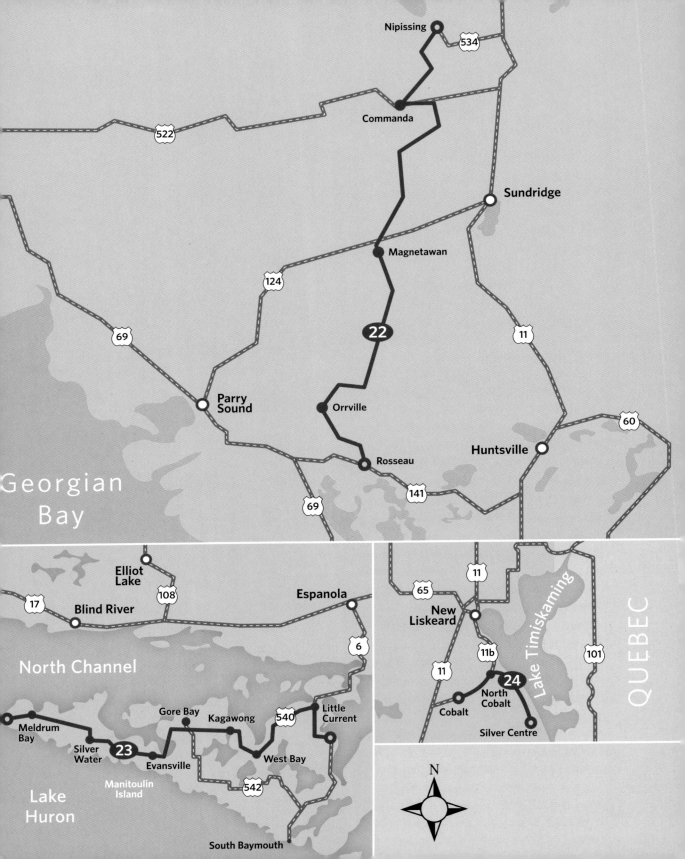

Section 4
Northern Ontario

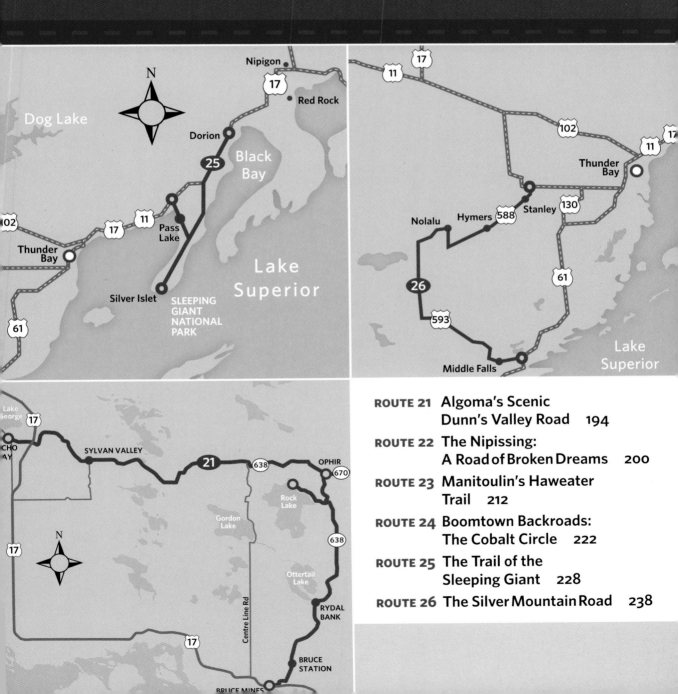

ROUTE 21 Algoma's Scenic Dunn's Valley Road 194

ROUTE 22 The Nipissing: A Road of Broken Dreams 200

ROUTE 23 Manitoulin's Haweater Trail 212

ROUTE 24 Boomtown Backroads: The Cobalt Circle 222

ROUTE 25 The Trail of the Sleeping Giant 228

ROUTE 26 The Silver Mountain Road 238

Here, amid the rugged Algoma mountains and the hidden lush valleys beyond Lake Huron's north shore, lies an opportunity to bypass the dreary Sudbury to Sault Ste. Marie portion of the Trans-Canada Highway. You don't add too many kilometres to the trip by taking this byway, and you get to drive through some magnificent mountain scenery with little villages in the valleys where you will want to slow down and enjoy the view. It's an area tinged with some of the North Shore's more interesting history.

Bruce Mines

Begin your tour in Bruce Mines, which straddles Highway 17 west of Sudbury. Despite the modern gas stations, fast food outlets and gift shops, Bruce Mines is the North Shore's oldest town and the oldest copper mining town in Canada.

Copper was one of the most valued trading commodities of the Ojibwe. A soft metal, copper could be gathered easily from the many surface deposits along the rocky shores of Lakes Huron and Superior. James Cuthbertson staked the first non-native mining claim at Bruce Mines in 1846, and a year later the Montreal Mining Company opened Canada's first copper mine.

Miners began to flock in from England and Scotland, and the rough-and-tumble little mining town of Bruce Mines grew quickly. By 1850 its population had climbed to more than 250. But as the demand for copper declined and the easy-to-mine small deposits ran dry, the mines gradually shut down. By 1876 the last of the copper mines had closed, but that did not mean the end of mining at Bruce Mines. The Mond Nickel Company purchased the mines and began shipping quartz-copper flux ore to Sudbury for refining.

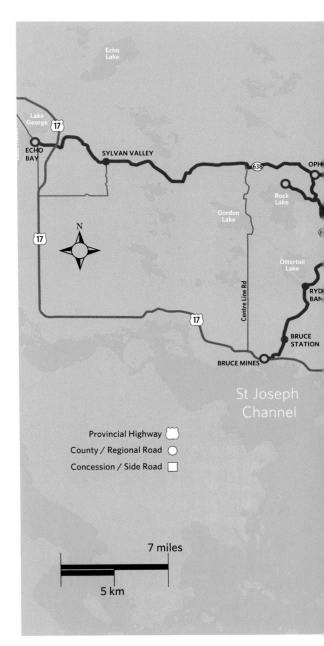

Provincial Highway
County / Regional Road
Concession / Side Road

7 miles

5 km

Opposite: Bruce Mines is the oldest copper mining town in Canada and the oldest town in the North Shore.

Leeburn still contains the tiny structure that was once Ontario's smallest general store.

In 1898 the Bruce Mines and Algoma Railway built a line to connect Bruce Mines with a newly opened copper mine on the shore of Rock Lake, 22 km to the north. But after a mere two decades of more loss than profit, the railway shut down.

To explore Bruce Mines, there are local walking-tour brochures that will guide you to the historical sites and structures along the town's old back streets. You can start with the museum itself, which is housed in a 1894 Presbyterian church, a picturesque wooden building with a crenellated steeple.

Across the highway from the museum, you can tour a replica of the Simpson Shaft, the site of Canada's first copper mine. Today the site resembles the mine as it may have looked during its height of operation. Back on the south side of the highway, walk east along Williams Street through the oldest part of Bruce Mines. Unfortunately, most of the early buildings that once stood here were destroyed by fire in 1917.

At the end of Williams Street, partly obscured by a young forest, are the weathered walls of the old town jail, built in 1887. Immediately east of the jail, now fenced off, is another of the town's many copper mine shafts.

Situated in shallow water behind the museum lies the cribbing of the original 1847 wharf. Then, if you drive east from the museum along Taylor Street you will find the Parker house, one of the town's oldest surviving buildings, which dates from 1867.

Bruce Mines to Rock Lake

To continue your driving tour, go north from the Trans-Canada Highway onto Highway 638. After 2 km, you reach the village of Bruce Station. After the Canadian Pacific Railway chose to locate its station outside of Bruce Mines, a satellite village grew up around the station, complete with its own main street and businesses. Now demolished, the Algoma Creamery stood on the corner of Bruce Station Road and the highway. Drive east for a short distance, and you will see the former post office and stores which stand opposite the now-vacant station grounds.

Return to Highway 638, turn right and cross the tracks. The next 5.5 km run past gently rolling pastures and modest farms. After you have travelled 3.2 km from the crossing, you can still make out the shrubby roadbed of the Bruce Mines and Algoma Railway as its crosses the highway. After another 3 km, you enter the quiet riverside hamlet of Rydall Bank.

Here the church is maintained by the local historical society. Built in 1907, it still houses an old pump organ and is listed on the Canadian Register of Historic Places. A plaque commemorates the bridge built over the Thessalon River and the settlers who entered the area to take up the farmlands after 1880. The steel bridge itself dates from 1911.

One of Bruce Mines' many heritage. The area includes the "Jail Trail" and the "Nip and Tuck," a trail that follows the route of the former rail line to the mines.

To find the plaque, take the lane through Rydall Bank Park. The lane briefly follows the old Bruce Mines and Algoma railway right-of-way. As you drive out of Rydall Bank, Highway 638 curves to the right and, you begin to see the looming mountains closing in on the little farm valleys.

About 12.5 km after leaving Rydall Bank, look for Old Mill Beach Road on your left. This side trip takes you to a wide public beach on the shore of Rock Lake. It is also the site of the mill that processed the ore from the Rock Lake mine. Around the picnic site, you may find evidence of rubble from the mill, but no early buildings have survived. The grounds here are spacious, and the view over the lake is worth a photo or two.

Rock Lake to Dunn's Valley

Continue north along Highway 638 to pass the Rock Lake Cemetery, a large cemetery considering the small population of the area today. When you reach Highway 670, a little over 2 km past the cemetery, turn right to reach scenic Dunn's Valley. The first section of this route leads through a pastoral valley surrounded by the steep, forested walls of the area's mountains. The mountains then converge to form a dark canyon through which the road winds until it opens out into Dunn's Valley.

From these gate-like cliffs, which loom nearly 100 metres above the flatlands below, Dunn's Valley opens before you. There is only one way in and one way out. Like the valley through which you just passed, it too is surrounded by the high hills of Algoma. Almost 10 km after leaving Highway 638, you come to the intersection of Nardi

Road and Skookum Road. Here you will see the school house, now vacant, and the church, now a private home, that together formed the centre of this isolated little settlement. Imagine for a moment the loneliness of the dozen or so valley families when the roads were but dirt trails and horse or foot the only means of travel.

Dunn's Valley to Leeburn Valley

Retrace your route to the intersection of Highway 670 and Highway 638.

North of the intersection, Highway 638 turns left at the hamlet of Ophir, which contains a former school as well as a church of more recent vintage. After driving for 3 km, you descend into another little valley and cross the Thessalon River before once more climbing into the hills. Less than 2 km later lies one of the more picturesque vales on this route, that of the Leeburn Valley.

From the top of the rocky ridge, the valley spreads out before you and, tucked into its folds, is the tiny hamlet of Leeburn. Following the closing of the mines in Bruce Mines, many settlers began to make their way inland. Several had relocated from the community of Kincardine on lower Lake Huron, others arrived directly from England or Scotland. During the winter, the lumber camps offered both work for the locals and markets to the area's farmers.

Here, in the wide fertile valley, Leeburn acquired two stores, a blacksmith, a church and a school, as well as two mills along the river. Two kilometres south, where the Bruce Mines and Algoma Railway crossed the Thessalon River, stood a flag stop and siding known as Leeburn Station. Of these vital early structures, only the church and a single store survive.

As the road bends to the right in the heart of the valley, follow the road to the left for a short side trip to the site of the Leeburn Station, and the

shores of Gordon Lake. Then, back in Leeburn, you can visit what was once Ontario's smallest general store. Smaller than the average garage, the little false-fronted wooden store operated since 1931, and it once supplied the residents of the valley. The church also stands nearby, although the school and the other stores have all been replaced with newer houses.

Leeburn Valley to Echo Bay

From the valley's western wall, there are even more interesting views up a little side valley to the north. Then you enter a miniature version of the Leeburn Valley before passing through a stretch of overgrown fields and abandoned farms. Finally, about

The scenery at Leeburn along the Dunn's Valley Road is a relaxing alternative to the busier Highway 17.

10 km after leaving the Leeburn store, you enter Sylvan Valley.

Although the scenery is less dramatic, this valley too was an enclave of farming in an otherwise mountainous area. After driving another 8 km, you begin to see the waters of the St. Marys River, which runs to Lake Huron, glittering in the distance. At this point, you are on the summit of a high sandy ridge that once formed the shoreline of a much older and much higher version of Lake Huron. Your descent to the flat farmlands below takes you onto what was once the bottom of the lake, where the finer lacustrine deposits account for some of the more fertile and stone-free soil in the area.

The road now passes an area of more prosperous farms and, after crossing the new Highway 17 bypass, enters the village of Echo Bay. Echo Bay lies on the old route of Highway 17 about 30 km west of Sault Ste. Marie.

This one-time port and railway station town is now primarily a dormitory community for those who work in Sault Ste. Marie. The station and most of the main street stores are gone and, newer homes now line the village streets. The only building of historic interest is the handsome wooden house that stands opposite the former station grounds.

22 The Nipissing: A Road of Broken Dreams

The Nipissing Road is a ghost town trail, a road of broken dreams. Once home to a settlement of hopeful pioneers, it is guarded today by their abandoned cabins and weathered barns. The road lies in the District of Parry Sound and winds along 120 km of gravel road from Rosseau on Highway 141 to Nipissing on Highway 534.

A ghost town trail has few facilities, so fill your lunch bag and gas tank in Rosseau, especially if you plan a tour of some of the side trails. Magnetawan, halfway along the route, has gas stations, shops and restaurants, but after that there is nothing until you reach Nipissing. Although most of the road is maintained, its condition varies. Some stretches are wide and well-kept; others are little more than two ruts plunging into dark woods, much as the pioneers might remember it.

What does the Nipissing Road offer? If you are an artist or photographer, the empty cabins and weathered barns feature unusual and rugged images. Cyclists and equestrians find the road peaceful and picturesque, while hikers can stroll down any number of old pioneer trails that have been closed to vehicles.

Opposite: The view near Commanda is typical of that seen along the Nipissing Road.

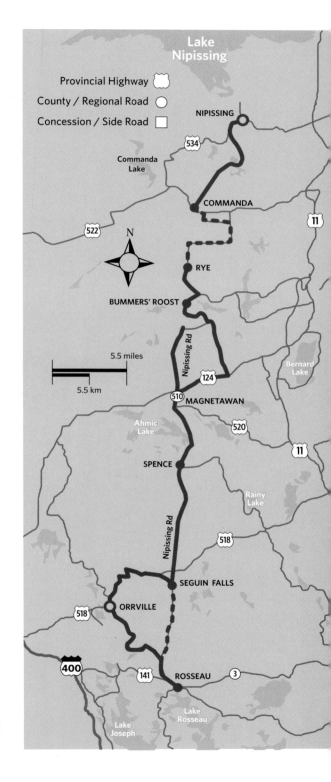

Poorly conceived government schemes are not just a modern-day phenomenon. The Nipissing Road was one of a network of colonization roads devised by the government of the Province of Canada in 1850 to settle the virgin uplands between the Ottawa River on the east and Georgian Bay on the west. Although these lands were touted as utopia for land-hungry immigrants, the roads were built mainly to help the influential lumber companies obtain the labour, the horses and the produce they would otherwise have lacked.

By 1877 the Nipissing Road was open between Lake Rosseau and Lake Nipissing, and the first of the thrice-weekly stages rattled into the new village of Nipissing. But with the forests laid waste and the fertile Canadian prairies ready for settlement, the Nipissing Road was doomed almost from the start. Settlers streamed away. Behind them they left overgrown bush farms and vacant villages.

Rosseau

Clinging to the granite shores of Lake Rosseau, the white farmhouses and shops of Rosseau village deserve a look before you start your drive. A century ago, Rosseau harboured the fleet of steamers that plied the bays and channels of Lakes Muskoka, Rosseau and Joseph. Settlers and investors disembarked here to follow the Parry Sound Road west to Parry Sound or the Nipissing Road north.

Tourists soon followed, and Rosseau survives now primarily as a summer cottage town. Of the houses, stores and churches that line the little town's few streets, most were built by pioneer labour and still display their early styles, although much of the clapboard siding has been replaced by aluminum. Historic markers line the route, explaining points of interest.

Rosseau to Orrville

Leave Rosseau along Highway 141 north. After 1 km beyond a small pioneer cemetery on the left, you will come to an intersection with a gravel road. This marks the start of the Nipissing Road itself and the site of a hamlet called Ashdown. Named after a pioneer family, Ashdown could once claim a store, an Orange hall, a blacksmith's shop and a hotel. Today, none survives. The landing for the Nipissing Road was on the shore of the lake near this point.

Turn right from Highway 141 onto the Nipissing Road and drive north for 1 km to a fork in the road. Take the left branch, McCauley Road. The original Nipissing Road followed the right branch; but after it bends right to become the Bear Cave Road, the Nipissing Road, which continues straight ahead, is little more than a bush trail at this point — suitable only for hikers or all-terrain vehicles. Follow the McCauley Road for 10 km to Orrville, keeping right at the Turtle Lake road and Star Lake road intersections respectively. This route takes you through the Turtle Valley, where fields of hay and oats bend to the breeze and beef cattle graze lazily in their pastures.

One of the first buildings that you see in Orrville is Campbell's blacksmith shop. Popular with local artists and photographers, this frame shop dates from the turn of the century. Its doors, however, have been closed for several years. Look also at the United church, a photogenic white frame building that dates from the days of pioneer worship. Throughout the community you will see other houses that bespeak their pioneer roots.

Orrville to Seguin Falls

At the stop sign after Star Lake Road bends left, turn right and follow Highway 518 east. Here young forests flank the road, reclaiming the exhausted soils of the old fields. After 11 km,

Now a popular cottage community, Rosseau marks the starting point for Nipissing Road travellers.

Highway 518 meets a T intersection, bringing you back into the original Nipissing Road. Although your route lies north, to the left, a side trip right leads to the ghost town of Seguin Falls. To take this side trip stay on Highway 518 for a few metres until it bends left, then follow the gravel road straight ahead for 1 km. The road twists around rock outcrops, and then you enter Seguin Falls: vacant cabins peer from their granite perches; a red brick schoolhouse is now a private residence; and, beyond the school, are the sites of the hotel, and railway crossing (now the Seguin Snowmobile Trail) and a cluster of old wooden houses that mark the centre of the one-time village.

Seguin Falls owes its birth to lumber king J.R. Booth. In 1896 this Ottawa millionaire acquired extensive timber limits in Algonquin Park, 160 km to the east. To tap his new riches, he extended the railway into the park and then on to Georgian Bay. By providing the shortest link between the upper Great Lakes and the Atlantic, he quickly captured the lucrative grain trade. For more than three decades, puffing steam engines strained under the loads of grain, lumber, manufactured goods and passengers. At the Nipissing Road crossing, the Spence Lumber Company erected a mill, which marked the beginning of Seguin Falls. The settlement grew to have a population of 500, with a general store, a post office, shops, a church, a school and the King George Hotel. The town prospered until 1933, when a trestle in Algonquin Park was wrecked, and, with the railway's life line severed, traffic almost vanished. With the lumber gone, the farms failed and the residents fled. Finally in 1954, the line was closed and the tracks lifted. When the hotel and its confectionery shut their doors forever, Seguin Falls became a ghost town. As you photograph the surviving buildings in Seguin Falls, remember that most are privately owned and that some are used seasonally. The King George Hotel stood beside the rail trail but burned down in 1989.

Seguin Falls to Magnetawan

Turn around at Seguin Falls, return to Highway 518, and continue north. For the next 25 km the road is wide and well maintained, although still gravel. Here it passes farmsteads and a once-bustling village. After 4 km, you pass the site of the original Seguin Falls. At first it was one of the many stopping places on the road, but most of its activities moved to be near Booth's railway when the first trains appeared. Today all original buildings are gone, and only a dirt trail leading west to the cemetery survives.

After 5 km, you will see on the right the St. John's pioneer cemetery. With its fading white headstones, some dating from 1876, the cemetery marks the site of the one-time village of Dufferin Bridge. A few metres beyond lies the Dufferin Methodist Cemetery, which tells a sad story. On the weathered tombstones of James and Janet Morden are the names of their six children, their ages between one-and-a-half years and ten years, who died between January 14 and January 19, 1902. The Ashton stone nearby lists four more children who died during the same period. The deadly ailment was diphtheria. With the nearest doctor more than two days away by foot, the children were doomed. It is a stark reminder, for a generation used to cars, computers and creature comforts, of the harsh conditions that faced settlers not so many years ago.

About 2 km farther on, the Nipissing Road intersects the Orange Valley Road. This was another branch colonization route, and it leads west over scenic hilltops for 10 km to Broadbent, a photographer's side trip if you have the time. This intersection also marks the site of the early village of North Seguin, again a place with no trace of its former activity.

Then follows a scene not unlike that which awed the Nipissing Road's first pioneer travellers. The road plunges into a dark, forbidding forest. Trees close in from both sides and meet overhead. Through this tunnel the trail twists one way and then another. It lurches over granite outcroppings and slogs through muddy swamps. Then, after 6 km, it brings you to Spence. Be sure to drop into the Cornball Store on your way.

Spence is described by an early traveller: "At the junction of the Ryerson and Nipissing Road is Spence post office, a good store, boarding house and public school." The boarding house became Simpson's Hotel, and Spence acquired a church and a population of 150. Today, the shells and foundations have mostly been replaced by new homes. The old red brick schoolhouse survives, and the hotel now rests in the Muskoka Pioneer Museum in Huntsville. A historical plaque marks the hotel's original site, and a photo depicts its before-and-after conditions.

North of Spence, the road widens and enters an area where more prosperous farms outlasted the demise of the road settlements. For 10 km, rolling fields and solid barns mingle with forested hills and new country homes as the road leads along the valley's flat floor to Magnetawan.

Magnetawan

Unlike the ghost towns of Spence and Seguin Falls, Magnetawan is very much alive. With its population of about 250, solid frame houses line the village's half-dozen streets, while shops and restaurants cluster by the bridges over the Magnetawan River. Overlooking the road, the historic "Church

Opposite: The Lake Rosseau Lighthouse rests on a shoal and is the subject of local efforts to save it.

Cemeteries often tell tales of harsh, even deadly, conditions along the Nipissing Road.

on the Rock" was the subject of an iconic painting by A.J. Casson. In a park beside the bridge a historical plaque commemorates the story of the Nipissing Road.

Situated at the junction of the Nipissing Road, the Ahmic Road and the Magnetawan Canal, Magnetawan grew quickly during the 19th century.

Settlers, many of them Swiss, crammed the steamers from Burks Falls and turned the valley from forest to farms. In 1925 the area's first hydro-electric plant whirred into life, powered by the falls in the river. Although commercial traffic on the canal ceased in the early 1950s, and the hydro plant fell silent soon after, Magnetawan continued to prosper.

The old plant, with its original generators still in place, is now a museum. It stands a few paces east of the Nipissing Road on Highway 510. The picturesque town invites you to linger, whether at the historic Magnetawan Grill or simply beside the waters of the river.

Magnetawan to Commanda

Leave Magnetawan north on Highways 520 and 510, which is the Nipissing Road alignment. Then, after 4 km, cross Highway 124 to stay on the Nipissing Road. Here, once more, the road is as the pioneer travellers might remember it. The forest is dark, as the route bends and twists around each obstacle. There are few clearings here and no old cabins. So dreadful was the soil that settlers shunned this area completely. Past the Youthdale Road, the Nipissing Road is no longer passable. If driving, you will need to return to Highway 124 and drive east to Pearceley Road and follow it north to Centre Road, where you turn left to get back to the Nipissing Road alignment.

After 18 km, there appears a clearing and a white frame house. This is the site of a one-time village, Mecunoma, and its famous hotel with the colourful name of Bummers' Roost. The original hotel burned in 1926, and today's house was built on the hotel foundations. This brings you to a T intersection with the Eagle Lake Road. Beyond

Opposite: A typical schoolhouse in a forest setting found on Ontario's pioneer roads.

the intersection, the Nipissing Road is no longer suitable for vehicles—so you should turn right on Eagle Lake Road and follow it for 1.5 km to the Rye Road, where you go left. After 2 km on this road, you will rejoin the original alignment of the Nipissing at the abandoned hamlet of Rye. Gone now are the store, post office and log hotels—some sources say there were as many as four hotels—and Rye today consists of a collapsing school and a cemetery.

An intersection 1.5 km north of the school marks the centre of the vanished hamlet. The white frame church was demolished in the mid-1980s, but the cemetery contains a number of white wooden crosses beside the headstones where many of the family names reflect the Germanic origins of the early pioneers.

As you travel north from this quiet intersection, you will pass the remains of a series of former bush farms, until the original road once more becomes impassable.

Beyond here the Nipissing Road once more becomes impassible for passenger vehicles. To continue on to the last portion of your route, return to Highway 124 and travel east to Highway 11. Then drive north and follow Highway 522, which will lead you back to the Nipissing Road and to the historic old general store in the ghost town of Commanda.

Commanda to Nipissing

Named for a local Ojibwa chief, Commanda is a small cluster of houses. Here, in 1885, James Arthur built the area's first general store. It was larger than most for a pioneer village—two storeys high, with a double porch and extensions to each side. Arthur distinguished his store with elaborate flourishes to its fretwork. Although most such buildings would have been replaced or severely altered, the Commanda store has survived five ownerships intact. Then in 1980, the Gurd Township and Area Historical Corporation purchased the building and refurbished it as a turn-of-the-century general store. The building reopened in 1982 as a "general store" museum that also features a restaurant and artisans' shop.

From the store follow Highway 522 back east and, after less than 1 km, turn left onto Alsace

The old general store in Commanda is now a unique general store museum.

The small community of Nipissing marked the end of the road, although few made it this far.

Road. Commanding a high, gravelly ridge is the Nipissing Road's only surviving farm community. Although stony, the soils here are deeper and they have allowed the farmers to grow hay and to graze beef cattle. At 5 km from Highway 522, the Alsace Road swings east away from Nipissing Road, which once more is a bush trail. After another 5 km, turn left at Wolfe Lake Road and drive a further 3 km to Highway 534. Turn right and follow the highway around steep hills and past modern rural residences. A left turn onto Highway 534 brings you into the road's final village, Nipissing. Both Highways 534 and 654 at this point trace the old colonization road alignment.

Nipissing remains small. Modern cottages and retirement homes now mingle with a school, houses and the log pioneer church that is now the Nipissing Township museum. During the village's short-lived heyday as a busy stagecoach terminus, stores and hotels sprouted on each corner. Today they are gone. No longer does Nipissing provide liquid refreshment for the weary traveller, but then, no longer does the journey from Rosseau take a full week as it did a century ago. Failed plans for two rail lines and a canal through the area would have created a city here instead of at North Bay.

Nipissing marks the end of your route. From here you can follow Highway 654 east to Highway 11 and home.

Overleaf: A frozen Lake Nippissing

Manitoulin Island is the world's largest freshwater island—120 km in length, though it narrows in places to just 2 km in width. It has more than 20 inland lakes and one of Ontario's longest dead-end highways. Highway 540, which is the backroad for this trip, is 145 km long and follows the cliffs and coves from Little Current at the island's eastern end to Manitoulin's western tip.

Despite its size, Manitoulin has no traditional road access. There are indeed only two approaches for drivers bound for Manitoulin Island. One is via Highway 6 south from the Trans-Canada Highway 17, 70 km west of Sudbury. This is a route noted for its high, scenic passes across the La Cloche Mountains, a rugged ridge of white quartzite. The access to the island, however, is not by a normal highway bridge, but rather by a paved and decommissioned CPR railway bridge.

The other approach is over the water. Ontario's largest car ferry, the *Chi-Cheemaun*, offers three daily sailings during the summer between Tobermory, at the tip of the Bruce Peninsula, and South Baymouth, on Highway 6, 65 km south of Little Current. Translated from the Ojibwa, the ferry's name means "Big Canoe."

Here is a territory that mainstream Ontario has only lately discovered. Despite proposals for mega developments, there remains a legacy of vanished sawmills and abandoned farmsteads. Many of the villages and towns have changed little since Manitoulin's boom period of the late 1880s, and they provide rustic subject material for photographers. High on Manitoulin's cliffs you will find hiking trails, lookouts and picnic tables, and, in their shadow, inland lakes for fishing, boating or swimming.

Opposite: A former railway swing bridge remains the only road access to the world's largest freshwater island.

Centuries ago, Manitoulin was a Native stronghold that its aboriginal inhabitants, the Ottawa, called Ekantoten. However, during the 17th century, the Iroquois incursions forced the Ottawa to flee to the shores of Lake Michigan, where they remained until 1836. In that year, the lieutenant-governor of Upper Canada, Sir Francis Bond Head, selected the large island as the centre of Native relocations. The scattered tribes returned, reluctantly at first, but by 1860 more than 1,300 Ottawa and Ojibwa were occupying a cluster of towns at the east end of the island.

But the haven was short-lived. Bowing to pressure from lumbermen and settlers, the Indian Branch sent William Bartlett and Charles Lindsay to take back the island. The Native peoples in return were to receive a paltry 10 hectares each. Not surprisingly, they refused. The strongest opposition came from the large contingent who occupied the Wikwemikong Peninsula. The next year William McDougall, commissioner of Crown lands, tried again, but he too was rebuffed. Only when he arbitrarily excluded the Wikwemikong from voting about ceding their lands did the other, smaller bands relent and move reluctantly to reserves. The Wikwemikongs, however, never yielded their lands, and today the Wikwemikong Peninsula remains Ontario's only unceded First Nations territory.

Then, between 1864 and 1879, the surveyors moved in, and by 1882 the government had sold 120,000 hectares, much of it to absentee speculators who resold it at several times its original price.

The first European settlements appeared in sheltered coves. By 1881 fishermen and lumbermen had set up mills and fishing stations in Little Current, Honora, Kagawong, Gore Bay, Cooks Dock and Michaels Bay. Early life was hard, and the tough berry, the haw berry, became a staple of the pioneer diet, so much so that the island's early farmers nicknamed each other the "haweaters." The name has survived to this day and now is used to promote tourism.

At first, only two roads linked the settlements: colonization trails from Michaels Bay, the island's first main port of entry on the south coast to Manitowaning, and to Gore Bay. But by the turn of century, farm concession roads had opened throughout the island, and the old pioneer trails were in parts completely abandoned while Michaels Bay itself became a ghost town.

Farming, fishing and forestry developed as mainstays for the island's economy, but each soon declined. Fire and overcutting combined to sweep the forests clean. Overfishing and the dreaded predator, the sea lamprey, defeated the fishery. And the stony and infertile soils that should never have been cultivated in the first place drove away most of the farmers. Since 1900 Manitoulin's population has risen from 10,000 to 13,000. The spectre of large development looms, and major projects now threaten the island's serenity.

Nevertheless, the picturesque vestiges of early settlement and the natural beauty of the cliffs and waters combine to make the Haweater Trail a wonderful way to explore the island.

Little Current

Manitoulin, the world's largest freshwater island, has the most unusual form of road access, an abandoned railway bridge. Built by the Algoma Eastern Railway, the Canadian Pacific Railway's predecessor, the bridge has been paved to allow autos. During navigation season it swings open for 10 minutes each hour to allow boats to pass.

The bridge leads to the island's main community, Little Current. From the south the highway enters Little Current on Manitowaning Road, an early colonization road. The town's main business district lines the shore on Water Street, where you

Kagawong is one of the route's most picturesque villages. Manitouwaning is now home to the historic CPR steamship Norisle located next to its dockside mill.

can watch the sleek American yachts glide to dock-side, fresh from a battle with the turbulent North Channel. Along the street are grocery stores, gift shops, the popular Anchor Inn tavern and offices of the *Manitoulin Expositor*, a community news-paper that has been published since 1879.

Little Current to Kagawong

The mighty rock ridge known as the Niagara Escarpment dips beneath the waters of Georgian Bay at the northern tip of the Bruce Peninsula and re-emerges to form the backbone of Manitoulin Island. The escarpment's cliffs form the island's north shore, ring its fjord-like bays and loom over its flat plains.

The first section of your trip follows the base of the escarpment and leads you to its highest lookouts and through its early ports. Your first lookout point, and one of the highest, lies close to Little Current. Follow Highway 6 south to 10 Mile Point lookout with ample parking and a gift shop (complete with haw berry jelly). Views here extend northward over the various channels that separate the island from the mainland, and to the gleaming white La Cloche Mountains. Continue south to Manitouwaning for the historic dockside complex that includes a former mill and decom-missioned CPR steamer the SS Norisle. Return to Little Current and follow Highway 540 west. Here, old farms mix with newer country homes until, after 2 km, the road enters the Sucker Creek First Nation territory. After 3 km, the road leaves the territory, traverses another small farming commu-nity and then meets the shoreline. For the next

6 km it follows the shoreline though, for most of this stretch, trees block the view. The road then bends south to Honora, where a handful of homes are all that remain of a once busy fishing and sawmilling port.

At 6 km south of Honora, Highway 540 meets the Bidwell Road and your access to the Cup and Saucer Trail, a hiking trail to the island's highest lookout point. The Cup and Saucer (named for its appearance) is a rock formation that looms high above the road. The trail is about 2 km long and includes steps and rails to help you up the steeper portions. The views from the top are panoramic. Below, to the east, lie the waters of Lake Manitou, and beyond that the farmlands of the eastern end of the island. To the west lie West Bay and the North Channel of Lake Huron. Allow about three hours for the hike.

Continuing west from the trail, the road brings you to the First Nation village of M'Chigeeng, the site of an early Native Canadian settlement called Mechocowedong. It is the island's most populous Native territory (Wikwemikong is the largest geographically) and, with its three art galleries, is one of Ontario's more important centres for First Nations artists. You can find their works in the Ojibwe Cultural Foundation, which you enter through a piece of stone artwork called "Bringing the Family Together." Across the road, the Immaculate Conception Church's architecture is meant to symbolize a tepee. Here, too, you will find galleries, craft shops and restaurants. Take a look especially at Lillian's Crafts and its stunning display of porcupine-quill baskets.

West of M'Chigeeng, Highway 540 swings inland for about 3 km and then turns straight north to cross a small agricultural plain. After 4 km, it bends west to the historic and picturesque village of Kagawong.

Kagawong

Kagawong lies about 1 km north of the highway on the shores of Mudge Bay. Like most of the island's cove villages, Kagawong began as a milling, fishing and shipping centre, but it had one more feature that the others lacked—water power. Just 2 km inland lies Lake Kagawong, from which a small river drains northward to the lip of a deep gorge. The 20 metre drop in the river powered early sawmills and later an electric powerhouse. Today it provides the focus for a small park beside the highway.

The village, a string of buildings along the road by the bay, contains some of the island's most appealing architecture. Here stand a former pulp mill, now the Old Mill Heritage Centre Museum, and a store, which is now the popular Manitoulin Chocolate Works. The Anglican church contains a pulpit made from the wreck of an old ship, while its stained-glass windows depict a ship and anchor. You can take a walking tour of the village; or you can continue your drive out to Maple Point and a scenic panorama of the North Channel Islands.

Kagawong to Gore Bay

From Kagawong, Highway 540 crosses a limestone plain to the island's first major town, and one of its most picturesque, Gore Bay. Gore Bay was once larger than Little Current, its future more promising. Today it has slid to second place. To enter Gore Bay, turn right from Highway 540 onto Highway 540B and drive 2 km into the town.

Gore Bay

One of Manitoulin's first European settlements, Gore Bay was the terminus of a colonization road from Michaels Bay on the south shore. By 1895 it had become not just a fishing and shipping port, but the centre of a prosperous farming community and the seat of the district court. Only a few

Gore Bay is a popular destination for boaters and tourists during the summer months.

buildings date from its early days, because in 1908 a fire razed most of the business district.

As Highway 542 enters the town it becomes Meredith Street, the business street where you will find most of the stores. Two blocks away on Phipps Street is the 1889 courthouse, which somehow escaped the flames. Beside it stands the jail built in 1895, which now houses the museum. Here you can look at a turn-of-the-century cell, as well as at early telephones and dental equipment.

Down on the water, you can visit the new tourist pavilion with its art gallery and tea room. Before leaving, drive out along East Bluff Road, or take West Bluff Road to Janet Head Park. Either route will reward you with sweeping vistas of the cliff-lined harbour and the wind-tossed waters of the North Channel.

Gore Bay to Silver Water

This section of the route traverses one of the island's most fertile plains, crosses a long causeway, and includes watery lookouts and a pair of ghost ports.

Continue west from Gore Bay on Highway 540. For 4.5 km, the road crosses fertile farming plains. Here you will pass some modern farms, their fields wide and green, herds of beef cattle lazily grazing. As Highway 540 bends sharply south, Highway 540A leads to the island township of Barrie Island, a low limestone plateau with two dozen farms. But keep on Highway 540 and follow it south toward Lake Wolsey.

The road continues through farm country for about 4 km and then enters the narrow peninsula that divides Bayfield Sound, a wide indentation of the North Channel, from Lake Wolsey. This 2 km long peninsula is separated from the south shore of the lake by a 1 km wide channel, which Highway 540 crosses on a scenic causeway. Off to the side is a roadside park that offers picnic facilities and a chance to fish. The south end of Lake Wolsey, which lies only 2 km from Manitoulin's south shore, marks the narrowest point of the island. Before crossing you can pause at Indian Point Bridge lookout to enjoy the view.

Continuing west on Highway 540 you pass through the communities of Evansville and Elizabeth Bay before arriving in the village of Silver Water.

Silver Water

Silver Water was once western Manitoulin's most important village, the retail centre for a busy farming area and for two ports. But the ports have vanished, along with their fishermen, sawmills and cabins, and many farms are now abandoned. Their decline affected the village and many of its original buildings are now gone. A few new homes have been added along with a newer general store.

If you are a history enthusiast, you may want to visit the vanished port of Cooks Dock. Tucked beneath a 100 metre cliff, it was at the turn of the century a fishing station and a lumber shipping port. To reach it, turn right on Cooks Dock Road and drive 5 km to the dock site.

Silver Water to Meldrum Bay

This, the last segment of the route, passes isolated pockets of farmlands, ventures into a tiny village of white houses on a green hillside, and ends at a curious lighthouse museum. It is as far as you go on Manitoulin.

From Silver Water, continue west on Highway 540. For 28 km the road traverses a rugged land of rock and forest. Overgrown clearings tell of futile farming efforts. Then on the right, as the road makes a sharp swing left, the blue waters of Meldrum Bay sparkle between the trees. A kilometre beyond that lies the village of Meldrum Bay. The bay from which the village derived its name is ringed with steep, forested hills. On the western shore are the church, hotel, stores and houses. Today, Meldrum Bay is home to only about 160 permanent residents, but at the turn of the century it contained a sawmill and a colony of fishermen. Now only the mill's foundations remain.

The community sees little traffic, and the pace is leisurely. Here you can visit the Meldrum Bay Country Store or enjoy a meal (or overnight stay) at the century-old Meldrum Bay Inn. And don't leave out the Net Shed Museum, a former net storage shed that is operated by the small but active Meldrum Bay Historical Society. It is open daily on alternating mornings and afternoons throughout the summer months and displays early photographs and fishing equipment.

The ambience of the place is to be enjoyed. Where else can you find yourself at the end of a 100 km long dead-end road? The tranquility and the maritime legacy combine to transport you back in time.

Meldrum Bay to Mississagi Lighthouse

From the village, rejoin Highway 540 for 1 km to a side road where a directional arrow points to the lighthouse. The dirt road crosses Manitoulin's most remote farming community and then, after 3 km, narrows and becomes a more rugged trail, twisting through the bush. After 5 km it emerges into a small, rocky clearing. Ahead stands the Mississagi Lighthouse. En route it will be hard to miss the Lafarge dolomite quarry, one of Ontario's largest, which ships their product on large ocean-going freighters.

The Mississagi Lighthouse is now a museum and campground office.

Built before the turn of the 19th century to guide ships along the channel between Manitoulin and Cockburn Islands, the lighthouse is now a museum. It is a squat wooden structure, painted the mandatory red and white. The attached keeper's cabin is furnished in a turn-of-the-century style and contains equipment that the keeper of the period used. The Mississagi Lighthouse tops a low limestone bluff, the crest of the Niagara Escarpment, just before it dips once more beneath Lake Huron's chilly waters.

From the light level, you can view the rocky shoreline below you and the distant form of the ghost island of Cockburn Island. There the main village of Tolsmaville is now a seasonal community. Its former concession roads have three dozen farms, all vacant, which tell of a once-bustling island community of farmers, fishermen and loggers who were forced to leave when the vital steamer service that linked them with the outside world was discontinued.

Overleaf: Sunset over Manitoulin Island.

24 Boomtown Backroads: The Cobalt Circle

A headframe marks the entrance into Cobalt.

More than ten years ago, a TV Ontario panel of historians (this author included) awarded Cobalt the designation, "Ontario's Most Historic Town"—and there was a reason for that. It was the silver discovery here in 1903 that spawned a world-famous silver rush creating a boomtown and giving the impetus for a railway and the opening of Ontario's northeast. This route explores that heritage, from the boomtown buildings in this unusual town to the skeletal remains of mine headframes that lurk amid the harsh rock knobs surrounding Cobalt. Thanks to the Cobalt Mining Museum, informative published walking and driving tours will lead the way.

n 1890 northeastern Ontario was touted for its farmland. From the north end of Lake Timiskaming, a flat plain of fine clays, the result of an ancient postglacial lake deposit spreads northwestward. The government of the day heavily promoted the area, which it dubbed the Clay Belt. With only steamers to get them there, settlers docked at places such as New Liskeard and Haileybury, still thriving communities today, and at other places that have vanished, like Hilliardtown and Tomstown.

To make colonization more attractive, the government laid plans to build a colonization railway to carry the settlers. In 1903 while scouting the woods for timber that the railway could use as ties, scouts James McKinley and Ernest Darragh found a dull grey rock that was inordinately heavy. Their discovery, by the shore of Long Lake (now Cobalt Lake), was silver. The rush was on.

Within just five years, more than 100 mines were clanging in the hills around the lake, while on the rocky shore boomed the town of Cobalt. The population grew quickly to 10,000, as simple cabins and gangly stores fought for valuable space on the steep hillsides. Despite local prohibition, Cobalt miners could be sure of satisfying their thirst at illegal booze cans called Blind Pigs. Little wonder that one of its heritage buildings is the Ontario Provincial Police's first lock-up. As prospectors wandered the hills, they uncovered more deposits. By 1909 Cobalt had a rival more than 40 km away, at Silver Centre.

But the small deposits of silver were soon exhausted. Later, as prices for silver plunged, the mines began to close, and by 1940 Cobalt's population had dwindled to fewer than 2,000. Silver Centre was abandoned completely, and it is now a ghost town.

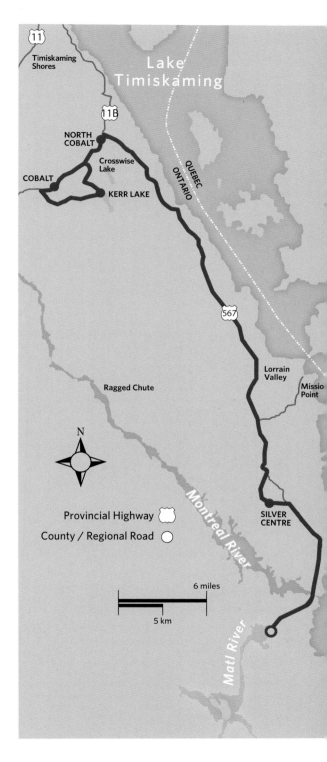

Cobalt retains much of its boomtown appearance.

Cobalt

By exploring Cobalt and its mining heritage, you will easily understand why TV Ontario's *Studio Two* program labelled Cobalt as "Ontario's Most Historic Town," a deserved designation of which the town's citizens are justly proud. With its twisting sidewalks, old wooden houses and early stores, Cobalt still looks like a boomtown. Although fires and demolitions have taken a heavy toll on its wonderful old buildings, enough remain that you can wander the streets and relive those glory days.

Start at the mining museum on Silver Street. It is one of North America's most celebrated mining museums, containing rare mining equipment, books on the romance of the rush, and Canada's largest collection of silver ore. It occupies the first office of the *Cobalt Nugget*, which during the peak of the boom had avid readers as far away as England and California. In the museum be sure to purchase the Heritage Silver Trail guide and the Cobalt Walking Trail Guide, both excellent.

Beside the museum is the present town hall, in the former YMCA building. Nearby gift and craft shops have moved into the old structures, while on the opposite side of the street is an old-time barber shop. While you're on Silver Street, check the schedule of the Classic Theatre. Built in 1920, the Classic was restored as a theatre in 1995.

Across from the museum, on the Willet Green Miller Memorial site, stands a headframe that was originally located in North Cobalt. The Pan Silver headframe was moved here in 1998 to house the Cobalt Historical Society. An outdoor heritage exhibit displays mining equipment and renderings depicting the town's heritage.

Behind the display and down by the tracks is the magnificent TNO railway station. Built to replace the TNO's original pattern-book station in 1908, the station contained a vaulted two-storey waiting room. After sitting empty for several years, it has been preserved and now is home to the town's welcome centre.

A few paces north of the museum, at the corner of Prospect and Silver Streets, is Cobalt's most unusual group of buildings. On the northeast corner is the Bank of Ottawa building, while on the northwest corner is a former grocery store. What makes this store so unusual is that it has a headframe sticking out of its roof. Anthony Giachino, who built it in 1926, decided to recycle the cool air from the depths of the then abandoned Coniagas mine shaft to cool his meat and vegetables.

On the southwest corner stands the Fraser Hotel, originally the Royal Exchange Building. The Bunker Museum moved here from its earlier home in the train station. Although massive compared with its neighbours today, several equally grand buildings once lined both Prospect and Lang Streets. Lang Street was once described as northern Ontario's premier shopping street with shops extending for more than 1 km. As a result of fires and demolitions, few remain. Prospect Street demonstrates the difficulty in town-building: it ends at a steep flight of stairs that leads to Cobalt Street, where many early homes reflect the boomtown style of housing, as do various other small back streets.

Farther east on Lang Street you come to the old town "square" and a historic grouping of buildings. As you near the new library you will find the firefighters' museum with a wall mural that shows you what Lang Street looked like in its glory days.

The Heritage Silver Trail

After you have followed the mining museum's walking tour, get back in the car to follow the Heritage Silver Trail guide for a circular tour through the barren hills around Cobalt and the sites of the many mines that operated there. Prepared by the Mining Museum and the Ontario government, the tour is a well-marked self-guiding drive. Start by driving east on Lang Street from the firefighters' museum.

Proceed a short distance to Ferland Street and, at the Miner's Tavern, turn right. Across the wooden bridge over the railway tracks stands the rusting headframe of the Right of Way Mine (so-called because it sits on the railway right-of-way), where three million ounces of silver were extracted. Here, where silver was mined from beneath the railway track, you will see a display of ancient mining machinery. Just beyond the bridge and on the left stands the legendary LaRose Blacksmith Shop where, legend has it, blacksmith Fred LaRose flung an axe at a fox. The axe chipped a rock, exposing what would become one the camp's richest ore bodies.

From the blacksmith's shop follow Kerr Lake Road, as it is called here, to Cross Lake Road, keeping right on Kerr Lake Road. This brings you to the Colonial Mine where you can arrange a tour with the mining museum. The route continues past the Nova Scotia Mine and mill site where operations ended in 1921. Just beyond the junction with Glenn Lake Road you will encounter one of Cobalt's more legendary mines, the Silver Sidewalk. The vein was literally the width of a sidewalk

The headframe from the former Buffalo Mine was used to keep produce cool when it was converted to a grocery store.

but plunged deep into the ground, as you will see from the viewing platform. From this location, the Beaver Temisk Road and the Penn Mill Road lead to other mine sites, where headframes yet loom above the forests—although these locations are not in the guidebook

Return to town by following the Kerr Lake Road back to the Glenn Lake Road and then Coleman Road. This will lead you to the McKinley Darragh mine site, where the town's first mill clanged into operation in 1903. A viewing platform here offers a look at the extensive ruins. The Coleman Road comes to a stop sign on Highway 11B, where a turn to the right leads back into town. The headframe that guards the entrance to the town here is the headframe and shaft for the Townsite Mine. Park here and follow the path to the "Glory Hole," which gives you a glimpse into an open pit. Highway 11B

leads you back to the mining museum. Overnight accommodation is available at the Silverland Motel on Lang Street beside which is Silver Cafe and Confectionery for a family-style meal.

Side Trip to Silver Centre

This section of the route leaves behind the scarred hillsides of Cobalt and leads you through a lush hidden valley with high, wooded hillsides and a valley floor of pastures and fields. Follow Highway 11B east from Cobalt for 4 km to Highway 567.

Turn right onto Highway 567 and follow it southeast through the rugged little village of North Cobalt and into a landscape of a rock and forest. After 7 km, the road bends south and enters the Lorrain Valley. The gentle pastoral scenes that you see during the next 20 km contrast starkly with the hard, forbidding bedrock that surrounds you.

At about 18 km from Highway 11B, a historical marker points down Old Mission Road to the shores of Lake Timiskaming and the site of an Oblate mission established in 1863 and now long-vanished. To continue on your southerly route, return to Highway 567 and turn left. After passing more farms and fields for 7 km, the road rises out of the valley onto a rocky plateau. A little over 2 km from Maidens Bay Camp Road on the left, look for a cindered road that branches right from Highway 567. This is the road to the ghost town of Silver Centre.

Silver Centre

As the Cobalt boom neared its peak in 1907, prospectors ventured farther afield and, in that year, discovered silver in these remote hills. Other mines quickly moved in, and the town of Silver Centre grew to a population of 700 with a streetcar connection to Cobalt and a hockey team of its own. Of the two dozen mines that worked the area, however, fewer than a half-dozen were profitable. By 1930 the silver boom had faded, and so had Silver Centre. As the mines closed, the rails were lifted and the road fell into disrepair.

Visitors can now view the Silver Sidewalk, thanks to a drive-it-yourself tour route.

Here, in 1925, you would have found stores and shops, a school, a theatre, a hockey rink, 50 houses and cabins and assorted mine structures. Silver Centre at its peak was home to 700 people. Sadly, the buildings were all moved or burned, and the regenerating forest hides most of what's left.

Silver Centre to Matabitchuan

From Silver Centre, Highway 567 continues another 13 km to its end at the Matabitchuan Dam. For 9 km the road winds across the forested highland that repulsed any efforts to settle it. Then it suddenly emerges from the woods and crosses a modern bridge. The lake to your right is the forebay for the Lower Notch Generating Station. The massive dam and powerhouse lie to your left, but are not clearly visible from the road. The pond created behind the dam backs 15 km up the Montreal River.

25 The Trail of the Sleeping Giant

A lake in Sleeping Giant Provincial Park.

Ontario's most famous rock formation is for many the Sleeping Giant of Thunder Bay. Arms folded across its chest, the figure consists of ancient limestone mesas that shape the Sibley Peninsula southeast of that Lakehead city. This trip uncovers the mysteries of the Sleeping Giant and probes the farming and fishing communities of this remote finger of land.

The route starts at Pearl on the Trans-Canada Highway, 50 km east of Thunder Bay, and runs south down the Sibley Peninsula and back for about 100 km.

This journey is for the hiker, the photographer and the ghost-town lover. Former fishing villages (reminiscent of the much-photographed Peggy's Cove in Nova Scotia) indent the east coast of the peninsula. Through the Sleeping Giant Provincial Park, the authorities have cut hiking trails to the lofty head and chest of the Sleeping Giant; and at the remote tip of the peninsula sits the site of Ontario's oldest, and richest, silver discovery—the ghost town of Silver Islet.

n 1845 silver was discovered on a small rocky islet 2 km off the tip of the Sibley Peninsula and it became the focus for the first European settlement in the area. Then in the mid-1880s the Canadian Pacific Railway hammered its rails across the neck of the peninsula. It was followed in 1903 by the Canadian Northern Railway, which paralleled it a few kilometres south. From the station villages of Pearl and Pass Lake, bush trails extended down the peninsula. Commercial fishing had been in full swing along the American shore since the fur-trading days of the 1820s and 1830s, but now the railways provided a means of shipping out the local catch. Soon most of the coves that could harbour a tug or a few skiffs had a small fishing station.

Farm settlement progressed much more slowly. Bush farms along the road to the railway stations gave way after the First World War to a settlement scheme to open up the peninsula's fertile post-glacial deposits near Pass Lake. It was to this plain in 1924 that the Ontario government invited 65 Danish settlers.

Although there were fewer farmers than fishermen, their activities are still evident on much of the peninsula's landscape. Tourism, however, has surpassed both farming and fishing as travellers pick through the amethyst mines near Pearl, hike the trails of the provincial park or settle for the summer into the miners' cabins in a ghost town.

Pearl to Johnsons Landing

The first portion of the route follows a one-time bush trail from Pearl, passes some bush farms and then leads into Johnsons Landing, the Peggy's Cove of the peninsula. From Pearl, drive south on Road 5. After less than 1 km, the road crosses the abandoned CNR right-of-way and then for 1 km follows the Pearl River, more a creek than a river. Along its banks you may see evidence of the early farms. The

Johnson Harbour is one of several attractive fishing coves on the Sibley Peninsula.

road then swings south and traverses a low, rolling landscape of young forest and overgrown clearings. Here the pockets of soil were small and infertile, and the bush farms were soon abandoned.

After 9 km, you will come to a T intersection. Your route lies to the right, but first turn left for a short trip to Johnsons Landing, reminiscent of Canada's maritime fishing villages perched on the smooth rocks that ring the small bay. Beyond the wooded inlet are the waters of Black Bay, a wide indentation of Lake Superior that contains some of the lake's best fishing.

Johnsons Landing to Silver Islet

The next section of the route leads through the prosperous Danish settlement to Squaw Bay, then through the Sleeping Giant Provincial Park to the legendary Silver Islet.

From the dead end at Johnsons Landing, return the way you came, and then turn left at the intersection. Suddenly the wide, level plain of the Danish farming community appears from the bush. Farm enlargements and abandonment of the fringe area have reduced the dozen and a half original farms to the half-dozen that carry on today.

From the first crossroads that you come to the road traverses the fertile farmland and, after 2 km, crosses a narrow wooden bridge. Look for a side road 1 km beyond the bridge. This side road, the Pass Lake Crossroad, leads west to Highway 587, the route you will take on your return. For the present, continue straight ahead. After 1 km, the road leaves the last of the farms and returns to Crown land. The road then continues to follow the bay. Summer cottages mingle with fishermen's cabins and even with the clearings of early farms.

Another 2 km bring you to the boundary of the Sleeping Giant Provincial Park, and, after a further 1 km, you come to a stop sign at Highway 587. Turn left to reach the campgrounds and trails for which the park has become famous.

At 3 km from the turn you will see on your right the starting point of a scenic drive through the park that provides you with spectacular views from the top of the mesa. The mesa is one of a group of mesas that forms the park's most famous feature, the Sleeping Giant.

Ojibwa legend claims that the shape is the form of a chief named Nanabozo (or Nanabijou), who was the son of the west wind. The chief had led his people to the peninsula to keep them safe from their traditional enemy, the Sioux, and it was here on a tiny rock shoal that they discovered silver. But to reveal its location, especially to the Europeans, meant retribution from the Great Spirit, so the chief swore his followers to secrecy. However, one of his subchiefs had secretly made jewellery from the metal, and, after the Sioux had captured him in battle, they led a group of Europeans to the islet. When the chief saw them coming, he called up a storm to send the canoes and their travellers to the cold depths of the lake. In punishment the Great Spirit turned Nanabozo to stone, the Sleeping Giant.

Geologists, however, have come up with a decidedly less colourful explanation. The rock mesa, they claim, is simply the remnant of a great limestone plateau whose sediments were laid down by an ancient sea. No matter how it got there, Ontario's most spectacular hiking trails lead to its lofty summits. To reach them, continue 12 km south on Highway 587 and ask for trail maps in the park office.

From the peaks of the mesa that tower here, 140 metres above the grey waters of the lake, you can see grain ships gliding in and out of Thunder Bay harbour, the wooded shoreline below and, in the distance, the shapes of other mesas.

Some surprisingly fertile soils attracted a colony of Danes to the Sibley Peninsula.

The main street of the ghost mining town of Silver Islet has changed little since its mine closed, although many of the cabins have become summer homes.

Silver Islet

From the park continue south on the highway. After 3 km, the road leaves the woods and enters a clearing. Then, in a long row, the cabins of the 100-year-old village of Silver Islet appear.

This was the site of Canada's richest silver strike. It all began in 1845 when Joseph Woods, who was exploring for copper, discovered an unusually rich silver vein on a rocky shoal 2 km from the tip of the peninsula. But there was no economical means of transporting the ore, and it lay idle until 1870, when Major William Sibley of Detroit bought the claim for what would be the bargain price of $250,000. He hired an engineer named William Frue to build retaining walls and to bring the mine into production. It seemed the spirit of Nanabozo grew restless and sent storms, tidal waves and ice to destroy Frue's breakwaters.

However, by 1873 Frue had constructed a barrier that withstood all that the Sleeping Giant could hurl at it, and production began.

On the islet Frue placed the mine buildings and bunkhouses; on the shore, a stamping mill with 50 stamps; and extending along a 2 km shoreline, 40 houses, a hotel, two churches, a store and a log jail. Within ten years, production exceeded $3 million, a figure that made it Canada's richest silver mine.

As the shafts edged out under the floor of the lake, huge coal-filled boilers were installed to pump out the perpetual leaks. By 1884 the peninsula had no more logs to feed the flames of the pumps, and all eyes looked southward for the form of the winter coal boat. The anxious residents could scarcely have known that, far over the horizon, the boat's captain, inebriated, had run the ship fast aground. Before he could free her, an early freeze clamped the vessel in ice for the winter. Silver Islet would get no coal. By March the flames in the boilers died and water began to fill the shafts. The mine was finished.

Miraculously, the town survived. Soon after the miners had fled, residents of the growing towns of Port Arthur and Fort William (the twin cities that are today's Thunder Bay) bought up the cabins as summer homes. Since then, successive owners have preserved, and in some cases replaced, the buildings of the town. The only structures to disappear are the mill, the mine buildings on the islet, the Catholic church, and the mansion of the mine's owner, Major Sibley.

As you enter the village, the first building you see is the log jail. It is Ontario's only surviving log jail and is privately preserved. Then the road enters the village proper and leads straight to the massive wooden store, now restored as a residence. From it the old miners' cabins, along with newer cottages, stretch along the shore. Their sturdy construction, and their distance from one another—a fire prevention measure—have combined to ensure their longevity.

Highway 587, more a lane, follows the shoreline to the left of the store. Still narrow, much as the miners might remember it, it is a one-way route east to west during the summer. Follow the road east along the shore. Lake Superior laps at your right, while the miners' cabins line the road on your left. As the road swings inland, the miners' graveyard lies about 100 metres into the bush to your left. To your right, far off the shore, you may be able to discern the low form of the shoal that produced Canada's richest silver mine.

Silver Islet to Pass Lake

The last segment of the route returns up the peninsula along a clifftop drive to the hamlet of Pass Lake. From there you can continue to the

The town cemetery for the ghost town of Silver Islet, abandoned a century ago. It is now a cottage community at the tip of the Sibley Peninsula.

deep Ouimet Canyon or to some of Canada's best amethyst-gathering sites.

About 1 km after the one-way road through Silver Islet leaves the shore, it reconnects with the two-way Highway 587. To return north, turn right and travel 30 km to Pass Lake. Alternatively, if it is open, you can embark on a scenic side trip to the park's clifftops.

Sleeping Giant Side Trip

Within the provincial park, follow the 9 km Thunder Bay Lookout Trail to a viewpoint 150 metres above the lake for stunning views of Caribou Island and the shores of Thunder Bay.

Return to Highway 587 and continue to the village of Pass Lake. Pass Lake, originally a station on the Canadian Northern Railway, became the focus for the Danish farm colony to its east, which was at one time famous for its strawberries. Seventy thousand quarts were shipped from the station in 1935 alone. Today the village contains

The Pass Lake railway trestle is among Ontario's loftiest railway bridges.

the squat, white Salem Lutheran Church that dates from the Danish migration, and Karen's Kountry Kitchen on the lake (opposite the abandoned railway right-of-way). The restaurant is the former station master's house. A few kilometres north you pass beneath the same rail, only here it hovers high above the roadway on what is northern Ontario's highest railway trestle.

More to See

A drive of 5 km north brings you back to the Trans-Canada Highway.

Canada's best amethyst deposits lie a few kilometres east. Most are privately owned, and the owners will allow you to collect on your own for a fee. The best pieces, however, usually make their way to the on-site gift shops first. To visit an operating mine complete with tours and a gift shop, follow

Highway 17 east to East Loon Lake Road and follow the directions to the Panorama Mine. The views along this long and twisting route give a clue as to how this interesting mine earned its name.

Side Trip to a "Grand Canyon"

You may also explore Ontario's own Grand Canyon. Ouimet Canyon is a 5 km long fissure that plunges 100 metres down into the ancient bedrock. So little sunlight reaches the bottom of the canyon that rare types of arctic vegetation—survivors of the ice age—grow undisturbed. To reach the canyon, drive east from Pearl for 10 km to the Ouimet Canyon Road and follow the Ouimet Canyon Provincial Park signs for another 10 km. This free park contains several kilometres of hiking trails, but be careful. There are few guardrails, and the footing can be slippery.

Indian Head at Ouimet Canyon Provincial Park.

For a more interactive canyon adventure, follow the signs along the Ouimet Canyon Road to Eagle Canyon, where two suspension foot bridges, including Canada's longest at 200 metres, suspends you more than 50 metres above the yawning canyon.

Overleaf: This suspension bridge crosses Eagle Canyon near Ouimet Canyon.

26 The Silver Mountain Road

The Kakabeka Falls on the Kaministiquia River are easily accessible for cars and campers.

West of the city of Thunder Bay lies a range of mountains that the Ojibwa call the Shuniah Weachu—Mountains of Silver. A series of soaring flat-top mesas, they spawned one of Ontario's first silver rushes. This 80 km route winds beneath their looming cliffs, taking you not only to the early silver mines, but also to waterfalls and valley villages, northwestern Ontario's first Finnish settlement, and a peek at the Ghost Railway to Nowhere.

The route starts at Kakabeka Falls, 30 km west of Thunder Bay on the Trans-Canada Highway 17, and follows paved secondary highways to Middle Falls, on the historic Pigeon River, Canada's boundary with the United States.

The early history of the Thunder Bay area is one of fur trading. Fort William began as a North West Company fur post in the closing years of the 18th century and became one of Ontario's largest trading posts. The fort has been carefully reconstructed, albeit on a different site, as a living museum. Its neighbour on the shore of Lake Superior, Prince Arthur's Landing, grew into a port where schooners called for furs and fish. In the 1880s, when the Canadian Pacific Railway was being constructed northwest from Lake Superior, these settlements grew into the towns of Fort William and Port Arthur. Nine decades later, they would amalgamate as the city of Thunder Bay. Thunder Bay is the highest city in Ontario's North, and is Ontario's tenth largest.

But the wealth of the fur was soon eclipsed by something far more spectacular—silver. In 1882 a local Ojibwa chief, Joseph L'Avocat, led prospector Oliver Daunais to the secret silver veins west of Thunder Bay, riches that until then the Native people had kept as closely guarded secrets. But the word got out, and the rush was on. Over the next 20 years, nearly a dozen mining camps were built in the mountains of silver. The largest were the twin towns of Silver Mountain East End and Silver Mountain West End. To gain access to them, the Silver Mountain Highway was built into the area, followed in 1891 by a little railway called the Port Arthur Duluth & Western (PDW) Railway but more fittingly nicknamed the "Poverty Agony Distress and Welfare" line. But the deposits were meagre and production disappointing. By 1910 the mines were silent.

When the mines closed, many of the miners, most of them immigrants from Finland, stayed on to clear small bush farms along the Silver Mountain Road. Others followed, expanding the clearings and lending the area a flavour of old Finland with distinctive Finnish barn and house

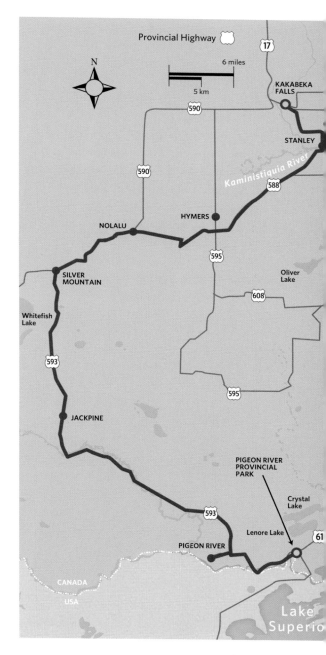

styles. Even as recently as the 1920s, new land was being broken along the Pigeon River, making the area one of Ontario's last true frontiers.

Kakabeka Falls to Hymers

This trip begins at a waterfall that has been called the Niagara of the North, and then follows the Silver Mountains to an obscure railway town. Well known to the early fur traders and Indians, Kakabeka Falls was the first difficult portage on the Kaministikwia River fur highway. Here, 30 km west of Lake Superior, the Kam drops 39 metres over a hard granite brink. Erosion has carved a gorge 3 km from the original lip of the escarpment. Beside the thundering cataract is a park that contains trails which follow the ancient portages used by Native peoples and, later, the voyageurs. The legend of Green Mantle tells of an Ojibwa princess, held by invading Sioux warriors, who led her captors over the brink of the falls to their deaths, and her own demise as well.

From the park, drive east on the Trans-Canada Highway for 4 km to Highway 588 and then turn south. The next 2 km lead you down the wall of the Kam Valley to a hamlet called Stanley. Once a busy junction on the PDW, Stanley can boast a pair of buildings that date from those steam-filled days. Along the north side of the river the rails have long been lifted, and Rosslyn Road follows the former rail bed.

Your route takes you south over the Kam River, where you will see a few of the prosperous farms on the silty soils of the river's flood plain. Across the bridge, at a T intersection, Highway 588 turns right to follow the old Silver Mountain Highway. Although it bears no resemblance to the bush trail first carved into the forests in the 1890s, Highway 588 still follows the route along the foot of the great mesas. After 3 km, the peaks loom close on your left. On your right are the small

overgrown clearings of the area's first bush farmers; some of them now contain the modern homes of the area's country dwellers.

At 12 km west from the Kam River bridge, you will enter Hymers. Originally a station on the PDW, it grew into a busy service town for the pioneer community. But when the railway closed here in 1954 and when better roads made Port Arthur and Fort William more accessible, many residents left. Today, without the newer homes of Thunder Bay's commuters, Hymers would be a ghost town.

To enter Hymers, turn right from 588 onto Highway 595 and drive down the wall of the Whitefish River Valley into the village. Before the bridge is a wooden mansion that was home to the family after whom the town was named. Across the small bridge is the village museum, housed in a wooden building that was originally the United church. The museum has displays of early pioneer implements, along with photographs of the town in its heyday. A few metres beyond the museum, Highway 595 turns right. This is the town's main intersection, where five stores, three blacksmith shops, two boarding houses and the PDW railway station once stood, giving the street its current name, Pee Dee Road.

Hymers to Nolalu

The next section of the route leaves Highway 588 to trace the original Silver Mountain Highway beneath red cliffs and into northwestern Ontario's Little Finland.

From the centre of Hymers, return to Highway 588, turn right and drive 5.5 km. Here at a stop sign the highway turns sharply right, while the Old Silver Mountain Highway follows a dirt road straight ahead. Follow the old road. This narrow trail winds past bush farms, many of which were started by unemployed miners on poor soils and

An early Finnish farmstead west of Thunder Bay.

are now sporting a few new country homes. Then the road swings into the shadow of a high, rocky mesa, which, with its vertical columns of rock, is called the Palisades.

After 5 km, you will come to a crossroad. Ahead of you, the old Silver Mountain route continues for another 1.5 km and then becomes passable only by four-wheel-drive vehicles. So you should turn right at the crossroads, crossing the bridge over the Silver Falls Creek. On this wide, sandy plain, a dozen Finnish farms—their barns still displaying distinctive round roofs—once operated.

After travelling 4 km from the crossroads, you will enter the valley of the Whitefish River once again and arrive at Nolalu. Originally a station on the PDW, its odd name came not from a town in far-off Finland, as many have surmised, but rather for its first postmaster, who named it after his lumber company, North Land Lumber (hence, No-La-Lu). The single village street beside the highway once shaded the railway track. Trains called three times a week, and the village became the focus for the Finnish farm community that surrounded it. Despite a decline in the rural population after the closing of the railway, the village has remained almost totally Finnish.

The PDW began as a Port Arthur effort to link with the coveted Canadian Pacific Railway in Fort William. Despite being thwarted by the CPR, its promoters built the line beyond Fort William and onward to the border with Minnesota, where they had expected to link with an American line proposed from Duluth. The American link was never built, and the PDW ended, literally, in the middle of nowhere.

A log chute by the falls on the Pigeon River.

Nolalu to Silver Mountain

The next section of your route follows the rail bed of the PDW, winding along the valley of the Whitefish River to Shuniah Weachu, the Mountain of Silver. From Nolalu, turn west onto Highway 588 and drive out of the village. More small bush farms peer from the young woodlots here. Although new country homes of commuters to Thunder Bay have replaced some the early farm homes, you may yet see examples of early Finnish houses and barns.

On the southwest corner of the junction with Highway 593 is the site of Silver Mountain station. Now a restaurant, its pyramid roof exemplifies a pattern devised by the PDW's later owners, the Canadian Northern Railway. Turn left here onto Highway 593.

Looming above the plain on the southeastern horizon is Silver Mountain itself. It was on this summit between 1890 and 1910 that the twin silver towns of Silver Mountain East End and Silver Mountain West End grew. Each contained not only mines and mills, but also hotels, stores and two dozen log cabins. But the mining activity was only sporadic; by 1910 it had ceased and the villages vanished.

Your route now ventures into a remote part of Ontario that was one of the province's last frontiers. Over the next 5 km, Highway 593 skirts the west end of the mountain and then enters the canyon of the Little Whitefish River. After 8 km, the river tumbles beside the road. After a few more kilometres, Highway 593 crosses the Arrow River, where the rural settlement of Jackpine is clustered. For

Opposite: On a cold day ice is forming from the water mist and covering everything around the High Falls waterfall on the Pigeon River.

Now a popular restaurant, the Silver Mountain station is the last to linger on the ill-fated PDW rail line.

the next 20 km the highway follows the valley of the Arrow River

Until the First World War, the valley of the Arrow River was unknown to all but a few trappers and loggers. But surveys showed a wide, apparently fertile, valley floor that could become a new farming community. Then, in the late 1920s and the early 1930s, with the Depression in full gear and bread lines growing in the cities of the south, the Ontario government threw open the flat soils of Devon Township to settlers. Many of the settlers were Finns, attracted by the proximity of the Finnish colonies of Suomi and Nolalu. Other settlers were simply trying to escape the Depression.

The last section of your route continues down the valley of the Arrow River and ends amid the spectacular mountains and waterfalls that mark the Pigeon River.

From the bridge over the Arrow River continue on Highway 593. For 5 km the road crosses the flat flood plain of the valley where overgrown clearings that mark failed efforts at farming are being overtaken by a young regenerating forest. The road then crosses the river once more and traverses a rolling, rocky countryside where the clearings of the bush farms become farther apart. After 10 km, at a T intersection, Highway 593 turns left, and the Old Pigeon River Road leads right for 2 km to the abandoned border crossing of Pigeon River.

The recorded history of the Pigeon River dates from the fur-trading days, when it was the highway to the west. Fur seekers, both French and Native peoples, paddled upstream to the fur grounds and returned laden with skins. But after the American Revolution, the Pigeon River became the new international border. Threats of customs duties forced the fur trappers to the Kam River, a more difficult route, but one that was free of international wrangling.

The area's first road had been built in the 1880s to bring mail from Duluth to the silver mines, but once the railways assumed this function the road fell into disrepair. It took until 1915 and angry petitions from area settlers to improve the road, but there was still no bridge. Rotary clubs in the Lakehead cities collected money to bridge the chasm, but because they had failed to complete an international agreement for the crossing, the bridge was dubbed the Outlaw Bridge.

Years later, during the 1950s and 1960s, when highways across Ontario were widened and improved, the westerly crossing of the Pigeon River was abandoned in favour of a new alignment 10 km east. The customs buildings were dismantled and moved. Among the foundations and vacant lots, fewer than a half-dozen buildings remain at the old crossing. And the Outlaw Bridge has vanished forever.

Return to Highway 593 and follow it east to Highway 61. The road crosses another rocky plain and for 6 km follows the north bank of the Pigeon River to Highway 61 and south to the entrance to Pigeon River Provincial Park, with its soaring mesas and hiking trails, to the more spectacular 30-metre-high Pigeon Falls. Trails also lead to Middle Falls. Although the falls are only 15 metres high, they are wide and the water thunders furiously into the eddies below. Portions of a rare early timber chute lie beside the falls. The Pigeon River is part of the Canadian Heritage River System Boundary Waters Voyageur Waterway.

Highway 593 ends at Highway 61. And so your route ends as it began, near some of Ontario's most picturesque waterfalls and amid some of its most magnificent mountain scenery. The highway will return you north to Thunder Bay, while the American border lies about 2 km south.

Index of Cities, Towns, Villages and Hamlets

Allanburg, 18
Ambleside, 54
Ameliasburg, 121
Andrewsville, 167
Ashdown, 202
Aurora, 96-97
Balaclava, 178
Baldwin, 91 Balsam, 104
Bancroft, 185-186, 188, 190-191
Bannockburn, 137
Barrie, 69
Barrow Bay, 65
Barry's Bay, 176, 182-183
Bath, 149
Bayfield, 50, 57, 59
Bedford Mills, 154
Belleville, 120
Bellrock, 138
Belmore, 54
Belwood, 38
Bewdley, 112, 114-115
Big Bay, 62, 143
Black Bank, 71
Black River Bridge, 125
Blair, 34
Bloomingdale, 35
Boulter, 189
Brampton, 101
Brantford, 22-23, 25, 31
Brechin, 94
Breslau, 31, 35
Brinkman's Corner, 66
Broadbent, 204
Bruce Mines, 195-198
Bruce Station, 196
Brucefield, 57

Brudenell, 179-180, 182-183
Brussels, 55
Buckstown, 100
Burgoyne, 52
Burketon Station, 107
Burritts Rapids, 165-167
Byng, 29
Cabot Head, 61, 65-66
Calabogie, 178
Caledonia, 26, 28
Camden East, 136
Camden, 133
Campbellcroft, 114
Cape Chin, 65
Cargill, 53
Carley Station, 81, 86
Carrying Place, 120
Cayuga, 28
Charlotteville, 45
Claremont Siding, 103
Claremont, 102-103
Clarkeville, 131
Clear Creek, 47
Clinton, 57
Clontarf, 179
Cobalt, 222, 223-227
Cobourg, 116-117
Colbeck, 40
Coldwater, 84
Colebrook, 137-138
Collingwood, 69, 73
Commanda, 201, 206, 208
Conestogo, 34, 36
Consecon, 125
Cooks Dock, 214
Coulson, 87

Craigmont, 189
Creighton, 86
Crowland, 19
Cumberland, 170-171
Dacre, 178-179, 182
Dain City, 19
Decker Hollow, 112
Demorestville, 120-122
Doon, 34
Dover Mills, 43
Dufferin Bridge, 204
Dunblane, 53
Dundalk, 40
Dunedin, 72
Dunnville, 15, 23, 29
Dyers Bay, 66
Eganville, 178
East Linton, 62
Echo Bay, 198-199
Edgar, 94
Egmondville, 56
Elizabeth Bay, 218
Elizabethville, 112
Elora, 22, 36-37
Emerald, 149
Esmonde, 179
Eugenia Falls, 74, 76-77
Evansville, 218
Eversley, 97-98
Farrell's Landing, 177
Fergus, 38-39
Ferguslea, 178
Fishers Glen, 44
Flesherton, 77
Formosa, 54
Fort Kente, 120

Fort Norfolk, 45
Fort Stewart, 188
Fort William, 233, 239
Foymount, 180
Galt, 32, 34
Garden Hill, 112, 114
Glen Huron, 72
Glen Major, 104, 106
Glen Morris, 32
Glen Tay, 157
Glenora, 124
Goderich, 51
Gore Bay, 214, 216-217
Gores Landing, 115-116
Grand Valley, 25, 38-40
Griersville, 76
Grovesend, 48
Guelph, 51
Haileybury, 223
Hamilton, 42
Harpurhey, 56
Harwood, 116
Hawkesbury, 174
Haydon, 107-108
Heathcote, 74, 76
Hemlock, 47
Hermon, 188
Hilliardtown, 223
Hogg, 62
Holland Landing, 90
Honora, 214, 216
Hope Bay, 64
Horning's Mills, 71
Houghton, 47
Huntsville, 204
Hymers, 240
Indiana, 28
Inverary, 153
Jackpine, 242
Jackson's Point, 93

Jacksonburg, 47
Johnsons Landing, 229-230
Kagawong, 214-216
Kars, 165
Keldon, 40
Kemble, 62
Kendal, 111
Keswick, 91
Kettleby, 98-99
Kilgorie, 71
Kimberley, 77
Kincardine, 198
Kingston, 141
Kingston, 9, 131, 138, 141-143, 145, 148, 152-153, 157, 163
Kirby, 103, 110-111
Kitchener, 22, 34, 59
L'Orignal, 170-171, 174
Lagoon City, 94
Lakeview, 48
Lavender, 72
Leeburn, 198
Lefaivre, 173-174
Leskard, 108-109
Lion's Head, 64-65
Little Current, 213-217
Lockton, 100
Madoc, 185
Magnetawan, 201, 204, 206
Manhard's Mills, 156
Manotick, 162, 164-165
Martinville, 84
Marysville, 145-147
Meaford, 69
Mecunoma, 206
Medonte, 87
Meldrum Bay, 218
Merrickville, 162, 167-169
Michaels Bay, 214
Middleport, 25-26

Midland, 82
Millhaven, 148
Mono Centre, 70
Monticello, 40
Mount St. Louis, 84
Mount St. Patrick, 178
Mountain Mills, 124
Mountain View, 121
Musclow, 190
Napanee, 130-136
Neals Corner, 46
New Carlow, 188, 190
New Hermon, 188
New Liskeard, 223
New Scotland, 100
Newburgh, 133-135
Newfoundout, 179-180
Newmarket, 89-90
Newport, 23, 25
Nipissing, 201, 208-209
Noble's Corners, 103
Nolalu, 240-242, 244
Normandale, 44-45
North Cobalt, 225-226
North Keppel, 62
North Seguin, 204
Northport, 122
Onondaga, 25
Ophir, 198
Orangeville, 68-70, 96-97, 101
Orillia, 94, 107
Orrville, 202
Oshawa, 103-104, 109
Owen Sound, 60-61, 69
Oxenden, 63
Paisley, 52-53
Palgrave, 99-100
Paris, 31-32
Parry Sound, 202
Pass Lake, 229, 233

Pearl, 229, 234
Perth Road, 152-154
Perth, 152-153, 157-160, 186
Peterborough, 114, 116
Picton, 119, 122-123, 125
Pinkerton, 53
Plainville, 115
Port Arthur, 233, 239
Port Bruce, 46, 48
Port Burwell, 48
Port Colborne, 15, 18-20
Port Credit, 69
Port Dalhouise, 16
Port Dover, 42-44
Port Hope, 114
Port Maitland, 28-29
Port McNicoll, 82
Port Metcalfe, 146
Port Robinson, 15, 18
Port Rowan, 45-47
Port Royal, 47
Port Ryerse, 44
Port Stanley, 42, 48
Port Weller, 15-16
Prinyer's Cove, 125
Prospect, 107
Queensville, 90
Raglan, 107
Rednersville, 120
Renfrew, 176-178
Richmond, 157
Roche's Point, 90-91, 93
Rockingham, 182
Rockland, 171-172
Rogues' Hollow, 134
Rosendale, 35
Rosseau, 201-203, 209
Rugby, 94
Ruskview, 71
Rye, 208

Saugeen, 53
Sault Ste. Marie, 195, 199
Seaforth, 55-57, 59
Seguin Falls, 202-204
Shanty Bay, 87, 89, 94-95
Shelburne, 69
Shrigley, 40
Silver Centre, 223, 227
Silver Islet, 228, 230, 232-233
Silver Mountain West End, 239, 242
Silver Water, 217-218
Simcoe, 44
Singhampton, 73
Smiths Falls, 169
South Baymouth, 213
Southampton, 50-52
Sparta, 48
Spence, 204
St. Catharines, 16-17
St. Thomas, 48-49
St. Williams, 45-46
Stanley, 240
Stella, 148
Strathcona, 133
Sudbury, 195, 213
Suomi, 244
Terra Nova, 71
Thorold, 17
Thunder Bay, 228, 231, 233, 238-240, 242, 245
Tobermory, 60, 66, 69, 213
Tolsmaville, 219
Tomstown, 223
Treadwell, 173
Trenton, 97, 120
Tyrone, 108-109
Vars, 172
Vasey, 82-83
Victoria Harbour, 81-82, 85

Violet Hill, 70-71
Vittoria, 45
Wainfleet, 15
Waldemar, 39
Walton, 55-56
Waterford, 114
Waubaushene, 80-82
Waupoos, 125
Welland, 15, 18-19
Wellington, 125, 165
Wendover, 172
West Montrose, 36
Westport, 153-154, 156
Wheatley, 43
Whitby, 103, 107, 109
Whitfield, 71
Wiarton, 61, 63-66
Wilno, 180, 183
Wingfield Basin, 66
Wroxeter, 54-55
Yarker, 136-137
York, 28

Index

"Birdhouse City," 125
"Clinton School Car," 57
"Forks of the Grand," 31
"Kissing Rock," 17
"Ontario's Venice," 94
"Roof of Ontario," 40, 73
"Talbot Trail," 44
"The Handmaid's Tale," 34

A

Ainley, William, 55
Albion Hills Conservation Area, 100
Algoma Eastern Railway, 214
Algoma's Scenic Dunn's Valley Road, 194-199
Algonquin Park, 183, 203
Allan, Charles, 37
American Revolutionary War, 23
Amherst Island, 142, 148-149
Andrews, Rufus, 167
Art Gallery of Ontario, 160
Arthur, James, 208
Augustinian Seminary (near Eversley), 98

B

Backus Heritage Conservation Area, 47
Backus Mill, 45
Baker, Edward, 146
Banks, James, 109
Bartlett, William, 214
Baverman, Judah, 72
Baxter Conservation Area, 165
Bay of Quinte Railway, 135-137
Bell, Alexander Graham, 25, 32
Benson, Sam, 131

Big Ben (horse), 160
Black Donald Mountains, 176, 178-179, 188-189
Boomtown Backroads: The Cobalt Circle, 222-227
Booth, John Rudolphus, 183, 203
Bostwick, John, 49
Boughton, Levi, 31-32
Boulton, James, 160
Brant, Chief Joseph, 23, 25
Breithaupt, William, 35
Briar's, The, 93
Brichta, G.J. and Philip, 93
Brock, Ira, 148
Brockville & Westport Railway, 156
Bruce's Cave Conservation Area, 62
Bruce Mines and Algoma Railway, 196
Bruce Peninsula Road, The, 60-67
Bruce Trail, 65, 68, 70, 100
Bunker Museum, 225
Burritt, Stephen and Daniel, 166
By, John, 157, 163, 167-168

C

Cabot Head lighthouse, 65
Calvin, Dileno Dexter, 147
Campbell, Robert, 100
Campbell, Thomas, 114
Canada Atlantic Railway, 172
Canadian National Railway, 137, 154, 171-172, 233, 242
Canadian Pacific Railway, 36, 80, 84, 103, 107, 174, 196, 198, 214, 241
Canadian Register of Historic Places, 196
Canadian Shield, 153, 185
Canada Southern Railway, 28
Canadian Wildlife Service, 125

Cape Croker Indian Reserve, 64
Capone, Al, 183
Cargill, Henry, 53-54
Carleton, Guy, 94
Carolinian forest, 32, 47
Carswell, Robert, 178
Casa Loma, 98
Casson, A. J., 206
Cataraqui Trail, 154
Central Ontario Railway, 188
Chalk, William, 56
Champlain, Samuel de, 94
Chateau Montebello, 174
Chiefswood, 25
Children of Peace, 90
Claremont Conservation Area, 104
Clarke, James, 131
Clarke, Robert, 131
Climbing Neptune's Staircase, 14-21
Cobalt Historical Society, 225
Cobalt Mining Museum, 222
Cobalt Nugget, 224
Cobourg and Peterborough Railway, 116
Coleman, Dr. T., 57
Cooper, James, 72
Copeland, Charles, 84
Credit Valley Railway, 38
Cuestas and Valleys, 68-77
Cumberland Heritage Museum, 172
Cuthbertson, James, 195

D

Dain City House Tavern, 19
Darragh, Ernest, 223
Daunais, Oliver, 239
de Brebeuf, Jean, 82
de Fenelon, Francois, 120
De La Roche, Mazo, 93
Demorest, William, 121

Dickinson, Moss Kent, 164
Dicky, Theron, 111
Doane, Thomas, 89
Doon School of Fine Art, 34
drumlins, 115
Dunlop, William "Tiger," 51
Dunning, Abijah, 171

E

Eastman, Adam and John, 165
Eaton, Lady, 98
Eaton, Sir, John, 98
Edinburgh Square Heritage and Cultural Centre, 26
Egan Chutes Provincial Park, 188
Elgin Military Museum, 47
Elora Gorge Conservation Area, 36-38
Erie Canal, 32
Essroc Cement Company, 123
Eugenia Falls, 74, 77
Eva Brook Donly Museum, 44
Everest, George, 93

F

Face of Farm Country, The, 50-59
Fathom Five National Marine Park, 60, 66
Ferguson Forest Centre, 165
Ferguson, Duncan, 178
Ferguson, James, 172
Ferried, Adam, 34
Flowerpot Island, 66-67
Foley Mountain Conservation Area, 157
Forester, 115
Forge and Anvil Museum, 48
Formosa Springs Brewery, 54
Fredenberg, William, 156
Freeman, Henry, 46
Frontenac II, 148

Frontenac-Howe Islander, 142
Frue, William, 232

G

Galt to Paris Rail Trail, 32
Galt, John, 51
Ganaraska Forest Centre, 112
Garden City Skyway, 16
Gellassy, William, 46
Giachino, Anthony, 225
Grand River Land Trust, 28
Grand Trunk Railway, 52, 172
Greig's Caves, 64
Guinness Book of World Records, 17
Gurd Township and Area Historical Corporation, 208
gypsum, (in Paris), 32

H

Hamilton & Northwest Railway, 100
Hayward, Gerald S., 116
Head, Francis Bond, 214
Hidden Treasures of the Erie Shore Road, The, 42-49
Hitchcock, Archibald, 146
Hood, John, 18
Horning, Lewis, 71
Howe Island, 142-144
Howells, Emily, 25

I

Irondale, Bancroft and Ottawa Railway, 188
Iroquois Beach Provincial Park, 47
Island Roads, 140-151

J

Jessup's Falls Conservation Area, 172
Johnson, George, 25
Johnson, Pauline, 25

K

Kakabeka Falls, 238, 240
Kelly, Archibald, 100
Kingston and Perth Road Company, 153

L

L'Avocat, Joseph, 239
La Cloche Mountains, 213, 215
Lake on the Mountain Provincial Park, 123
Lake Simcoe Steeple Chase, The, 88-95
Lalemant, Gabriel, 82
LaRose, Fred, 225
Leacock, Stephen, 93
Lefaivre, Hercule, 171
Lefaivre, Pierre, 171, 173
Lindsay, Charles, 214
Lindsay, James, 165
Little Bluff Conservation Area, 125
Little Cataraqui Creek Conservation Area, 153
London, St. Thomas & Port Stanley Railway, 48
Long Point, 47
Loyalists, 9, 125
Luther Marsh Conservation Area, 40
Lymburner, Horace and Robert, 66
Lyon, Robert, 160

M

Macaulay Mountain Conservation Area, 125
MacCaulley, William, 123
MacDonald, Archibald, 124
MacPherson, Allan, 131-132

Manitoulin Chocolate Works, 216
Manitoulin's Haweater Trail, 212-221
Marine Rail Heritage Centre, 61
Marston, John, 174
Martin, Jasper, 84
Marylake Shrine, 98
Mason, John, 44
Matheson, Roderick, 157
Maitland, Peregrine, 91
McDougall Mill Museum, 177
McDougall, John, 177
McDougall, William, 214
McKinley, James, 223
McNeil, Alexander, 64
McPherson, William, 26
Mennonite country, 35-36
Merrick, Stephen, 168
Merritt, William Hamilton, 15, 23, 168
Midland Railway, 114
Miller, George, 136
Miller, Ian, 160
Ministry of Natural Resources, 84, 124
Mohawk Indian Residential School, 25
Mond Nickel Company, 195
Mono Cliffs Provincial Park, 70
Montreal Mining Company, 195
Moore, William, 122
Morden, James and Janet, 204
MS Chi Cheemaun, 66
murals, historic (in Welland), 18-19
Murray Canal, 119-120
Murray, Thomas, 120
Muskoka Pioneer Museum, 204

N

Napanee River Road, The, 130-139
Net Shed Museum, 218
Newburgh Academy, 135
Niagara Escarpment Commission, 70, 73

Niagara Escarpment, 17, 101, 215, 219
Niagara River, 15
Nipissing: A Road of Broken Dreams, The, 200-213
North West Company, 239

O

O'Brien, Edward, 95
Oak Ridges Moraine, 97
Ojibwa, (submarine), 47
Old Stone Church National Historic Site,
    (St. Andrew's), 93
Ontario & Quebec Railway, 103, 107, 157
Opeongo Pioneer Road, The, 176-183
Ottawa River Road, The, 170-175

P

Parks Canada, 163, 166, 168
Payne, Manuel, 49
Pellatt, Sir Henry, 98
Pelton, William, 46
Perry, David, 134
Perth Road, The, 152-161
Pigeon River Provincial Park, 245
Port Arthur Duluth & Western Railway, 239-241
Port Maitland lighthouse, 29
Port Robinson Park, 18
Port Stanley Terminal Railway, 49
Prince Edward Point National Wildlife Area, 125
Princess Sodalite Mine, 188
Purple Woods Conservation Area, 107

Q

Quaker Meeting House, 48 89
Quaker village, (Sparta), 48
Queen's Bush, 51
Quest for Fire, (movie), 64
Quinte Shore Road, The, 118-127

R

Rathbun Lumber Company, 138
Redner, Henry, 120
Remarkable Highlands of Hastings, The, 184-191
Rice Lake Road, The, 110-117
Richardson, A. H., 107
Richardson, Arthur H., 112
Rideau Canal, 153, 156-157, 162-163, 165, 167
Rideau River Road, The, 162-169
Rideau Valley Conservation Authority, 164
Ridge Road East, The, 102-109
Ridge Road West, The, 96-101
River Rat Race, 77
Robinson, Peter, 116
Rose House Museum, 125
Royal Mohawk Chapel, 25
Ruthven Park, 28
Ryerse, Sam, 44

S

Sandbanks Provincial Park, 125
Saugeen Bluffs Conservation Area, 53
Sawatsky, Dan, 18
Seneca College, 98
Shade, Absalom, 23, 32
Sharon Temple, 90-91
Sibbald, Susan, 93
Sibbald Point Provincial Park, 93
Sibley, William, 232
Silver Mountain Road, The, 238-245
Simcoe, John, 93
Sleeping Giant Provincial Park, 228-237
South Bay Mariners' Museum, 125
South Norfolk Railway, 46
Sowden, Samuel, 31
Spence Lumber Company, 203
Spirit Rock Conservation Area, 64
SS Keewatin, 82, 83

Steelton, 18
Steeple Chase (book), 106
Stennett, Walter, 91
Studio Two (television program), 224

T

Talbot, Thomas, 43
Tay Canal, 157
Templin Gardens, 39
Tett, Benjamin, 154
Thompson, David, 28
Thompson, John, 133-134
Those Surprising Simcoe County Highlands, 80-87
To the Source of the Grand, 30-41
Toronto, Grey & Bruce Railway, 54
Trail of the Sleeping Giant, The, 228-237
Tranquility of the Grand River Road, The, 22-29
Treadwell, Nathaniel, 171, 174
Trent Canal, 115
Trouve, Claude, 120
Turkey Point, 45
Tyrone Mill, 108-109

U

United Empire Loyalists, 9, 43

V

Vader, David, 136
Van Alstine, Peter, 124
Van Egmond Foundation, 57
Van Egmond, Constant, 56-57
Van Norman, Joseph, 44
Vankoughnet, Peter, 177
Vanstone, William, 55

W

War of 1812, 43, 81, 93, 120
Watson, Homer, 34
Watson, John, 182
Weese, John, 120
Welland Canal, 14-21
Wellington County Museum and Archives, 38
Wellington, Grey & Bruce Railway, 51-53, 55
Whitmarsh, Eleazer, 168
Willson, David, 90
Wilson, John, 160
Wolfe Island Railway and Canal Company, 145
Wolfe Island, 142, 145-146
Wolfe Islander III, 145
Wolfe Islander, 147
Woodland Cultural Centre, 25
Woods, Joseph, 232
World Heritage Site, 163

Y

York Pioneer and Historical Society, 90

Photo Credits

All photographs are courtesy of the author, Ron Brown, except for the following:

Cover: Bottom - Muskoka Stock Photos/
  Shutterstock.com
Back cover: 2nd row right - George Walker;
  3rd row - Leo Bruce/Dreamstime.com;
Bottom - Meg Wallace Photography/
  Shutterstock.com
Pg 2: Muskoka Stock Photos/Shutterstock.com
Pg 5: Chris Collins/Shutterstock.com
Pg 6: © iStockphoto.com
Pg 8: David P. Lewis/Shutterstock.com
Pg 10: Elena Elisseeva/Shutterstock.com
Pg 13: SF photo/Shutterstock.com
Pg 14: SurangaSL/Shutterstock.com
Pg 19: Chris Robart
Pg 24: SF photo/Shutterstock.com
Pg 27: SF photo/Shutterstock.com
Pg 29: SF photo/Shutterstock.com
Pg 32: JHVEPhoto/Shutterstock.com
Pg 33: SF photo/Shutterstock.com
Pg 35: Tom Worsley/Shutterstock.com
Pg 36: Elijah Lovkoff/Shutterstock.com
Pg 37: Elijah Lovkoff/Shutterstock.com
Pgs 38-39: JHVEPhoto/Shutterstock.com
Pg 58: Christopher Meder/Shutterstock.com
Pg 60: Mark52/Shutterstock.com
Pg 67: Viktorus/Shutterstock.com
Pg 75: © George Fischer Photography

Pg 79: SF photo/Shutterstock.com
Pg 88: George Walker
Pg 90: George Walker
Pg 105: pavels/Shutterstock.com
Pg 113: SF photo/Shutterstock.com
Pgs 116-17: © iStockphoto.com
Pgs 126-27: © iStockphoto.com
Pg 140: SF photo/Shutterstock.com
Pg 150-51: SF photo/shutterstock.com
Pg 159: David P. Lewis/Shutterstock.com
Pg 160: Leo Bruce/Dreamstime.com
Pg 162: Paul McKinnon/Shutterstock.com
Pg 164: Paul McKinnon/Shutterstock.com
Pgs 168-69: David P. Lewis/Shutterstock.com
Pg 187: © George Fischer Photography
Pg 194: George Cragg
Pg 197: George Cragg
Pg 205: Meg Wallace Photography/
  Shutterstock.com
Pg 207: Judy Tiessen/Dreamstime.com
Pgs 210-11: © iStockphoto.com/gladassfanny
Pg 212: John Goldstein/Shutterstock.com
Pg 217: SF photo/Shutterstock.com
Pgs 220-21: Christopher Meder/Shutterstock.com
Pg 228: pavels/Shutterstock.com
Pg 235: David P. Lewis/Shutterstock.com
Pgs 236-37: Wolf Mountain Images/
  Shutterstock.com
Pg 238: © Hartley Millson
Pg 243: Owl Mountain/Shutterstock.com